# A New Life of Dante

Stephen Bemrose is a lecturer in Italian at the University of Exeter.

Cover image: *Ritratto di Dante*, by Andrea del Castagno (Uffizi Gallery, Florence). Reproduced by kind permission of the Ministero per i Beni Culturali e Ambientali.

# A NEW LIFE OF DANTE

*Stephen Bemrose*

UNIVERSITY
*of*
EXETER
PRESS

First published in 2000 by
University of Exeter Press
Reed Hall, Streatham Drive
Exeter EX4 4QR
UK
*www.exeterpress.co.uk*

Reprinted with revisions 2009

**British Library Cataloguing in Publication Data**
A catalogue record for this book is available
from the British Library.

Paperback ISBN 978 0 85989 845 4

Typeset in 11/13pt Sabon
by XL Publishing Services, Tiverton

Printed in Great Britain by Short Run Press Ltd, Exeter

For

KISSANPOIKA

# Contents

# Preface for the 2009 re-issue

It is now close on a decade since this book was first published. My aim was to offer something readable, accessible and useful to a fairly wide audience—not just university students, but any non-specialist reader keen to find out something, or something more, about Dante. I think it is fair to say, on the basis of 'feedback' of all sorts, that my aim has succeeded. Interest in Dante from all angles continues unabated, and I am persuaded that the time is right for the book to make a reappearance. The text is substantially unaltered. Nothing has occurred in the ever-lively field of Dante studies to move me to change my mind, and the differences from the 2000 volume are chiefly a matter of minor correction and clarification, bibliographical updating and a few chronological adjustments—these last being appropriate for a book that now belongs to the dawn of a new century, rather than the end of the previous one. I hope that what I have written will continue to be found useful, perhaps even stimulating or catalytic.

April 2009                                                SB, Exeter

# Preface to the original edition

My aim in this book has been to provide an accessible account of Dante Alighieri's life, interwoven with considerable discussion of his writings.

Accessible to whom? To university students certainly, but also to any curious, intelligent, English-speaking (but non-specialist) reader at the end of the twentieth century. Therefore, no prior knowledge is assumed of Graeco-Roman civilization, nor of Christian history or doctrine, nor indeed of medieval Europe. Moreover all quotations in Italian or Latin have been fully translated, the translations being my own unless otherwise indicated.

I have tried to cover the whole of Dante's life, and the following areas in particular: his early career as a lyric poet and his enthusiasm for philosophy; his involvement in the political life of Florence; the power struggles leading to his exile; his increasingly isolated wanderings, during which his idiosyncratic political thought steadily evolved; his response to Emperor Henry VII's abortive invasion of Italy; his association with the della Scala family of Verona; his final years in Ravenna. As to his writings, apart from providing a broad yet selective survey of his masterpiece the *Divine Comedy*, I have paid attention to his 'minor' works (some of them not widely known), in particular the *De Vulgari Eloquentia*, the *Convivio*, the *Monarchia* and the political letters. My aim throughout has been to present Dante as an intensely philosophical writer as well as a socio-political one, and to keep in view both these aspects of his personality and work—in so far as they can be separated.

I am of course immeasurably indebted to the work of a great many earlier and contemporary scholars, far more so than may be apparent from those specifically cited in the text and notes, or included in the Bibliography. Perhaps the most important debts have been to Barbi, Boyde, Foster, Nardi, Padoan, Petrocchi and Took. Of those known to me personally, and who have read all or part of the manuscript, I am especially grateful for valuable advice and encouragement from Dr John Took of University College London and from my Exeter colleagues Dr Mark Davie and Professor Paul Diffley. But the greatest debt of all is expressed in the dedication.

July 1999                                                        Stephen Bemrose
                                                                        Exeter

# A List of Dante's Works
# and the Editions Used in this Book

## List of Dante's Works

*Rime* (the Italian lyric poems; *c*.1283–*c*.1308)
*\*Detto d'Amore* (Italian verse; *c*.1286)
*\*Fiore* (sequence of Italian sonnets; 1286)
*Vita Nuova* (anthology of Italian lyric poems, with Italian prose commentary; *c*.1293–95)
*De Vulgari Eloquentia* (Latin prose; 1303–4)
*Convivio* (Italian prose; 1304–8?)
*Epistolae* (Latin prose letters; 1304–*c*.1316)
*Divina Commedia—Inferno, Purgatorio, Paradiso* (Italian verse; probably not begun before 1307 and completed by 1320–21)
*Monarchia* (Latin prose; 1317?)
*Eclogues* (Latin verse; 1319–21)
*Quaestio de aqua et terra* (Latin prose; 1320)

\* attribution to Dante disputed by many experts

## Editions Used in this Book

For quotations from and references to Dante the following critical editions have been used:

*Rime*, ed. K. Foster and P. Boyde as *Dante's Lyric Poetry*, 2 vols (Oxford: Clarendon Press, 1967).
*Detto d'Amore* and *Fiore*, ed. G. Contini as *Il Fiore e Il Detto d'Amore attribuibili a Dante Alighieri* (Milan: Mondadori, 1984).
*Vita Nuova*, ed. D. De Robertis in *Opere minori*, 2 vols (Milan-Naples: Ricciardi, 1980), I/1, pp. 1–247.

*De vulgari eloquentia*, ed. P.V. Mengaldo in *Opere minori* (Milan-Naples: Ricciardi, 1979), II, pp. 3–237.

*Convivio*, ed. C. Vasoli and D. De Robertis in *Opere minori* (Milan-Naples: Ricciardi, 1988), I/2, pp. xi–c; 3–1108.

*Epistole*, ed. A. Frugoni and G. Brugnoli in *Opere minori* (Milan-Naples: Ricciardi, 1979), II, pp. 505–643.

*Divina Commedia*, ed. G. Petrocchi as *La Commedia secondo l'antica vulgata*, 4 vols (Florence: Casa Editrice Le Lettere, 1994[2]).

*Monarchia*, ed. P.G. Ricci (Milan: Mondadori, 1965).

*Egloge*, ed. E. Cecchini in *Opere minori* (Milan-Naples: Ricciardi, 1979), II, pp. 645–89.

*Questio de aqua et terra*, ed. F. Mazzoni in *Opere minori* (Milan-Naples: Ricciardi, 1979), II, pp. 691–880.

## Abbreviations

The following standard abbreviations have been used:

| | | | |
|---|---|---|---|
| *Inf.* | *Inferno* | *Conv.* | *Convivio* |
| *Purg.* | *Purgatorio* | *Mon.* | *Monarchia* |
| *Par.* | *Paradiso* | ED | *Enciclopedia dantesca* |
| DVE | *De vulgari eloquentia* | | |

# A Guide to Further Reading in English

## 1. The 'Divine Comedy'

(a) Editions and Translations

The best Italian edition is *La Divina Commedia*, edited by U. Bosco and G. Reggio, 3 vols. (Florence: Le Monnier, 1980). Still very valuable is *La Divina commedia*, ed. N. Sapegno, 3 vols (Florence: La Nuova Italia, 1968).

Of bilingual Italian and English versions the best is *The Divine Comedy*, ed. and trans. C.S. Singleton, 6 vols (Princeton: Princeton University Press, 1970–75). On a smaller scale, but still useful, is *The Divine Comedy of Dante Alighieri*, trans. J.D. Sinclair, 3 vols (London: Oxford University Press, 1971). Of the many English verse translations, the most helpful are the two in the Penguin Classics series, by D. Sayers and B. Reynolds (Harmondsworth: Penguin, 1949–62) and more recently by M. Musa (Harmondsworth: Penguin, 1984–86). In all these volumes, especially Bosco-Reggio and Singleton, there is a wealth of information, and not just for the general reader or beginner. Indispensable for those wishing to enquire more deeply into the *Comedy* is the *Enciclopedia dantesca*, ed. U. Bosco, 6 vols (Rome: Istituto dell'Enciclopedia Italiana, 1970–78). For those without Italian there is still much to be gained from *A Dictionary of Proper Names and Notable Matters in the Works of Dante*, by P. Toynbee, rev. C.S. Singleton (Oxford: Clarendon Press, 1968), and now the excellent *Dante Encyclopedia*, ed. R. Lansing (New York: Garland, 2000).

(b) *Inferno*: Criticism

An excellent short essay on the first *cantica* is Foster's classic 'An Introduction to the *Inferno*' in *The Two Dantes and Other Studies*, pp. 1–14 (London: Darton, Longman and Todd, 1977). Far more extensive, though on a more mundane level, is W. Fowlie, *A Reading of Dante's 'Inferno'* (Chicago and London: University of Chicago Press, 1981). Also helpful is A.K. Cassell, *Dante's Fearful Art of Justice* (Toronto-London: University of Toronto Press, 1984).

(c) *Purgatorio*: Criticism
Among modern studies concentrating on the *Purgatorio*, mention may be made of: P. Armour, *The Door of Purgatory: A Study of Multiple Symbolism in Dante's 'Purgatorio'* (Oxford: Clarendon Press, 1983); P. Armour, *Dante's Griffin and the History of the World* (London: Oxford University Press, 1989); D. Cervigni, *Dante's Poetry of Dreams* (Florence: Olschki, 1986); F. Fergusson, *Dante's Drama of the Mind: A Modern Reading of 'Purgatorio'* (Princeton: Princeton University Press, 1953); J.T. Schnapp, 'Introduction to *Purgatorio*' in *The Cambridge Companion to Dante*, ed. R. Jacoff, pp. 192–207 (Cambridge: Cambridge University Press, 1993).

(d) *Paradiso*: Criticism
A brief selection of works on the *Paradiso:* J. Freccero, 'An Introduction to the *Paradiso*' in *Dante: The Poetics of Conversion*, ed. R. Jacoff, pp. 209–20 (Cambridge, Mass.: Harvard University Press, 1986); R. Jacoff, 'An Introduction to *Paradiso*' in *The Cambridge Companion to Dante*, pp. 208–25; J.A. Mazzeo, *Structure and Thought in the 'Paradiso'* (Ithaca, New York: Cornell University Press, 1958); J.T. Schnapp, *The Transfiguration of History at the Center of Dante's 'Paradise'* (Princeton: Princeton University Press, 1986).

*2. Minor Works*
As to the more important of these, the most useful English translations, whether in bilingual editions or not, are the following:

*Rime*, edited by K. Foster and P. Boyde as *Dante's Lyric Poetry*, 2 vols (Oxford: Clarendon Press, 1967)
*La Vita Nuova (Poems of Youth)*, translated by B. Reynolds (Harmondsworth: Penguin, 1969); *Vita Nuova*, translated by M. Musa (London: Oxford University Press, 1992). Also very useful is *Vita Nuova*, edited by J. Petrie and J. Salmons (Dublin: Belfield Italian Library, 1994); this does not include a translation, but the helpful notes are in English and there is a glossary and a

vocabulary. A good parallel-text edition is *Vita Nuova*, translated by D.S. Cervigni and E. Vasta (Notre Dame, Indiana-London: University of Notre Dame Press, 1995).

*De Vulgari Eloquentia: Literature in the Vernacular*, translated by S. Purcell (Cheadle, Cheshire: Carcanet Press, 1981); *De Vulgari Eloquentia*, edited and translated in a parallel- text edition by S. Botterill (Cambridge: Cambridge University Press, 1995).

*Convivio: Dante: The Banquet, translated with introduction and notes*, by C. Ryan (Saratoga, California: ANMA Libri, 1989).

*Epistolae: Dantis Alagherii Epistolae: The Letters of Dante*, edited and translated by P. Toynbee (Oxford: Clarendon Press, 1920).

*Monarchia*, translated and edited by P. Shaw (Cambridge: Cambridge University Press, 1995).

*Eclogues*: in P.H. Wicksteed and E.G. Gardner, *Dante and Giovanni del Virgilio* (London: Constable,1902).


## 3. Criticism

Of the mass of critical writings on all aspects of Dante (not just biographical ones), perhaps the following very brief selection includes works most likely to help the inquiring reader go further and deeper. Some are a good deal more specialised than others. All, however, are in English.

Bergin, T.G., *An Approach to Dante* (London: The Bodley Head, 1965).

Boyde, P., *Dante Philomythes and Philosopher: Man in the Cosmos* (Cambridge: Cambridge University Press, 1981).

Boyde, P., *Human Vices and Human Worth in Dante's 'Comedy'* (Cambridge: Cambridge University Press, 2002).

Boyde, P., *Perception and Passion in Dante's 'Comedy'* (Cambridge: Cambridge University Press, 1993).

Cosmo, U., translated by D. Moore as *A Handbook to Dante Studies* (Oxford: Blackwell, 1950). (Originally published as *Guida a Dante*.)

Davis, C.T., *Dante and the Idea of Rome* (Oxford: Clarendon Press, 1957).

D'Entreves, A.P., *Dante as a Political Thinker* (Oxford: Clarendon Press, 1952).

Ferrante, J.M., *The Political Vision of the 'Divine Comedy'* (Princeton: Princeton University Press, 1984).

Foster, K., *The Two Dantes and Other Studies* (London: Darton, Longman and Todd, 1977).

Freccero, J., *Dante: The Poetics of Conversion*, ed. R. Jacoff (Cambridge, Mass: Harvard University Press, 1986).

Hollander, R., *Allegory in Dante's 'Commedia'* (Princeton: Princeton University Press, 1969).

Holmes, G., *Dante* (Oxford: Clarendon Press, 1980).

Kirkpatrick, R., *Dante: 'The Divine Comedy'* (Cambridge: Cambridge University Press, 1987).

Singleton, C.S., *An Essay on the 'Vita nuova'* (Cambridge, Mass: Harvard University Press, 1949, repr. Baltimore: The Johns Hopkins University Press, 1977).

Singleton, C.S., *Dante's 'Commedia': Elements of Structure*, Dante Studies 1 (Cambridge, Mass: Harvard University Press, 1954, repr. Baltimore: The Johns Hopkins University Press, 1977).

Singleton, C.S., *Journey to Beatrice*, Dante Studies 2 (Cambridge, Mass: Harvard University Press, 1958, repr. Baltimore: The Johns Hopkins University Press, 1977).

Took, J.F., *Dante, Lyric Poet and Philosopher: An Introduction to the Minor Works* (Oxford: Clarendon Press, 1990).

On Dante's late-medieval context (historical, political and intellectual):

Gilson, E., *History of Christian Philosophy in the Middle Ages* (New York: Random House, 1954).

Hyde, J.K., *Society and Politics in Medieval Italy: The Evolution of the Civil Life, 1000–1350* (London: Macmillan, 1973).

Larner, J., *Italy in the Age of Dante and Petrarch, 1216–1380* (London and New York: Longman, 1980).

Leff, G., *Medieval Thought from Saint Augustine to Ockham* (Harmondsworth: Penguin, 1958).

Lewis, C.S., *The Discarded Image* (Cambridge: Cambridge University Press, 1968).

Runciman, S., *The Sicilian Vespers* (Harmondsworth: Penguin, 1960).

Schevill, F., *History of Florence from the Founding of the City through the Renaissance* (New York: Harcourt Brace, 1936).

Waley, D., *The Italian City-Republics* (London: Weidenfeld and Nicolson, 1969).

# Guelph and Ghibelline,
## a Prefatory Note

There is something impalpable, protean almost, about these two terms. That they denote, very crudely, allegiance to the Pope or the Emperor respectively is acceptable as far as it goes, but that is not far enough. It would be more accurate to say that in many central and north Italian cities, traditional political and clan divisions tended, during the course of the thirteenth century, to be polarized, in a way that they might otherwise not have been. This was owing to the presence, or rather existence, of the medieval Empire. The so-called Holy Roman Empire, that is, whose rulers were for the most part German princes. The emperors, no longer present on Italian soil after 1250, still exercised south of the Alps something akin to the influence of an electromagnetic field. The various emergent, or already emerged, communes were by the mid-1200s often characterized by pro- or anti-Imperialist traditions. The Hohenstaufen Emperor Frederick II (Barbarossa's grandson) had established his court at Palermo in 1220. From then until his death in 1250 the Imperial presence in the Italian peninsula presented a strong challenge to those communes and other political entities that favoured the Papal cause, or indeed pursued an independent line. Even after Frederick's death, Imperial power continued in Italy for nearly two decades. Under his illegitimate son Manfred (not himself an emperor), Imperial fortunes waxed in Tuscany and north-western Italy, and it was only after the papal-backed victories of Charles d'Anjou at Benevento (1266) and Tagliacozzo (1268) that Hohenstaufen power in Italy was at an end. Manfred was killed at Benevento and, after the latter victory, Charles beheaded the Hohenstaufen boy-king Conradin, aged sixteen.

By this time the Italian terms *Guelfo* and *Ghibellino* had rapidly gained currency. They are first attested in Florence in the 1240s, but in fact they hark back to the rivalry, already acute early in the twelfth century, between two powerful German dynasties. Thus

*Guelfo* derives from the Saxon *Welf* family, dukes of Bavaria and fierce enemies of the Hohenstaufen. *Ghibellino* comes from *Waiblingen*, one of the Hohenstaufen castles. Both German names were used as battle cries, it seems, perhaps as early as the Battle of Weinsberg (1140).[1] By the later thirteenth century, many Italian towns had their Guelph and Ghibelline factions, often with their own officials and a party structure. Historians have rightly stressed the local nature of many of these organizations, pointing out that their rivalries were intrinsic to the particular social and political traditions of the town in question, and often had only a tenuous link with the political stances associated with their party labels. Indeed there came to be sharp divisions, often centred on families or groups of families, within the broad Guelph traditions of certain cities: thus in Florence and Pistoia at the beginning of the fourteenth century the struggle between 'White' and 'Black' Guelphs had quite eclipsed the earlier Guelph-Ghibelline conflicts. Having said this, there was after 1268 a clear Papal interest, at times closely linked with the French House of Anjou, present and active in Italian political life. There was also an Imperialist sphere of influence, operating from a distance—with two short-lived exceptions early in the fourteenth century, when Emperors Henry VII and Lewis IV launched ill-fated military expeditions.

How does Dante fit in? Politically active in Guelph Florence, he was banished in 1302 by the Black faction (backed by Pope Boniface VIII) but quite soon estranged himself from his fellow White Guelph exiles. These frequently made common cause with expatriate Ghibellines in their various manoeuvres against the victorious Blacks. Dante too was far from ill-disposed towards the Ghibellines. It is true that the idiosyncratic system of political thought he evolved during the first decade or so of exile shows a transcendence of Guelph-Ghibelline factionalism,[2] yet it would be futile to try to distance Dante from Imperialism. His political letters of 1310–11 (V–VII) are vehemently in favour of the Emperor. And his great treatise, the *Monarchia*, is a passionate assertion of the legitimacy, desirability and necessity of a world monarchy. Although the *Monarchia* may be regarded as primarily a theoretical statement, the letters are a response to a particular political situation. Henry VII had 'descended' into Italy, as the chroniclers quaintly put it. In other words, he had invaded. Some cities offered him immediate homage, some procrastinated, others like Florence resisted, causing Dante in his fiery Letter VI to rail against what he saw as his native city's insolence.

Dante was never in any formal sense a Ghibelline. But the exiled writer of the political letters and the *Monarchia* was most certainly an Imperialist. He would not at this stage have aligned himself closely with any narrow group of expatriate Florentine Ghibellines. Yet in so far as they, like all Ghibellines, supported the Imperial cause, and especially when that cause seemed, with Henry's arrival, to be in the ascendant, Dante would surely have felt an affinity with them. Given his intimacy with great Ghibelline warlords, in particular Can Grande della Scala (and maybe also Uguccione della Faggiuola), we may justly label him a 'ghibelline'—with a small 'g'. Of course we need not label him at all. But it is clear where his sympathies lay. It was not the bitterness of exile that turned him, in defiance of his better judgement, against Florence and Guelphism. It would be more plausible to argue that he was only ever a Guelph because of family tradition, and because the only route to political advancement in Florence at the end of the thirteenth century was via the *Parte Guelfa*. Indeed, I think that when early in the nineteenth century the great lyric poet Foscolo, who revered Dante, called him 'the fugitive Ghibelline' (*il Ghibellin fuggiasco*) he was not wide of the mark.[3]

# 1

# A Florentine Childhood
## (1265–1283)

Dante Alighieri was born in medieval Florence into a family of the minor nobility who, like many of their kind, were of Guelph allegiance. As an opening sentence this may seem harmless enough, but it leaves much unsaid and may not mean a great deal to the non-specialist reader. So perhaps we should begin again.

Thirteenth-century Italy, of which the city-republic of Florence was a part, was utterly different from the modern unified nation-state which has existed for the past century and a quarter. It was also very different from, say, the High Renaissance (early sixteenth-century) Italy of Machiavelli or Raphael, dominated by five large political entities (whose government was generally of an aristocratic kind) and vulnerable to foreign military intervention on an unprecedented scale. Again, medieval Italy shows marked differences from medieval France or England or Germany. Three particular points may be stressed here. First, commercial life was of paramount importance in thirteenth-century Italy. Second, the peninsula, most markedly in its central and northern areas (and particularly Tuscany and Lombardy), was highly urbanized. Third, there was a flourishing lay culture; the long-standing notion that in the Middle Ages all learning was firmly in the hands of the Church, such that society consisted of a literate clergy and an illiterate laity, is quite false when applied to Dante's Italy. Indeed it is often wide of the mark north of the Alps. These three distinctive features of medieval Italy are closely interrelated. But the prominence of the towns is in many respects the key to the character of Dante's Italy. Population statistics are crude, but not without significance. Suffice it to say here that in 1300, the year in which the action of Dante's *Divine Comedy* is set, there were at least twenty-six towns of over 10,000 inhabitants in the Italian peninsula. The kingdom of France and the duchy of Burgundy between them had at this time fewer than twenty such towns, and the various German states less than ten. In England there were just two (London and Bristol).[1] Commercial and financial activity flourished in central and northern Italy as nowhere else in Europe, except Paris, London and Cologne, and this had led to rapid population growth in the century and a half up to 1300. The expanding city walls of many an Italian town during the period bear striking witness to this process.

Historians often refer to the thirteenth century as the great age of the Italian communes. Many, though by no means all, of the central and northern towns were republics, certain categories of whose citizens were able to play a direct part in civic and political life. The origin of the communes is often obscure, but in general it is true to say they arose in the eleventh and twelfth centuries, in conditions of turmoil consequent upon the collapse of the old Italian kingdom (a shaky structure dating back to the time of the Lombards). In the course of the thirteenth century the political, social and cultural life of the communes developed rapidly, and certain characteristic institutions of government and administration emerged. These include the offices of *podestà* (roughly equivalent to 'chief magistrate') and *capitano del popolo* (a representative of middle-class interests), and in the case of Florence and other cities the small group of officials known as *priori* (priors). Moreover in certain cities—Florence is a prime example again—the major guilds of traders and professional people exercised a great deal of political power.

A brief word should be said at this point about the aristocracy, the class into which Dante was born. A reader familiar only with feudal England after the Norman conquest might well be misled by the sentence with which this chapter began. The Italian nobility of Dante's time did not necessarily live in fortified manors or castles. It was quite normal for them to reside much of the time in the towns, though they frequently owned property in the *contado*, the countryside surrounding their city. Nor did they necessarily live on the proceeds of their estates. Indeed, they were frequently involved in trade, if only as investors. The three classes of *grandi* or *magnati* (the nobility); *borghesia* or *popolo grasso* (the middle classes); and the *popolo minuto* (the common people) are not to be thought of as watertight compartments. The close relations between the *grandi* and the leading merchants led to marriages which crossed what was

2

often only a thin dividing line. Upward social mobility was an increasing phenomenon. But Dante's own family was by no means rich, and had probably undergone something of a socio-economic decline in the thirteenth century. Certainly both his father and grandfather had at one time acted as moneylenders (though this is not something the poet is keen to tell us about). Apart from their house in Florence, the family seem to have possessed no property other than two farms at nearby Camerata and Pagnolle, together with a couple of smallholdings. In fact Dante's father, Alighiero II di Bellincione, was no powerful baron but a businessman and small landowner who operated in Florence and in and around the neighbouring commune of Prato. He was never active in politics and when his party, the Florentine Guelphs, were defeated by their Ghibelline enemies in 1260 he was not considered worth exiling. Thus although many prominent Guelphs and their families were unable to return to their native city until after the Ghibellines were themselves defeated in 1266, Dante's family were in Florence throughout the 1260s and it was there, in May 1265, that the poet was born.

Documents pertaining to the Alighieri family at this time are not exactly plentiful, but what there are have been exhaustively collected and studied by a number of eminent Italian scholars during the course of the twentieth century.[2] The most authoritative recent judgements are those of Petrocchi.[3] On the basis of such documentation as exists, Dante's father Alighiero II (born about 1220) was married twice. His first wife Bella (possibly of the Abati family) bore him Dante and later a daughter, whose name is not known. Bella died quite soon, perhaps when Dante was as young as five and certainly when he was no more than eight. Alighiero was soon remarried, to Lapa Cialuffi, who bore him a son and daughter, Francesco and Gaetana (or 'Tana'). So Dante had a sister and two half-siblings. Very little is known about his childhood, and inevitably all sorts of legends and conjectures have arisen. Might the eight-year-old have witnessed the grand ceremonies of June 1273, when Pope Gregory X and the French prince, Charles d'Anjou (brother of the late St Louis), met in Florence in an attempt to pacify the still fractious Guelphs and Ghibellines? There is no means of knowing. The first date commonly reckoned to be of significance in Dante's life is 1274, the year when the nine-year-old boy is supposed first to have met Beatrice, the beloved inspiration

3

of much of his youthful verse, and later to become, in the *Divine Comedy*, his guide through the heavens. But this date is attested only in Dante's collection of poetry with prose commentaries called the *Vita Nuova*, which will be discussed in the next chapter. The first independent document concerning the young Dante is the legal instrument (*instrumentum dotis*) dated 9 January 1277, by which he was betrothed to Gemma Donati, of a Florentine family rather more prominent than the Alighieri. Such childhood betrothals were not at all uncommon in aristocratic or mercantile families. The marriage in due course took place, most probably in 1285. However, not once is Dante's wife mentioned in his writings (unlike Beatrice).

Certainly Gemma cannot help us to understand Dante's work, but a knowledge of his education can. Although we have some information about Dante's studies after 1290 (see Chapter 3), we unfortunately know nothing for sure about what he learnt as a child. Although Florence was not at this time a university city, education was widely diffused and basic literacy high. Referring to a somewhat later period (the early fourteenth century), the contemporary Florentine chronicler Villani estimated that between 8,000 and 10,000 children received elementary education, with 1,000–1,200 attending 'abacus schools' (these provided numeracy skills for commerce) and some 550–600 going on to a further training in logic, as well as Latin.[4] In fact, as much as half the male population of Florence may have received some kind of schooling. Elementary education was in the hands of the numerous *doctores puerorum*, private individuals who taught not only reading and writing but also Latin grammar. We can only presume that Dante's first studies were of this kind.[5] Perhaps it should be explained that neither in his childhood nor at any later stage did Dante learn Greek. Knowledge of Greek in the medieval West was uncommon, and the full-scale revival of Greek studies had to wait until the fifteenth century. Although Dante did attend certain ecclesiastical centres of learning later on, he was taught in his childhood and adolescence by laymen. But apart from formal instruction in Latin grammar, Dante would have learnt a great deal about lay culture, not least vernacular poetry and prose, in a more informal manner. Florence was characterized at this time by a lively interest in the relatively recent tradition of Italian verse, which for practical purposes dates only from the 1220s. Moreover, the Florence of

4

Dante's youth was an international trading centre whose merchants, with their many business trips abroad, brought home with them the fruits of their contact with other languages and cultures. Of special importance here are the contacts with France, both northern and southern. These matters will be the concern of the earlier part of the chapter which now follows.

# 2

# Beatrice and the *Vita Nuova*
## (1283–1295)

### (i) Early Influences: The Medieval Lyric; Brunetto Latini; the Roman Poets

Dante's earliest writing, indeed his entire literary output up until his exile at the age of thirty-six, consisted of lyric poems in Italian (together with vernacular prose commentaries on some of them). His first poem can probably be dated to the year 1283, and for the rest of the 1280s his output was substantial. Some thirty-one of these poems he later assembled in an anthology interspersed with prose. This was the *Vita Nuova*, the extraordinary account of his love for Beatrice Portinari, composed probably in 1293–95. Before considering this work, and the poems that preceded it, a very brief sketch of Italian poetry prior to Dante may be helpful.

Italian emerged as a literary language markedly later than, say, Anglo-Saxon, Old French or Provençal. It was not until the 1220s that the first lyric verse was written. Most of this was the product of the so-called *Scuola Siciliana*, or Sicilian School, a group of love poets resident at or associated with the court established at Palermo in 1220 by the half-German, half-Norman Emperor Frederick II. These poets owed a great deal to the flourishing tradition of troubadour poetry written in southern France from about 1100 until late in the thirteenth century. Not only did the Sicilians adapt many of the well-known Provençal themes, such as the lover as servant or vassal of his (typically distant and unreciprocating) lady, but they also modelled much of their vocabulary on the quasi-technical terminology of the troubadours. Compared to the vast corpus of Provençal verse (over 600 manuscripts of the twelfth and thirteenth centuries have survived), the Sicilians produced little—though it seems they invented the sonnet. But then their *Scuola* was short-lived. After the Emperor's death in 1250 there was a period of political upheaval, although the court was continued under his sons Conrad IV and Manfred. The chief focus of poetic activity in Italy now moved north: the literary history of the mid-century is dominated by the so-called Siculo-Tuscan, or simply Tuscan, School. Here the cities of Arezzo and Lucca (not quite at this stage Florence) are the most important. The central figure is Guittone d'Arezzo, whose large and varied corpus of poetry was not confined to amorous themes and exercised a powerful influence in the 1260s and 1270s. Indeed, it influenced Dante's earliest poems in the 1280s, notwithstanding his later strictures against Guittone. A number of other poets from central Italy are generally referred to as the *Guittoniani*, among them Bonagiunta da Lucca. We encounter his spirit in the *Divine Comedy* (*Purg.* XXIV, 49–63), talking to Dante about his and Dante's own poetry, to the manifest advantage of the latter! Contemporary with Bonagiunta was Guido Guinizelli of Bologna. Although happily acknowledging his poetic debt to Guittone, he displays a number of stylistic and thematic features, and here chiefly his emphasis on the ennobling power of love. These were early on identified, notably by Dante himself, as looking forward. What they looked forward to was the next major stage in Italian literature: the emergence of the *Dolce Stil Novo* (or 'Sweet New Style')—the phrase is Dante's own.

The *Stil Novo* poets were a small group of young Tuscans, including some Florentine aristocrats, most of whom were known to one another personally. They strove to achieve a certain purity of diction, rigorously eliminating from their verse all Gallicisms, Provençalisms and Latinisms, and most of them, though not all, shared common views as to the nature of love. An awareness that they were doing, or trying to do, something novel is evident, but it may be going too far to describe this loose, informal group of Stilnovists as a literary movement. Dante himself belonged to the group in the 1280s; its chief exponent, however, was Guido Cavalcanti, Dante's senior by some ten years. Dante's close friendship with Guido dates from around 1283. He referred to him as 'il primo amico' ('my best friend'), and it is to him that the *Vita Nuova* was dedicated. Cavalcanti was not only an outstanding poet but also very interested in philosophical matters, though he wrote no philosophical works as such. It is generally supposed that he exerted a strong formative influence upon the young Dante.

An equally important, though very different, influence was exercised by an older Florentine, Brunetto Latini (born about 1220). Readers of the *Divine Comedy* will remember that Dante meets Brunetto almost halfway through Hell, among the spirits of those who in their earthly lives had (apparently) been guilty of sodomy (*Inf.* XV, 22–124). However, I am not here concerned with the difficult questions raised by that literary encounter, but with Brunetto's important role in the Florentine culture of his time.[1] He was a bourgeois, and by profession a notary, a member of that flourishing breed which in thirteenth-century Italy catered for the increasingly complex legal and administrative demands of the communes. He was also a 'rhetorician', skilled in the vital diplomatic art of writing official letters, in accordance with certain elaborate conventions, or formal rules of expression. Some grounding in rhetoric, the art of effective verbal expression, was a standard component of medieval education at this time. By 1253 Brunetto held a position of considerable importance: he was Secretary and Letter-writer to the governing council of Florence. He might have continued in this administrative role, had not his life been dramatically changed, as Dante's was to be, by political events.

After the 1260 Ghibelline military victory at Montaperti, Brunetto, who at the time of the battle was on his way back from a mission in Spain, decided to take refuge in France. Here he remained for over five years, in various locations from Montpellier to Paris. Although he found notarial employment, this period of exile is famous as the occasion for Brunetto's most extensive work, an encyclopaedia, written in French: the *Livres dou Tresor*. This was not intended for scholars, but for literate merchants and others who wanted relatively easy access to some notions of rhetoric, ethics, politics, history, natural science and so forth. The book's contents are not original and derive from well-known authorities; Brunetto was above all a communicator and teacher.

A further political development, the momentous defeat of the Ghibelline forces in 1266 at Benevento, enabled Brunetto to return to Florence, where he was once again in the forefront of civic life until his death in 1294. He also continued writing in the vernacular: his Italian didactic poem the *Tesoretto* aimed, like the *Tresor*, to present knowledge in an easily assimilable form. He turned his attention to the ancient world as well: his *Rettorica* is an Italian translation, with commentary, of part of Cicero's *De inventione*. He is mentioned by contemporary chroniclers as having played a key role in the development of Florentine learning. If this seems surprising, it should be remembered that thirteenth-century Florence was not a centre of higher education like Bologna or Padua. Brunetto, then, was far more than just another professional notary and rhetorician; he was an encyclopaedist in the vernacular, a purveyor of general learning to the literate and intelligent who were not themselves scholars. In this respect his aims were not dissimilar to those of Dante himself, as stated in the opening lines of his philosophical treatise the *Convivio*. Here Dante explains that his purpose is to instruct those who have not the time for study, owing to their family and civic duties ('la cura familiare e civile'). That Dante was enormously endebted to Brunetto is beyond question, though it is no longer generally held that he was in any formal sense the young poet's tutor.

Together with these medieval influences there was the ancient world, chiefly represented in this stage of Dante's development by the Roman poets. His first acquaintance with classical literature would have occurred as part of his youthful training in grammar. No doubt anthologies, mnemonic couplets and so forth played their part, but it is clear that Dante had firsthand knowledge, which over the years was to become extensive, of the major ancient poets then accessible in Italy. It has been established that thirteenth-century Italian education included a core curriculum of Virgil, Ovid and Horace, with the frequent addition of Lucan and/or Statius.[2] In fact Dante, whose reading of all these authors was to continue well after his exile in 1302, pays especial tribute to them in the *Divine Comedy*. One of the most notable passages in the *Inferno* (IV, 79–105) describes his meeting in the circle of Limbo (the abode of the virtuous pagans) with a *bella scola*, a distinguished coterie consisting precisely of his guide Virgil, together with Horace, Ovid and Lucan. To these Romans Dante adds the name of Homer himself, the supreme poet (*poeta sovrano*). To Virgil's delighted approval, the group welcome Dante as a sixth among their circle of wisdom. Statius too would undoubtedly have been present here, but Dante apparently believed him to have been a Christian, and so we find him in the *Purgatorio*, where he appears as a major character from Canto XXI onwards. And during Virgil's conversation with him in Canto XXII (13–15; 97–105), the literary roll-call of Limbo is extended to include Juvenal, Terence, Caecilius, Plautus, Varius and Persius. Although Dante's knowledge of some of these may have been slight (indeed Caecilius' works did not survive and Plautus was practically unknown in Dante's day), the influence of the *bella scola* of master poets (Statius included) is very evident throughout his writings. Virgil exerted far and away the most profound and wide-ranging influence. Indeed Virgil as a character in the *Comedy* acknowledges that Dante knew the *Aeneid* in its entirety (*Inf.* XX, 114). In addition to this thorough command of the great epic, he was also very familiar with Virgil's *Eclogues*. He knew several of Ovid's works, besides his *Metamorphoses*, as well as the *Thebaid* and the *Pharsalia*—the epics of Statius and Lucan respectively.[3] Horace's imprint was the slightest. It is worth repeating the statistical findings of Moore's classic study, written a century ago.[4] Moore found that in Dante's writings as a whole there were about 200 quotations from, or allusions and references to, Virgil, about 100 to Ovid, some 50 to Lucan, 30–40 to Statius and just 10–20 in the case of Horace. Only the Vulgate Bible and Aristotle figure more prominently than Virgil. Already in the 1280s Dante had embarked upon the study of Latin poetry, something that was to prove one of the most fruitful engagements in European literature.

## (ii) The *Detto d'Amore* and the *Fiore*

I return now to Dante's own writing in the 1280s. Apart from lyric poetry in the Stilnovist manner, it is possible that in his very early twenties (perhaps by the end of 1286) he wrote the *Detto d'Amore* and the *Fiore*. Both of these are controversial, in the sense of having given rise to controversy over their authorship. Both exist in a single manuscript source only and remained unpublished until late in the nineteenth century. They are the only works of any importance to have been seriously proposed this century for admission to the canon of Dante's writings. Their attribution to Dante has been fiercely contested, partly on stylistic grounds, and partly owing to their subject matter. The battle has raged for years and has tended to be highly technical, so that even a brief résumé of it would be beyond the scope and purpose of the present book. However, many leading *Dantisti* now agree with the view of the authoritative Gianfranco Contini, namely that these poems are the authentic

10

work of Dante.[5] They both represent the results of his early contact with French culture, and more specifically with one of the greatest vernacular enterprises in the Middle Ages, the *Roman de la Rose* (the *Romance of the Rose*).

This massive amatory epic (which is much more besides) runs to over 22,000 lines, and was written in northern French (not Provençal) from roughly 1230 to 1280. The first 4,000 lines or so are the work of Guillaume de Lorris (who died about 1237) and the rest we owe to Jean de Meun. By contrast with the *Divine Comedy*, the principal narrative technique employed by both authors is that of bald personification allegory. The characters in the poem, that is to say, are named after and are representative of certain moral abstractions or psychological dispositions. So it is that the lover-protagonist encounters in a dream such characters as *Oiseuse* (Idleness), *Courteisie* (Courtesy), *Bel Acueil* (Fair Welcome), *Malebouche* (Calumny), *Jalousie* (Jealousy) and so on. Having been introduced by the god of Love to the prospect of the amorous rewards consequent upon perseverance, the Lover, after various mishaps, manages to kiss (briefly) the Rose, the object of his desire. Shortly afterwards Guillaume's section of the poem (which is considerably more refined and restrained than its sequel) ends. Jean de Meun's learned and, according to one line of inter-pretation, worldly-wise continuation recounts the Lover's subse-quent vicissitudes with much scholarly digression. *Raison* (Reason) finally fails to dissuade the Lover from what she sees as his foolish resolve, and with the help of *Amis* (Friend) and *Fauxsemblant* (Deception), the Lover finally plucks the Rose. The thin veil of allegory notwithstanding, the physical consummation of love—deflowering, indeed—is here voluptuously celebrated. This all-too-brief summary cannot possibly convey the richness and variety of the *Rose*, which has now been the object of widely differing critical attention for over a hundred years.

The question for us is, how does Dante relate to this extraordi-nary poem? There can be no doubt that he knew it well—there are reminiscences and echoes of it almost throughout his undisputed writings, from the *Vita Nuova* to the *Purgatorio*. But with the *Detto d'Amore* and the *Fiore* we are dealing not with reminiscences but with a free and imaginative re-working of the matter of the French romance. The *Detto*, generally presumed to be the earlier of the two works, is based only on de Lorris' section of the *Rose*. It is

11

written in seven-syllable couplets, the very same metre as Brunetto's *Tesoretto*,[6] and shows considerable mastery of and delight in the technical difficulties and challenges of Italian verse. As John Took has observed, it looks back to Guittone d'Arezzo, whilst having much of the *Dolce Stil Novo* about it. And as Took goes on to say, the interest of the *Detto* lies not so much in narrative as in psychological and emotional self-analysis.[7]

The *Fiore* is a much more substantial piece. Consisting of no less than 232 sonnets, it covers, in a skilfully condensed adaptation, the entire narrative of the *Roman de la Rose* (albeit shorn of certain episodes, such as the long speeches of Nature and Genius). In interpreting Dante's poem, critics have tended to emphasize the worldly cynicism, the exaltation of self-interest, the apparently exuberant subversion of the idealistic elements of so-called courtly love—all of which typify Jean de Meun's section of the *Rose*. This line of interpretation sees the *Fiore* as 'an exercise in bourgeois "realism", urban, comic, and reductionist'.[8] 'Bourgeois' here is simply being used to indicate a lay, urban outlook, sceptical of courtly-chivalric idealism, an outlook surely prevalent in the Florence of the 1280s, and one which we have no reason to suppose a young poet (albeit of aristocratic origins) would not have been receptive of or sympathetic towards. Took himself, however, inclines to the different view that Dante's purpose in the *Fiore* is to invite the reader to ponder the tension between two different types of love: the aim is to pose a moral problem, not to subvert a set of values. But however we are to interpret the *Fiore* it is, as Took again so aptly observes, a response to what must have been for Dante a highly impressive vernacular poem: the *Rose*, in all its encyclopaedic variety, reflecting a diversity of ancient and medieval thought, from Boethius to St Bernard of Clairvaux. The *Rose* represented 'a challenge, an invitation to do as much again, and more besides, in Italian'.[9] The 232 sonnets are Dante's response to that challenge. Their ethos and tone may indeed be different from the *Dolce Stil Novo* poems, whether those included in the *Vita Nuova* or not, but this is not a valid reason for denying that Dante could have written them. In fact two groups of poems that are indisputably his, dating from the same time as the *Vita Nuova* (or a little later) are markedly different from it in style and content. These are the earthily comic *Tenzone* with Forese Donati (an exchange of six sonnets, three from each poet) and the so-called *rime petrose* (or 'stony' poems).

12

## (iii) From Bologna to Caprona

It would appear that around the time of the completion of the *Fiore* Dante spent a period of perhaps a few months in Bologna, probably late 1286 to early 1287. This may well have been his first experience of a non-Florentine milieu (although many believe he was briefly involved in a military excursion in 1285, which will be discussed shortly). And Bologna would certainly have been the first major city, other than that of his birth, with which Dante came into contact. Evidence for his presence in Bologna is threefold, not all of it equally persuasive. First there is the famous sonnet 'Non mi poriano già mai fare ammenda' ('[My eyes] will never make amends to me') in which mention is made of the Garisenda, the well-known tower in Bologna. This poem is not about the tower, but about love: Dante reproves his eyes for gazing upon the great tower and in so doing missing the chance of beholding a lady of surpassing beauty and reputation. Of course this does not prove that Dante did see the Garisenda in person, and it certainly tells us nothing about when he may have done so. But the second piece of evidence may well do. The Bolognese Enrichetto delle Querce, another notary, made his own transcription of this sonnet of Dante's to fill up the space in a legal document, datable to the second half of 1287. So the poem was known in Bologna by then—a time when Dante's youthful verse does not appear otherwise to have been known outside Florence—and this *may* suggest he was in Bologna in person. Thirdly, several of his lyric poems that can be dated to around this time show stylistic and thematic differences from his very first verse (still influenced by Guittone) as well as from the *Detto* and the *Fiore*. These poems in fact show the influence of the Bolognese poet Guinizelli. They are considered to be an intermediate stage between Dante's very earliest 'Guittonian' lyrics and the poetry of the later 1280s, which shows the full influence of Cavalcanti and the Florentine *Stil Novo*. Critics have therefore seen in the 'Bolognese' poems further evidence that Dante did visit Bologna at this time.

The purpose of the visit remains obscure. It is not unreasonable to conjecture that, apart from contacts with the Bolognese poets, and perhaps with the young Cino da Pistoia, who may already have been studying law there, Dante would have frequented the company of various fellow-Florentines present in the city at the time (including a relative of Cavalcanti). But despite enthusiastic efforts

13

by some Italian scholars earlier this century, there is no evidence that he ever attended the famous university. In fact over the years numerous critics have striven to give Dante a degree, or at any rate to credit him with a period of university study. So, apart from the Bologna conjecture (not in itself an implausible one), we have had the Paris theory and indeed the Oxford hypothesis—this last being especially dear to Gladstone, who found it agreeable to believe that the poet he so loved had attended his own beloved university.[10] Yet there is not one shred of evidence that Dante ever set foot outside central and northern Italy. Nor are these conjectures as to Dante's involvement in higher education remotely necessary. The breadth and depth of learning so apparent in his later works is partly (though only partly) explicable in terms of his semi-formal studies in Florence in the early 1290s. But, much more importantly, he was in the final analysis self-taught. So are all great men of learning.

Turning now away from literary and intellectual matters, and on to a more public aspect of Dante's life in the later 1280s, he was not yet active in politics, but his first (and in all probability only) military experience belongs to these years. It is a possibility, though nothing more, that he was involved in a small Florentine expeditionary force in late 1285 to early 1286 (about a year before the visit to Bologna). In autumn 1285 hostilities had broken out between the two Tuscan cities of Siena and Arezzo. The latter persuaded the inhabitants of the small town of Poggio Santa Cecilia, in Sienese territory, to rebel against Siena and sent them considerable military assistance. Siena responded by laying siege to the town and requesting help from Florence. This request was granted, and at the end of November a force of one hundred Florentine cavalry rode southward. The date of their return to Florence is not known, but it seems they were involved only in the initial stages of the siege, for perhaps a matter of weeks, rather than months. (In fact the castle of Poggio Santa Cecilia did not fall to the Sienese until April 1286.) There is no reason why a young man of Dante's class should not have taken part, though it has to be said that the conjecture that he did so rests exclusively on a passage from the *Vita Nuova* (IX, 1–4). Here Dante, referring it seems to this period, speaks of being obliged to leave Florence for a time, in the company of many fellow-citizens.

But although the Poggio Santa Cecilia episode must remain open to question, scholars no longer doubt Dante's involvement in two campaigns in 1289. The first concerned Arezzo once again, and was the culmination of the war of 1288–89 between that city and Florence. The principal causes of the conflict were, first, the animosity between Arezzo (by now staunchly Ghibelline) and Florence (by now under Guelph control for over twenty years), and second, doubtless at least as important, the fact that Arezzo barred an important trade route between Florence and Rome. Preparations for conflict on a far larger scale than that of the Poggio Santa Cecilia expedition were probably well under way in Florence during 1287, and it may even be that Dante's return from Bologna in that year indicates that he was recalled. The climax of the war was the battle of Campaldino (a plain to the north of Arezzo) on 11 June 1289. This ended in bloody defeat for the Aretines. The Florentine forces were commanded jointly by Corso Donati and Vieri de' Cerchi (two *grandi* who, as we shall see, found themselves only a few years later as the heads of two violently opposed factions within the Florentine Guelph party). Arezzo's Ghibelline troops were led by Buonconte da Montefeltro, who was himself killed in the battle. (In the *Purgatorio* [V, 85–129] his soul converses with Dante, vividly describing the battlefield scene.)

Was Dante there? The evidence here rests partly on a passage in the *Inferno* (XXII, 1–9), where Dante claims to have seen as an eye-witness military action in the territory of Arezzo. More striking is the testimony of Leonardo Bruni, the Florentine scholar and politician whose biography of Dante dates from the 1430s. Here he quotes in Italian from the text of an otherwise unknown letter (the original, now lost, would probably have been in Latin) in which Dante briefly alludes to the battle. He states that he was not a novice in military matters (this might refer to Poggio Santa Cecilia, or simply to a period of training), but he was very frightened, an emotion which gave way to great joy at the massive defeat of Arezzo's forces: 'la parte ghibellina fu quasi del tutto morta e disfatta' ('the Ghibellines were almost all killed or vanquished').[11] Though it is possible that the letter is an invention of Bruni's, the consensus now is that it is genuine: many readers have detected an unmistakeable ring of truth in it. Shortly after Campaldino, it seems Dante took part in further military action, in western Tuscany, near Pisa. Troops from Pisa and Lucca as well as from Florence were involved. The campaign centred on the fortress of Caprona. This had previously been held by Judge Nino Visconti, an exiled Pisan

Guelph allied to the Guelph city of Lucca. But it was then retaken in the summer of 1289 by Guido da Montefeltro (Bonconte's redoubtable father, then in his mid-sixties) on behalf of Ghibelline Pisa. (Both Nino and Guido are to loom large as characters in the *Divine Comedy*.[12]) Lucca asked its Guelph ally Florence for help. Although briefly tied down with the aftermath of Campaldino, the Florentines were soon able to detach a considerable part of their force in eastern Tuscany. Some 400 cavalry and 2,000 infantry set off westward, probably in late July. This expeditionary force helped Judge Visconti and the Lucchesi to retake Caprona on 16 August. It is held that Dante was among those 400 knights, and indeed there is a direct 'eyewitness' reference to the siege in the *Inferno* (XXI, 94–96), a much more specific reference in fact than the allusion to Arezzo in the following canto. To sum up, 1289 was a year of outward, as well as inward, activity for Dante; it saw him in the saddle, as well as at the desk.

### (iv) Beatrice

1289 also saw the death of Beatrice's father: Folco Portinari died on 31 December. Discussion of the identity and history of Beatrice is of necessity brief, given the paucity of hard information about her. This need not unduly concern the reader of Dante, however, for the Beatrice of the *Vita Nuova* and the *Divine Comedy* is, of course, a literary creature. That does not mean there was no real Beatrice lying behind Dante's poetic creation. His two great fourteenth-century successors in Italian literature, Petrarch and Boccaccio, celebrated in their writings their love for Laura and Fiammetta respectively. Much time has been wasted in hypotheses as to the identity of these ladies, if indeed they existed. But from the earliest days of Dante criticism, it has been held that there was a real Beatrice, and that it was possible to identify her. The question 'Who was Beatrice?' had already been asked by Benvenuto da Imola, in his Latin commentary written in the 1370s, half a century after Dante's death. 'Sed quae est ista Beatrix?' asks Benvenuto, and proceeds to assure us that she was really and truly ('realiter et vere') a Florentine lady of great beauty.[13] He does not mention her family, but Boccaccio does.

Giovanni Boccaccio was not only the foremost of medieval Italian story-tellers; he was also (among many other things) the first professional Dante scholar. In the last year or so of his life (1373–74) he was employed by the Commune of Florence to give public *Lecturae Dantis,* that is readings from the *Divine Comedy* and explanatory lectures upon those readings. (Thus was inaugurated something of a fashion; it has been intermittent, but today, more than six centuries after Boccaccio's death, *Lecturae Dantis* take place in many centres around the world.) Boccaccio tells us that Dante's Beatrice was Bice, daughter of Folco Portinari, and that she was married to Simone de' Bardi. Or rather, he told this to a public audience in Florence, in the course of one of his *Lecturae.*[14] The Portinari and the Bardi had both been prominent Florentine families (far more so than the Alighieri, incidentally) and were still prominent in the Florence of the 1370s. Boccaccio is frequently fanciful when far from home, so to speak, but it is unlikely that his public identification of Beatrice with Folco's daughter would have gone unchallenged if untrue. Accepting, then, this traditional identification of Beatrice, we have the following meagre data. 1287 (probably)—marriage of Beatrice Portinari to Simone de' Bardi, a member of the very wealthy Florentine family who founded the Bardi banking house (it was of European importance, but crashed in 1345 when Edward III of England declined to repay his Hundred Years' War debts[15]). December 1289—death of Folco Portinari (an outstanding citizen of Florence, who had held high political office three times in the 1280s). 8 June 1290—death of Beatrice herself, at the age of twenty-four. Little more can be said with any degree of certainty about Beatrice de' Portinari. It is high time that we looked at her as she appears in the *Vita Nuova*, which is however not about her, but about Dante.

## (v) The *Vita Nuova*

Although the precise date of the *Vita Nuova* is not known, it was clearly written after Beatrice's death, and most probably in the period 1293–95. Some of the poems in it were written at least ten years previously. To call it an anthology might be misleading if that term were taken as suggesting something miscellaneous, a mere collecting together of Dante's verse. The thirty-one *Vita Nuova* poems are a deliberate selection from those Dante had written in the previous decade or so, amounting to more than twice that number. He scrupulously discarded any that were not central to (or might interfere with) his theme. Ostensibly that theme is the origin and development of Dante's love for Beatrice; more subtly it is the development of his understanding of love itself. The poems are not presented in isolation; they are linked by expository passages of highly sophisticated prose. Each poem is accompanied by an account of the circumstances that led to its composition and a brief analysis of its structure and meaning.

This amazingly rich little book (it is called a *libello* in the first of its forty-two short chapters) begins with an account of Dante's first sight of Beatrice, when he was aged nine and she eight. He does not see her again for nine years: the number nine has a special symbolic significance throughout the *Vita Nuova*. She now honours him with her greeting; he is filled with joy but later she is aloof, and he is devastated. But he subsequently finds fulfilment simply in praising her, without hope of reward. His poems of praise begin before her death and continue after it. However, more than a year after her death, Dante is in some undefined sense consoled by a mysterious and unnamed noble lady, a *donna gentile*. This episode notwithstanding, he returns to his post-mortem devotion to Beatrice, and the *libello* ends with a momentous reaffirmation of his commitment to praise her. From the very beginning Beatrice is presented not only as a paragon of beauty but also as supremely virtuous. She has a beneficial, indeed a spiritually curative, effect upon those whom she greets. Her very name is no accident: she is, literally, one who blesses (a *beatrix*). This is so apparent, we are told, that many referred to her as 'Beatrice' even though they did not know this was in fact her name. Throughout the book she is surrounded by religious imagery, if that is not putting it too mildly. Before her death she is eagerly awaited by the angels in Heaven, a Heaven whose only defect is the lack of her presence. And when she does die, not only does Dante break off one of his longer poems after just the first stanza, but he begins the next chapter (XXVIII) with an unexpected and highly dramatic Biblical quotation: 'Quomodo sedet sola civitas plena populo! facta est quasi vidua domina gentium' ('How lonely sits the once populous city! She who was Queen of the nations is become as a widow'). Nothing less than the opening of the prophet Jeremiah's Lamentations will do to convey the poet's sense of loss. The final poem of the *Vita Nuova* shows us Beatrice in Heaven, resplendent and the recipient of celestial honour. The final prose chapter shows us Dante planning to lavish upon her an unprecedented kind of poetic honour.

Moving on, let us focus briefly on what seems to be most novel in the *Vita Nuova*. Its novelty is underlined by its deliberate structure. The events narrated, misty and aethereal as they generally seem, are in fact organized in two cycles, the second of which broadly corresponds with, and mirrors, the first. At the beginning of the *libello* Dante appears as a fairly conventional courtly lover. His joy derives from Beatrice's greeting (the word 'salutation', for those with an interest in etymology, would however do greater justice to the Italian *saluto*). This greeting is his sole reward. There is no question of a kiss, let alone anything more; we are a long way from the ethos of the *Fiore*. But before long this joyous equilibrium is shattered. In Chapter X Dante relates how Beatrice denied him her greeting, her salutation. To put it more bluntly, she cut him in the street. This leads to grief on his part, and a somewhat self-centred lamentation of her coldness, her apparent mockery of his love. In the all-important Chapter XVIII, however, we have a breakthrough: the first of Dante's two great discoveries about the nature of love. He tells us that he was in the company of certain noble ladies ('gentili donne'), who had come to know of his love for Beatrice. She, fortunately, was not present, for by this stage Dante found her proximity too much to endure. One of the unnamed ladies asks Dante the aim of his most unusual ('novissimo') love. He explains that formerly Beatrice's salutation had been the end of all his desires, the source of his bliss ('beatitudine'). But now, he adds, that salutation is withheld. Yet the god of Love has relocated, so to speak, the source of his bliss in something he cannot be deprived of. When pressed to identify this new source he simply says: 'In quelle parole che lodano la donna mia' ('In those words with which I praise my Lady'). He then tells us that thenceforth he proposed to adopt a new subject matter for his poetry: the praise of 'questa gentilissima' and nothing else. Indeed in the very next chapter we have the first of the 'praise poems', the great *canzone* 'Donne ch'avete intelletto d'amore' ('O you ladies who understand love'). So the eighteenth chapter is a watershed. Dante has come to a new conception of love. No longer is it a bargain: far from expecting something in reward for his love, he realizes that his love poetry is its own reward. Thus ends the first of the two structural cycles.

The second begins with Dante once again in a state of joy and equilibrium, now writing poems of praise. This inner state, however, is shattered, once again by an external event: death deprives him of Beatrice. Again, he falls into a state of grief and lamentation. His poetry seems insufficient to sustain him, and he fears that being now cut off from his beloved, his love will waver. Indeed in this weak state he is prey to the enigmatic *donna gentile*. But the symmetry is re-established at the very end of the work, with the final sonnet 'Oltre la spera' ('Beyond the sphere'). Here Dante comes upon his second discovery about the nature of love. Beatrice is now glorified in Heaven, more beautiful and virtuous than ever. But far from being cut off from her, Dante can send his sighs soaring up beyond the outermost of the physical heavens, beyond the limits of the material cosmos, to where she gazes on God. His love will survive her physical death: that is the new understanding, the 'intelligenza nova', that the god of Love has vouchsafed to him. At the end of the first cycle, he had resolved to praise Beatrice in his verse. Now he goes further: if God grant that he may live a few more years, he hopes to say of Beatrice things that have never been said about any other woman. (He did live more than a few more years and he did say them—in the *Divine Comedy*.) That then is an outline of a fundamental pattern (not the only one) governing the *Vita Nuova*: two successive external blows are overcome by two internal discoveries. Or as Boyde, one of the foremost modern interpreters of Dante, has put it: 'Paradise is twice lost from external causes, and twice regained through a deeper understanding of love coming from within'.[16]

# 3
# The Consolation of Philosophy
## (1290–1296)

### (i) Boethius and Cicero

This chapter begins a little before the compilation of the *Vita Nuova* and seeks mainly to investigate Dante's very rapid and thorough absorption in philosophical inquiries, something which took place shortly after Beatrice's death. It is as well to clarify at the outset what is meant by 'philosophy' in a medieval context. A modern reader will readily associate 'philosophy' with a certain kind of intellectual investigation, based upon general principles, into such areas as logic, ethics, language and meaning, the relationship between the human mind and the body, the problem of human freedom of choice and action, and so forth. Now all these areas were also, to a greater or lesser extent, the concern of medieval thinkers, but in the thirteenth century, and for hundreds of years thereafter, the term 'philosophy' was understood to cover a far wider field than it does today. In particular, it included the natural sciences (which used to be known in English as Natural Philosophy). So for Dante philosophy would have included astronomy, geography and physiology (*inter alia*), as well as logic, ethics and metaphysics. Another important difference concerns the methodology of medieval philosophers: a great deal of their speculation took as its starting-point the pronouncements of an earlier authoritative writer (an *auctoritas*) which were then commented and elaborated upon. Aristotle is the example *par excellence* here. This approach is quite alien to post-Renaissance philosophy, which sees itself as proceeding in a sceptical manner from a bare minimum of pre-suppositions or self-evident truths. So different has medieval philosophy seemed both from that of the modern world and from that of antiquity, that in many British universities undergraduate courses dealing with the history of Western philosophy jump straight from Plato and Aristotle to the seventeenth-century writings of Descartes, a leap of very nearly 2,000 years.[1]

So much by way of preliminary clarification. Although Dante's wide learning is not made fully apparent until after his exile from Florence in 1302 (in the *Convivio*, in the *Monarchia* and not least in the *Divine Comedy* itself), it seems that his basic grounding in philosophy was achieved in a highly intensive period of study in the early 1290s. As a child and a youth, he would have learnt Latin and also the rudiments of what were then called the Liberal Arts (seven subjects which constituted the backbone of medieval education, namely: Grammar, Dialectic, Rhetoric, Arithmetic, Music, Geometry and Astronomy). Cavalcanti and Brunetto Latini would doubtless have alerted him to many questions looking beyond the basic curriculum of the Liberal Arts to more properly speculative areas. But Dante himself tells us that his real initiation into philosophy occurred only in the early 1290s, when he was over twenty-five. The key text here is from the *Convivio*, Dante's first work of philosophy in the full medieval sense of the word. In the *Convivio* (II, xii, 1–7) he tells us that after Beatrice's death (June 1290) he was at first inconsolable. Yet after a little while ('alquanto tempo') he sought consolation, not from other people, nor from himself, but from reading works that had in the past consoled others. He refers specifically to two works by Latin authors, Cicero and the considerably later Boethius. These writings made such an impression upon him that he was fired with enthusiasm for philosophy, which he began to imagine as a compassionate lady ('una donna gentile ... in atto ... misericordioso'). He then began to frequent those places where (in Florence at any rate) this *donna gentile* was most in evidence, namely the schools run by members of the religious orders ('le scuole de li religiosi'). He also attended certain undefined 'disputations by philosophers' ('le disputazioni de li filosofanti'). Such was Dante's enthusiasm for this new kind of intellectual absorption and fulfilment (evidently going far beyond his previous experience) that he continued in it for about two and a half years, at the end of which time love for philosophy had driven out every other thought from his mind. Despite some intricate scholarly discussion as to which precise period Dante is referring to in this passage, there is no doubt that we are dealing with the years 1291–93.

This intriguing retrospective chapter from the *Convivio* invites further comment. Let us start with Dante's two consoling books, and first with the *De Consolatione Philosophiae* (*On the Consolation of Philosophy*) by Severinus Boethius. Its author was a Roman philosopher and statesman from late antiquity. In fact he lived after the fall of the Roman Empire and rose to become a leading administrator of the Ostrogothic Emperor Theodoric the Great. He was probably a Christian and certainly an intellectual, thoroughly involved with the revived form of Hellenistic philosophy known as neo-Platonism. Accused by political opponents of conniving with the Senate against Theodoric, Boethius was deprived of his official status, imprisoned (in Pavia) and executed in AD 524. He is famous for his translations from Aristotle, but above all for the *De Consolatione*, five books of Latin prose and verse written during his imprisonment. The work begins with the apparition of Philosophy, personified as a noble and radiant lady, who consoles him in the face of death; in fact the whole treatise is cast in the form of a dialogue between Boethius and his consoler. This personification was not Boethius' original invention; in what are known as the Sapiential Books of the Old Testament (particularly Proverbs 8 and Wisdom 8–9) we find a female personification of Wisdom (*Sophia* in Greek). And 'philosophy' originally meant precisely the love of wisdom. Boethius' philosophical treatise was one of the most widely-read books throughout the Middle Ages and beyond. It was translated into many languages, including Italian and French, as well as various forms of English: King Alfred the Great produced an Anglo-Saxon version, and Chaucer one in Middle English. In fact, Alfred was not the only English monarch to do so, since Elizabeth I later joined the distinguished company with her Boethius of 1593.

Dante's second author was Cicero, the Roman statesman and great master of Latin prose, who lived in the first century BC. Though not himself an original philosopher, he was one of the main channels through which Greek thought and culture were transmitted to the Roman world. The particular Ciceronian text that Dante now tackled was, like Boethius' work, concerned with the therapeutic power of philosophy. Entitled *De Amicitia* (*On Friendship*), it is also sometimes known as the *Laelius*, since it contains Cicero's account of the consolatory advice given by Laelius to his sons-in-law, following the death of his friend Scipio Africanus the Younger. Dante frankly admits that he found Boethius and Cicero hard at

first, but on the basis of his grounding in Latin ('l'arte di gram-
matica') and a modicum of his own native wit ('un poco di mio
ingegno'), he made such progress as he could. Dante's difficulties
are likely to have been due not to inadequate Latin (as some have
thought), but simply to his unfamiliarity at this stage with philosophical works of this kind. Having said that, it should be realized
that both these works are far more accessible than the intricate and
highly technical philosophical and theological treatises of Dante's
own century, with which, however, he was quite soon to feel at
home. But the real importance of Boethius and Cicero for Dante at
this time was that reading them unlocked a door, so to speak. As
Dante puts it in the *Convivio* (II, xii, 5), just as someone looking
for silver may unexpectedly discover gold, so he found much more
than comfort in his grief: he glimpsed a new world of learning via
the thinkers and doctrines mentioned by Boethius and Cicero, and
he came to realize that philosophy was a thing supreme ('somma
cosa'). I know of no better gloss on Dante's words than what
Kenelm Foster wrote in 1965: 'He found he had entered a marvellous new world; real, yet grander than any dream: both translucent
and mysterious: an immense unfathomable *order* of parts in a
whole, with at its centre a luminous experience which from now
on became the deepest spring and motive of his life—the experience of his own mind seeing truth.'[2]

## (ii) Aristotelianism and the Friars

Inspired by this new intuitive understanding of the greatness and
beauty of philosophy, Dante then began to attend 'le scuole de li
religiosi', schools run by members of the religious orders. Which
schools were these and who were the *religiosi*? There is little or no
doubt that Dante is here referring primarily to the teaching activities of the Franciscan and Dominican friars, at their Florentine
churches of Santa Croce and Santa Maria Novella respectively.[3] It
should be made quite clear that attendance at these schools in no
sense implied any formal or informal involvement with the religious
orders in question. There is no implication here that Dante was a
potential Franciscan or Dominican novice (he was in any case
married by now), nor even that he might have entered those minor
religious orders from which married men were not debarred. Dante
remained a layman throughout his life. The religious orders in thir-

teenth-century Florence offered instruction on a wide variety of subjects, by no means all theological in any strict sense, and laymen were freely admitted. These schools are not, then, to be confused with seminaries.

A word should be said at this point about the Franciscans and Dominicans. The emergence of these two religious organizations was by far the most significant new feature of the Western Church in the thirteenth century. Both these orders of friars were in many respects different from the older monastic orders, notably in that, unlike many monks, the friars did not isolate themselves in communities apart from the life of lay folk. On the contrary, they deliberately established their churches and 'convents' (i.e. residential communities) in towns, and from the very first their lives were closely involved with those of the laity. Founded at the beginning of the thirteenth century by St Francis of Assisi and his slightly older Spanish contemporary St Dominic, the new orders of friars were very soon recognized formally by Pope Honorius III. They quickly expanded and became a powerful influence in the Church, often to the dislike of the monastic orders and the ordinary ('secular') clergy. The dynamism of the earliest followers of Saints Francis and Dominic can only be compared to that of the Jesuits in the sixteenth century. Both the new orders were strongly committed to learning and teaching, the latter function going far beyond the traditional task of preaching to the faithful. The most intellectually able Dominicans and Franciscans were at the forefront of academic life, among them some of the greatest minds of the century, including Albertus Magnus, Thomas Aquinas, Bonaventure and Roger Bacon. The great towns and universities of thirteenth-century Europe were the focus of Dominican and Franciscan endeavour and achievement. In the words of Richard Southern: 'Without the towns the friars would never have come into existence; without the universities they would never have become great.'[4] Within a few decades of their foundation the new orders had secured positions of prime importance in the University of Paris, then the greatest centre of learning in the West: by 1234 no fewer than nine of its fifteen doctors of divinity were Dominicans. Florence had no university for the friars to take over, so they soon set up schools of their own. Their energetic expansion in the city is reflected in their building programmes: the Franciscans' little church of Santa Croce, which they had acquired in 1228, was soon enlarged, as was the Dominicans' Santa Maria Novella. This had been acquired by the new order in 1221, and underwent major reconstruction; by 1279 it had attained its present-day grandiose proportions. (It should be pointed out that a number of other religious groups, not all of them especially associated with teaching, expanded their Florentine churches about this time, among them the Cistercians, Servites and Carmelites.)

As a young man, then, Dante frequented the recently-established centres of learning at Santa Croce and Santa Maria Novella. The Augustinians too had a rather smaller school at their church of Santo Spirito, and this also he may have attended. The clerics teaching at these churches were by no means all natives of Florence; indeed, the new religious orders were essentially international in character. They included a number of scholars with full university training, some of whom had studied in Paris. In the early 1290s the leading figure at Santa Croce was Pier di Giovanni Olivi. His counterpart at Santa Maria Novella was Remigio de' Girolami, a far less original thinker, but probably more influential as a teacher than Olivi. Both men were more than competent to initiate intelligent non-specialists such as Dante into the world of thirteenth-century learning. The reader may want to know something more of what that involved, in what Southern has called 'the most intellectual century of the Middle Ages'.[5]

To a very large extent the academic life of the later Middle Ages, and of the thirteenth century especially, was dominated by ancient Greek and (later) Arabic writings. It would be an exaggeration to say that the Scriptures and Aristotle were the two great authorities of the time, but not an over-exaggeration. (Plato's philosophical dialogues were little known in the medieval West.) Aristotle's wide-ranging works date from the fourth century BC and cover astronomy, meteorology, psychology, zoology, botany and much besides, as well as what one would today regard as the more obviously philosophical territory of logic, ethics and metaphysics. They were at an early stage the subject of learned commentaries, at first by Greeks, and later by scholars from the length and breadth of the medieval Islamic world. The latter included Ibn Sīnā (Avicenna to the Christian West) who was born in AD 980 in what is now Uzbekistan, and Ibn Rushd (or Averroes), a Moor living in twelfth-century Spain. The stimulus of Aristotle's thought came late to the Christian West, however. Even in Dante's time it was a relatively recent phenomenon. During the early medieval period, the half-millennium following the fall of the Roman Empire in the fifth century (once known as the Dark Ages), the West was cut off from all but certain Aristotelian works on logic, let alone the prolific speculations of Muslim thinkers. As far as Aristotle is concerned, nothing was known except those parts of the *Organon* (his logical writings) that had been skilfully translated into Latin by Boethius. It is worth reiterating that the medieval West's knowledge of Greek learning was indirect, via Latin translations: expertise in the Greek language itself was uncommon until the fifteenth century.

This cultural isolation of the earlier medieval West was dramatically transformed in little more than fifty years, as a result of the industry of the mid-twelfth-century Spanish translators based around Toledo and of their counterparts in Sicily, who were also translating into Latin, but a little later. By the very early 1200s a considerable corpus of Aristotelian texts was available, including most of the *Organon*, as well as treatises on metaphysics, physics, cosmology, psychology and rhetoric. (The Toledo 'workshop' had also produced Latin versions of the leading Islamic thinkers.) Many of these twelfth-century translations were not, however, made from Greek but from Arabic manuscripts, and in some cases these in turn had been translated from Syriac versions of Aristotle. In fact the earliest Western contact with Aristotle was in an indirect, imperfect and sometimes even garbled form. Later in the thirteenth century much was done to expand and revise the Latin Aristotelian corpus by individuals who were able to translate direct from Greek, among them the Englishman Robert Grosseteste (Bishop of Lincoln) and more importantly Thomas Aquinas' Flemish friend William of Moerbeke (who became Archbishop of Corinth).

Despite the inaccuracies and uncertainties of the new Aristotelian texts, they were seized upon by the university intelligentsia from the outset, especially in Paris. And from the outset they were the cause of considerable disquiet. Certain of the pagan Aristotle's tenets were plainly at odds with Christian belief; for instance, his universe was an eternal one—it had always existed and had not been created out of nothing by God at the beginning of time. Furthermore, Aristotle denied (or certainly seemed to deny) the survival after death of each individual human soul. Although many great thinkers of the time strove to incorporate as much Aristotelianism as possible within a Christian account of the world and man's place in it (the most outstanding of these thinkers was to be Aquinas), the new learning was nonetheless regarded by many conservatives as dangerous. Twice, in 1210 and 1215, the redoubtable Pope Innocent III issued decrees forbidding the Parisian scholars to read the physical and metaphysical books of Aristotle, together with certain commentaries upon them (probably Avicenna's). Pope Gregory IX protested similarly in the 1220s and 1230s, as did Innocent IV in 1245. These pronouncements seem to have been successfully, perhaps even cheerfully, ignored. Indeed there was a group of Paris intellectuals whose assimilation of Aristotle went far beyond that of Aquinas: the so-called Latin Averroists. Their mentor was the commentator Averroes, whose concern had been to lay bare what he saw as the true meaning of the Aristotelian texts, without seeking to reconcile them with a 'revealed' religion (in his case Islam). The Averroists seem to have gone too far, so to speak, and a few of them were actually persecuted by the Church authorities. In 1277 the Bishop of Paris felt obliged to condemn solemnly no less than 219 propositions, then apparently current in the Arts Faculty of the University. Many of these were at least loosely 'Averroist', including one to the effect that happiness is to be had in this life and not in another, and even the view that the Christian religion is an obstacle to progress in knowledge. Yet despite all the polemic and controversy, clear echoes of which are found in Dante's work, a great deal of the new Aristotelian and Graeco-Arabic learning did come to be accepted as a key part of the medieval Christian world-view. In Foster's words: 'The second half of the thirteenth century, when Dante grew to manhood, saw the general acceptance as the chief sources of philosophical and scientific culture for every educated European, whether cleric or layman, of the works of Aristotle and of his Greek and Arabic commentators'.[6]

This then was the intellectual world which Dante first encountered in the Florentine 'scuole de li religiosi'. By the time he came to write the *Convivio*, more than ten years after this initial period of intense study, his knowledge of ancient and medieval thought was wide-ranging indeed. He was extensively acquainted with Aristotle (in direct translation and via numerous medieval commentators—there are over eighty references to him in the *Convivio*), as he was with Aquinas and with his teacher Albertus Magnus (St Albert the Great). He was also in touch with strains of thought deriving from Plato. He did not of course read Plato in the original, and probably had only a slight acquaintance with those few of Plato's works then available in Latin. But he obtained a good deal of indirect data about Plato and Platonism from Cicero, Augustine, Boethius, Aquinas and others. It is impossible to say just what he read when, but the earlier 1290s were clearly crucial for his intellectual development; it was then that that initial, wonderful insight into the nature and potential of philosophy occurred. It would seem that after his period of attendance at Santa Croce and Santa Maria Novella, Dante continued to apply himself assiduously to learning. We know from the *Convivio* (III, ix, 15) that in the same year he wrote the important allegorical *canzone* 'Amor che ne la mente mi ragiona' ('Love speaking to me in my mind') his eyesight was so badly affected by prolonged study that he had to rest in cool and dark places, bathing his eyes with pure water. Fortunately his sight recovered. The year in question is uncertain, but probably between 1295 and 1298. Dante's pursuit of philosophy was arduous as well as a source of delight. Some of the questions he pondered seem to have been intellectually taxing in the extreme: in a well-known *Convivio* passage (IV, i, 8) he says that at one point he withdrew temporarily from further philosophical study because he was so perplexed by the question of God's understanding of (or, according to some, His creation of) Prime Matter. This highly technical problem was the subject of one of the many thirteenth-century debates between philosophers of different schools or traditions. There is no reason to suppose it untypical of Dante's concerns during this period; it may simply be an extreme case—extreme in the degree of Dante's puzzlement. It would seem that by the mid-1290s he was quite familiar with the kinds of question that exercised the so-called scholastic philosophers, the 'schoolmen' of the time, even though he would not have involved himself in all the technicalities of those professionals.

### (iii) Dante's Earliest Philosophical Poems

Now Dante was not merely reading philosophy at this time. Here we must return to his literary output, and in particular to three groups of poems written about the time the *Vita Nuova* was compiled, or perhaps as much as a year after its completion. The three groups are very different, and all are quite unlike the poetry of the *Vita Nuova*. The poems in the first group are the direct result of Dante's immersion in philosophy. These are often called 'allegorical and doctrinal poems'. The latter description is the more important, for although some (the earlier ones) use the technique of allegory, all are 'doctrinal', in the sense of being didactic poems, intended to impart instruction. The first is 'Voi che 'ntendendo il terzo ciel movete' ('O you who move the third heaven by intellection') and is addressed to the angelic spirits widely believed in Dante's day to cause the movements of the heavens; more precisely, to those angels moving the planet Venus, thought to influence the course of earthly love. But this *canzone* (datable to a period between August 1293 and early 1294) is not about Dante's love for any earthly woman; it recounts the turning-point in his life when he became enamoured of Philosophy, here represented allegorically as a beautiful lady. At least, that is how Dante was to interpret the poem in the *Convivio*. For, together with 'Amor che ne la mente mi ragiona' ('Love speaking to me in my mind'), it is the subject of an extensive commentary in the later treatise; the interpretation of the two poems takes up the whole of Books II and III. Both poems are concerned with a new experience, the devotion to philosophy, with all its concomitant problems and difficulties, even setbacks, and both express this theme in terms of a *donna gentile*, Philosophy personified.

Closely related in subject matter and literary technique are the *ballata* 'Voi che savete ragionar d'Amore' ('O you who know how to discourse upon Love')—which in fact preceded 'Amor che ne la mente' —and the two sonnets 'Parole mie che per lo mondo siete' ('Words of mine that have [wandered] the world') and 'O dolci rime che parlando andate' ('O sweet verses that speak [of the noble lady]'). The first two of these poems stress Dante's fear and awe in the face of Philosophy, and her apparent haughtiness and indifference towards him—standard elements of erotic verse, here being used to convey the intractability and elusiveness of many philosophical problems. In 'Parole mie' this leads Dante to go so far as to renounce his new-found love, but in 'O dolci rime' his commitment is re-affirmed. Now all these philosophical poems still use the conventions and style of the *Dolce Stil Novo*. These may or may not have been apt for relating the vicissitudes of Dante's rapport with Philosophy, but there is no doubt that he consciously chose to discard and move beyond them when a little later he tackled the direct exposition of philosophical themes in two substantial and elaborate *canzoni*, 'Le dolci rime d'amor ch'i' solia' ('The sweet rhymes of love which I used to [seek out in my thoughts]') and 'Poscia ch'Amor del tutto m'ha lasciato' ('Since Love has abandoned me utterly'). Both these are overtly didactic pieces, concerned with ethical matters; the first seeks to probe the true nature of nobility (*gentilezza*) in people, and the second investigates *leggiadria*, for which no one single word will do in modern English, though 'charm', 'elegance' and 'grace' are all related to it. What is new in literary terms about both these *canzoni* is that Dante has gone beyond the allegorical use of the *Stil Novo* manner; 'Le dolci rime' begins with an explicit statement that it is appropriate, in view of the subject matter now being tackled, to abandon the 'sweet rhymes'. Dante evidently considered this *canzone* to be of great importance; it was to become the springboard for the thorough and wide-ranging exposition to which Book IV of the *Convivio* (the longest of its four books) is devoted. It is very likely that 'Poscia ch'Amor del tutto' was also intended for a *Convivio* commentary. Originally, so Dante tells us, the *Convivio* was to have expounded fourteen of his poems. But it remains unfinished. If, as seems probable, Dante abandoned it, in 1307 or 1308, in order to proceed with the *Inferno*, then few if any will think an uncompleted *Convivio* too high a price to pay.

## (iv) The *Tenzone* with Forese

We come now to a very different trio of poems, different from the doctrinal verse and from the *Vita Nuova*, though written at roughly the same period. Some time between 1293 and 1296 Dante engaged in a *tenzone*; the term is of Provençal derivation and refers to an exchange of poems, often in the nature of a disputation or debate, between two or more poets. Dante's three sonnets in this *tenzone* were addressed to Forese Donati, who replied with three of his own. Forese, related to Dante's wife Gemma, was an apparently rakish and witty companion of Dante's youth and young manhood. Whereas some thirteenth-century *tenzoni* were on such lofty matters as the true nature of love or virtue, this one between Dante and Forese is characterized by mutual vituperation of a far from elevated kind. Dante accuses Forese of neglecting his wife (and perhaps also of impotence), of gluttony, theft and illegitimacy. Forese in turn scorns Dante's alleged humiliating and ridiculous poverty, obscurely insults his father, and accuses Dante of cowardice. Clearly the two were firm friends.

Now the style and subject matter of these poems is far indeed from the *Vita Nuova*. It is not that long since they occasioned a good deal of strait-laced embarrassment on the part of critics. Foster and Boyde point out in their masterly 1967 edition of all Dante's lyric poems that the only previous complete English version of the lyrics (1906) dismisses the *tenzone* as having 'no artistic value'. It makes no attempt to explain these poems, and even declines to reproduce their original text, which it does in the case of all the other lyrics. Some Italian scholars of that period were similarly dismissive.[7] But what Dante was doing in the *tenzone* (apart from amusing his fellow-poet and friend) was making a deliberate, and in fact very skilful, excursion into the 'comic' or low style. The impression may have been given that Italian poetry in Dante's time was exclusively concerned with an aethereal, idealized kind of love or, as in Dante's own doctrinal verse, with weighty ethical or other philosophical matters. But alongside all this were poems celebrating physical love, poems subversive of courtly ideals, poems of invective and abuse, employing coarse and down-to-earth language, spicy and colloquial. There were in fact two distinct genres, each formalized with its own special set of conventions determining content, language and style. As Foster and Boyde emphasize, 'both traditions were "literary" and ... both were recognised in the literary theory of the day'.[8]

The *tenzone* sonnets look forward to the low, comic style, the grim and earthy black humour of certain of the later *Inferno* passages (especially Cantos XXI–XXII and Canto XXX), just as they can be related retrospectively to the *Fiore*. In fact now that the latter is widely accepted as Dante's authentic work, the *tenzone* with Forese should come as less of a surprise. But it need never have caused embarrassment. In the *Purgatorio* (XXIII, 37–133) Dante meets the spirit of Forese, who had died in 1296, expiating—appropriately—the sin of gluttony. Although in their encounter Dante appears to regret his past friendship with Forese (and he does seem to be making specific amends for things said in the three sonnets), there is no reason to suppose that he did not find both friendship and poetic exchange highly diverting at the time. If a more 'human'

Dante emerges from these verses than from some other parts of his work, then so be it. The critics were made for the poet, and not vice versa.

## (v) The *Rime Petrose*

Quite unlike the *tenzone*, and equally far removed from the *Vita Nuova* and the *Dolce Stil*, is the third group of distinctive mid-1290s poems. These are the four so-called *rime petrose* (literally, 'stony' or 'rock-like' poems).[9] Probably all written late in 1296, or shortly thereafter, they are remarkable for their poetic technique, their style and—in the final poem of the quartet—their subject matter. The poems owe their title to the recurrent word *petra* ('stone'), used in various ways, but primarily to refer to an unnamed beautiful young lady (her youth is emphasized) who is stony-hearted towards Dante. (It is otiose to speculate as to whether she existed in reality, or merely in the reality of Dante's imagination.) Unrequited love is a theme endemic in medieval (perhaps in all) love poetry, but here it is combined—in the fourth of these poems—with the theme of vengeance.

Before we come to this distinctive feature, a word needs to be said about the *rime petrose* as literary artefacts. They are an experiment, exercises in 'hard' poetry, poems which are not easily accessible to the reader, and in which the poet deliberately sets himself arduous technical problems of versification. The first and fourth poems are *canzoni*, by this time a well-established poetic form in Italian, while the middle two are *sestine*, the *sestina* being a rarer and technically taxing form which originated in Provençal verse. In fact all four of the *petrose* poems owe a great deal to southern French troubadour poetry in its highest stage of development. Dante's earliest contacts with Provençal were probably indirect, via his reading of the Sicilian and Siculo-Tuscan poets, whose work bears the mark of a substantial troubadour influence. It is not known when Dante began to read troubadour verse at first hand, but there is little or no doubt that he had done so when he came to write the *rime petrose*. They echo the style of, and may indeed have been intended as a kind of homage to, one great troubadour above all: Arnaut Daniel.

Arnaut flourished around the year 1200, the high point of that distinctive southern French culture soon to be eclipsed in the aftermath of a major political and religious upheaval—the two early thirteenth-century Albigensian Crusades, which resulted eventually in southern France's political and cultural subservience to the French monarchy. Arnaut was in his own day the acknowledged master of the *trobar ric* and *trobar clus* styles—literally the 'rich' style (with its delight in recherché vocabulary, and particularly in difficult and challenging rhyme-words) and the 'closed' style (in which initial difficulty of comprehension is held to be a virtue rather than a vice, a tribute to the hard work of the poet and a challenge to the reader to work hard as well). Both styles overlapped, not surprisingly; both were to be found in the same poems. Arnaut is one of several poets whose soul is to be encountered by Dante during his journey through Purgatory. Their meeting is the occasion for Dante, as poet, to demonstrate to us his own skill in writing Provençal verse (*Purg.* XXVI, 136–48).

The four *petrose* lyrics are intended to be a technical *tour de force* in the manner of Arnaut. The details of the verse technique are outside our scope, but there is space to convey some idea of the content and flavour of the final *canzone* 'Così nel mio parlar voglio esser aspro' ('I want to be as harsh in my language ...'). The language and subject-matter of this poem are of a violence quite unparalleled in Dante outside the pages of the *Inferno*. Dante wants to make his language as harsh as is the behaviour towards him of the 'bella petra', the 'beautiful stone', whose excruciating combination of disdain and power to enthral he has lamented in the previous three poems. Here he evokes the young girl's cruelty more vividly than ever: she herself is immune to love (or to his love), for she has armour-plated her body with jasper; yet she rains deadly blows upon Dante which no shield of his can withstand; she wields (or perhaps *is*) a pitiless iron file rasping his very life away; in short she is a murderous assassin and robber. After four stanzas of this, Dante turns to vengeance. At first he wishes that the god of Love would split open the heart of the stone lady, who has so lacerated his own heart. But then he imagines himself as the avenger and gives vent to an unexpected fantasy of erotic violence: if only he could grasp in his hand the beautiful locks of blond hair which have so tormented him, then he would show no mercy. Indeed, he would be like a playful bear. Even though now he is whipped by those locks, he would then avenge himself a thousandfold. The *canzone* ends with a *congedo*, a few brief closing lines, in which Dante

addresses his poem (as was conventional). But whereas most
*congedi* commend the poem to the lady or other recipient with
words of praise or apology, or something similarly ingratiating, this
poem is urged to drive an arrow through the cruel girl's heart. The
poem ends uncompromisingly: 'ché bell'onor s'acquista in far
vendetta' ('for one acquires great honour by taking revenge'). All
these sentiments are conveyed in deliberately unusual language. We
are a long way, and purposefully so, from the sweetness of the
*Dolce Stil Novo*. Strange and 'harsh' words abound, especially
rhyme-words. Some knowledge of Italian is required to appreciate
this point, of course, but suffice it to say that words like *spezzan,
scemi, scorza, bruca, guizzo, rimbalza, squatra* and *scudiscio* are
hitherto unknown in Dante, and form part of a bold stylistic experiment. And as Foster and Boyde point out, another distinctive
element in this poem is the high preponderance of concrete nouns,
by contrast with the *Vita Nuova* verse, where abstract nouns predominate.[10]

These three groups of post-*Vita Nuova* poems bear witness to
new intellectual experiences and new stylistic enterprises; they
expand Dante's poetic world far beyond the Beatrician and other
verse of his first literary decade.


## (vi) Charles Martel

Before we leave the Dante of the early to mid-1290s, mention
should be made of an episode in 1294 which is linked to the earliest
of the doctrinal poems referred to above. 'Voi che 'ntendendo' was
written in late 1293 or early in 1294, and it seems very likely that
one of the first to read it, or hear it read aloud, was a young French
prince, Charles Martel. Charles was the son of Charles II, King of
Naples and Count of Anjou, and the grandson of the great Charles
I, who had conquered Naples and Sicily, and defeated the Imperial
Hohenstaufen dynasty in Italy. Charles Martel was the titular king
of Hungary, a title bestowed on him by his mother, daughter of
King Stephen IV of Hungary. He never in fact ruled over that
country, power having been seized by Andrew III, Stephen's cousin.
Early in March 1294 Charles paid an official visit to Florence. He
stayed for three weeks and was joined in due course by his parents,
Charles II and Mary of Hungary. The commune of Florence, by
this time solidly Guelph and broadly a supporter of the House of

Anjou and its activities in Italian territory, received the young prince with elaborate ceremony and sent out an advance welcoming party of well-born young Florentines, headed by Vieri de' Cerchi's son Giano, who was roughly the same age as Dante. It is generally accepted that Dante took part in this courtly delegation, which became an adjunct to Charles' retinue for the next few weeks. This was not an official diplomatic mission, but something more ceremonial than political; at any rate it was not crucially strategic, and the rulers of the commune could safely delegate it to young men of good birth who were at the time excluded from political office. At all events, Dante seems to have formed a close friendship with Charles Martel during their brief acquaintance. This was not to be renewed, for Charles died in Naples the following year, aged twenty-four. But like so many who figure in the story of Dante's life, he was to reappear in the *Divine Comedy (Par.* VIII, 31–IX, 9). Here his spirit speaks to Dante in friendly terms, and at the very beginning of their exchange he quotes the opening line of 'Voi che 'ntendendo'. His long speech to Dante that follows is about history and politics, not poetry, but the direct reference to Dante's *canzone* is certainly not fortuitous, and may well be intended to re-evoke the events of March 1294. That Charles was a lover of poetry and also intellectually gifted is attested independently of Dante.

This chapter has focused on Dante's studies and poetry in the years following the death of Beatrice. In the next chapter we shall see him in another role—not back in the saddle, as in 1289, but in the council chamber. The young man of letters and amateur of philosophy is about to embark upon his political career.

# 4

# Guilds and Government
## Dante the Politician
## (1295–1300)

### (i) The Florentine Political System

Dante entered actively and officially into Florentine political life in November 1295, at the age of thirty. To say that he became a member of the Special Council of the *Capitano del Popolo* (literally, 'Captain of the People') is to convey singularly little to most modern readers. Here some survey of the immediately pertinent historical background is essential. Our concern is with the particular forms of government that had evolved in Florence by this time, not in respect of day-to-day administrative procedures, but with special reference to the changing involvement in government of different social classes in the 1280s and 1290s.[1] The Ghibelline-Guelph conflicts are not of immediate relevance here, but one possible misunderstanding should be dispelled at the outset. It has already been noted that Florentine society at this time can broadly be divided into three strata: the *grandi*, or magnates; the *popolo grasso*, or merchants, professionals and other guildsmen; and the *popolo minuto*, the common people, to all intents and purposes excluded from power. Now it should not be thought that the *grandi* are automatically to be associated with the Ghibellines, the supporters, broadly speaking, of the German Emperors' claims to power in Italy. Nor should the middle class be presumed to support the Guelph cause, which by the late thirteenth century had become allied with the cause of the papacy and the House of Anjou. There is some degree of truth in the association of the two social classes with the two supra-municipal political parties, but to equate the two would be misleading.

By the time Dante came onto the political scene, Florence had two leading officials (apart from the very powerful priors, of whom more anon). These were the *podestà* ('chief magistrate') and the *capitano del popolo* (a representative of the middle—not the lower—classes). The term *popolo* is often misunderstood. It was frequently used, without further qualification, to indicate the mercantile class, but in order to distinguish these people from the *popolo minuto* we also find them referred to as the *popolo grasso* (*grasso* literally meaning 'fat'; clearly not a term referring to the poor). Those holding the office of *podestà* were often career men, legally-trained officials serving a six-month term of office in one city before moving on to another (being ineligible for re-appointment in the same place). It was in fact a requirement for them to be outsiders, and not from some immediately neighbouring commune, at that. The *podestà* who was to condemn Dante to death in 1302 was Cante de' Gabrielli, originally from Gubbio, in Umbria. Both *podestà* and *capitano* each had two councils of their own, a general and a special one. The largest was the *podestà*'s General Council (300 members) and the smallest the thirty-six-strong Special Council of the *capitano*, which Dante joined for the stipulated six-month period in 1295 (the *capitano* himself served for a year).

In addition to the four councils of the *podestà* and *capitano*, there was the *Consiglio dei Cento* (the Council of One Hundred). In all, there were 676 conciliar seats. Members of the five councils were elected, though the franchise was far from universal. Since each councillor served for six months only, and since no one was allowed to serve on more than one council at a time, and since by no means all outgoing councillors would have been, or have wished to be, immediately elected to a different council, this suggests that in any one year a thousand citizens (a very conservative estimate) would have participated in the government of the commune. Around the year 1300 the total adult male population of Florence was roughly 36,000; at least one in thirty-six of these, then, would have been a council member in any one year, and as a proportion of those in fact eligible for such a position, the figure would be far higher.

Now if all this sounds too democratic to be true, then perhaps it is. The deliberations of the councils were far from devoid of importance, yet for over a decade before Dante served on his first council, the real executive power had lain with a much smaller body: the priors (the term has no religious connotations whatever). This group of initially three, then six (and for a time seven) men gave overall direction to the government of the Florentine commune. The institution of the priorate dates from 1282 and is indicative of the rise to political power of the guilds (especially the seven leading ones). For the priors were drawn exclusively from the guilds and only guild members could vote for them. It should be stressed that by this time the major guilds wielded enormous commercial and financial power, both at home and abroad. As to the latter, the trading guilds of many Italian cities, not just Florence, had established flourishing enclaves in ports in the Eastern Mediterranean and the Near East, sometimes with their own churches. And at home they had their own bureaucracy, extending even to their own courts or tribunals. The 1282 innovations in Florence were simply the translation onto the political stage of the *de facto* economic power of the *arti maggiori*, that is, the major guilds. There were seven of these, representing: judges and lawyers; cloth importers and finishers; wool merchants; silk merchants; bankers; furriers; physicians and apothecaries. The first three priors took office on 15 June 1282; one was from the cloth importers' guild, one from the wool merchants', one from the bankers'. Their numbers were almost immediately increased to six, one from each *sesto*, or district, of the city. Although at first dominated by the *arti maggiori*, the priorate was extended in 1287 to the five *arti medie*, the middle-ranking guilds. But the *popolo minuto* (some of whom belonged to the humble *arti minori*) were excluded. And, after 1293, so were the *grandi*, the aristocrats.

## (ii) Giano della Bella's Reforms

Tension between merchants and *grandi* was considerable, as it was too between the 'ordinary' merchants and an increasingly oligarchic priorate of quasi-*grandi*. In January 1293 there was enacted a series of legal provisions known as the *Ordinamenti di Giustizia* ('Ordinances of Justice'). These were largely the brainchild of Giano della Bella, a vigorous supporter of the *popolani*, that is the middle classes (though himself of noble birth), and were designed to strengthen the role of the priors, whilst ensuring they were of the approved socio-economic complexion, and whilst at the same time imposing political and legal restraints on the *grandi*. The *Ordinamenti* decreed that after each prior had completed his short period of office (a mere two months) he was not to be re-eligible for that office for two years; furthermore the priors were to act as a single body, accepting the principle of collective responsibility for their decisions and giving interviews as a group. They were even required to reside together, away from their families. There was now a formal ban on the appointment of any of the *grandi* to this office, and some seventy-two families were named as belonging to this politically proscribed class. They were either long-established aristocrats, or powerful bankers and merchants, who, though guildsmen, were by now considered as in effect magnates, and therefore to be excluded from government. The *grandi* (both traditional and parvenus) were the object, moreover, of amendments to the criminal law: the financial penalties imposed on a magnate guilty of harming the person or property of a *popolano* were far more severe than those such a victim would suffer if convicted of a similar offence. The *grandi* were forbidden to raise fines from among their families or supporters, and the mere oath of a member of an alleged victim's family was considered valid evidence against a magnate. Such anti-aristocratic financial discrimination by a ruling mercantile class was not uncommon in the thirteenth-century communes. In 1279 bizarre steps were taken in Padua whereby a large group of alleged pro-Imperialists, clearly straightforward political enemies of those then in power in that city, were elevated to the rank of knighthood so that they might be taxed more heavily, even though they were not exactly rich.[2]

The Florentine *Ordinamenti* were further strengthened in 1293–94, particularly while Giano della Bella himself was one of the priors (February–April 1293). The situation was potentially explosive. Men like Corso Donati and Vieri de' Cerchi, the commanders at Campaldino (Corso at least could be called the hero of that battle), belonged to the magnate class. Yet they were excluded from government. Had all the aristocrats been of only moderate means, like the Alighieri, this exclusion would not have been of much consequence. But it was precisely because families like the Donati and Cerchi were immensely influential and rich (not all the city's money was in merchant hands) that their political proscription was dangerous for the stability of the commune. It was not very long before concessions and compromise were thought to be prudent. In July 1295, as a result of elaborate manoeuvres by the magnates and some of the less radical guildsmen, the *Ordinamenti di Giustizia* were modified. Involved in these manoeuvres was the recently-elected Boniface VIII, that remarkable pope who will be the subject of much of our next chapter. Giano della Bella's power had already waned, and in fact in February 1295 he had been obliged to leave Florence. He went to France, never to return.

## (iii) Dante's Political Début

The new modifications to the 1293 *Ordinamenti* were partly concerned with the criminal law, but much more importantly, they allowed the aristocracy a role in government. Political power was still to be reserved for the *popolani*, but by a splendid piece of Florentine ingenuity, the *grandi* could now be considered part of the merchant class, provided they enrolled in one of the guilds. It was not necessary actually to practise the trade or profession concerned. This was the loophole Dante quickly took advantage of; at an unknown date in the summer of 1295 he enrolled in the Guild of Physicians and Apothecaries. This and the Guild of Judges and Notaries were what might be called the 'intellectual' guilds. Dante's guild also ran the Florentine bookselling trade, but that has nothing to do with his choice to join it. He would have scorned the selling of books, and indeed throughout his life maintained something of an aristocratic contempt for trade (anachronistically aristocratic in the Italy of his day). Dante's choice of this guild probably had to do with his already keen interest in the natural sciences, medicine included; membership of it would have enabled him to mix with specialists in this field. More importantly of course, it was his entrée into public life, into a political career that was to last just over six years, until his exile from Florence. It might be wondered why the still young poet and scholar wanted to be active politically. However unusual it may be for artists and intellectuals to become politicians in our own century, in the medieval Italian communes it was considered entirely appropriate that intelligent and articulate, indeed learned, men should participate in government. There was a strong sense of civic duty in this regard. Moreover, had Dante needed any encouragement in this direction, he would surely have got it from Cavalcanti, by now an ardent supporter of the Cerchi faction (about which more anon). An even stronger influence would have been Brunetto Latini, who had died the previous year, and who had held all manner of public offices in the commune (he was one of the priors in 1287).

Dante's first official position in the Florentine government, as a member of the Special Council of the *Capitano del Popolo*, lasted from 1 November 1295 to 30 April 1296. He is not recorded as having made any special contribution to the decisions of this council, but that his opinion was already valued at this early stage may be inferred from the fact that on 14 December (a mere six weeks after taking his seat as councillor) he was part of an *ad hoc* group of *savi* (literally, 'wise men'). This group had been convened to examine no less a matter than the procedure for electing the priors. Dante spoke during the 14 December meeting, though what he said is not recorded in detail.[3] From May until the end of September of the following year he was a member of the Council of One Hundred. On 5 July 1296 Dante made a speech to this body in favour of a package of administrative and legal proposals.[4] Two of these are of interest. The first sought to forbid any attempt to welcome into the city a group of recent exiles from neighbouring Pistoia; it was feared that their presence might be a catalyst for even greater civil unrest in ever-fractious Florence. The second proposal sought to confer full power on the priors and the *Gonfaloniere di Giustizia* (who between them constituted the *signoria*) to proceed against anyone assaulting, or even insulting, members of the *popolano* class who were holders of public office. It will come as no surprise that this measure was aimed above all at the magnates ('et maxime magnates'): the inter-class aggression which Giano della Bella's *Ordinamenti* were designed (one-sidedly) to suppress was still a problem. Indeed, relatively few of the magnate class, whether old-established nobles or the new *grandi*, had condescended to do what Dante did, and join a guild. They were thus still excluded from official positions in the commune, and this rankled with many.

Dante is known to have served again on one of the councils for a six-month period in 1297, though the details are unclear. Nothing precise is known about his political activities in 1298 or 1299, not least because the official minutes of the commune's councils from July 1298 to February 1301 have been lost (to the frustration of many historians, and Dante scholars in particular!). No doubt had he been appointed or elected to any especially prominent position, this would have been noted in documents other than those records now lost. Boccaccio was surely exaggerating when he wrote that nothing was decided without consulting Dante.[5] But it is highly likely he continued to be active in political life during these last years of the 1290s, since in May 1300 he embarked on the first of his missions as a diplomat (more were to follow, both before and after his exile) and in June 1300, shortly after his thirty-fifth birthday, he was to achieve his highest office, as one of the six priors. It might be as well to point out here that all these political positions were unpaid, unlike those of the *podestà* and *capitano del popolo*, which were stipendiary. Although in the years immediately following the death of Dante's father in 1283 the Alighieri seem to have been comfortable enough financially, in the later 1290s both Dante and Francesco, his younger half-brother, had to take out loans.[6] Francesco was barely twenty, and had not yet established himself as the most economically successful of the family; he turned out to have entrepreneurial skills that Dante himself did not, or chose not to, possess.

Dante's role in Florentine politics, then, was a respectable and respected one, culminating after only four and a half years in diplomacy and the priorate. As Petrocchi has pointed out, all this was a result of Dante's personal prestige.[7] Within the small circle of Florence's political and intellectual élite, his talents would have been recognized by 1295. His political career owed nothing to his family connections, nor to his position (certainly not a prominent one) within the Guelph party, the *Parte Guelfa*. And now for more about the Florentine *Parte Guelfa*.

## (iv) Guelphs and Guelphs

As has been explained, from 1282 onward chief executive power rested with the priors, roughly speaking the political arm of the major guilds. But the *Parte Guelfa* itself continued to exercise considerable influence. It was one of a number of political societies that by around 1250 had become prominent in certain Tuscan cities. These societies had their own *capitani*, their own councils, and their own funds—often very substantial. After the brief period of Ghibelline rule from 1260 to 1266, Florence was in broad political terms decidedly Guelph. The political life of the commune was under direct Guelph party control from 1267 to 1280, during which time the leader of the party (the Guelph *capitano*) and its councils were officially part of the government. Constitutionally this changed in 1280, but the party's prestige and influence did not. By now the *Parte Guelfa* was very wealthy, not only because it had the backing of prominent merchants and bankers, but also because it had acquired the property of its Ghibelline enemies, exiled in 1266 and 1267. In fact it made substantial loans to the commune, not without strings attached. The loans meant in practice that the policies pursued by the priors tended to harmonize with the aims of the party. When Giano's *Ordinamenti* were introduced in 1293 they aimed in part at weakening the influence of the *Parte Guelfa* (whose leadership was from the magnate class) over the priors (supposedly the guardians of the middle-class interest). Indeed, one of Giano's aims was to nationalize the party's assets, but he fell from power before anything was done in this respect.[8]

The *Parte Guelfa* continued to be of great importance in Florentine politics; although in constitutional theory it was just a pressure group, it was an immensely powerful one. After 1266 the Ghibellines were never again to wield power in Florence, but it should not be thought that all was plain sailing for their Guelph successors. By the time Dante was involved in politics, the chief internal causes of Florentine tension were not just the continuing hostility between *popolani* and magnates, but more overtly and urgently the bitter factional rivalry within the Guelph party itself. By 1300 the contemporary chroniclers were referring to the conflict between so-called 'Black' and 'White' Guelphs. These labels do not tell us much. It is more helpful to say that by the mid-1290s two powerful factions had clearly evolved, associated with and indeed led by Corso Donati and Vieri de' Cerchi, the victors of Campaldino. Their factions were in due course to be known as the Blacks and the Whites respectively.

The Donati and the Cerchi, like so many really bitter enemies, were close neighbours; both families had their principal residences in the Porta San Pietro quarter and both, moreover, were (like the Alighieri) part of the San Martino *popolo* (i.e. parish—the word *popolo* has several meanings) within that quarter. The Donati were old-established aristocrats, and Corso himself is frequently spoken of by contemporaries as the embodiment of an overbearing, indeed arrogant patrician demeanour. Though considerably more elevated socially and economically than the Alighieri, they were far less wealthy than the Cerchi, prominent bankers who had now gained the magnate ranks, having emerged from social (though not financial) obscurity as late as the 1250s. It might be thought that the rivalry between Donati and Cerchi factions is to be seen as a conflict between the old nobility and the *nouveaux riches* (against the latter of whom Dante was to inveigh so vehemently in the *Divine Comedy*[9]). But, typically, the matter is more complex. Doubtless the animosity between aristocrat and parvenu had a good deal to do with Corso's dislike for Vieri, and vice versa. But in fact Corso's faction became associated not with his fellow noblemen but with the wealthiest of the major guildsmen (bankers and rich merchants), whilst Vieri's attracted, together with many of the *nouveaux riches* certainly, members of the older aristocratic families, including eventually Dante.

A most overt supporter of the Cerchi was Cavalcanti, well-known as an outspoken enemy of Corso. According to the chronicler Dino Compagni (our only source, unfortunately), Corso took unsuccessful steps to murder Dante's friend and fellow-poet while he was on a pilgrimage to the Spanish shrine of St James at Compostela. On his arrival back in Florence Cavalcanti, on horseback, attacked Corso in the street. He was repulsed, suffering minor injury as a result of the stones hurled at him by Donati supporters.[10] He was subsequently fined 1,200 florins by the commune for his assault upon Corso. This would seem to be a minor example of an all too frequent occurrence.

As time went on, political differences between the Donati and the Cerchi emerged in the area of Florence's foreign policy. By the time the labels 'Black' and 'White' came to be used, these differences were very clear. The Donati/Blacks were the more staunchly Guelph in the traditional sense, that is, they supported the papacy and the House of Anjou. The Cerchi/Whites were what might be called 'moderate' Guelphs, and sought to promote policies independent of those of the papacy and not subservient to the interests of Anjou. This 'ideological divergence', if that is not too grand an expression, turns out (as so often) to have a strong economic basis. It is no accident that many of the Blacks had financial interests in the Kingdom of Naples (now ruled by Charles II, Count of Anjou) and in France itself. They had good reason to favour continuing the traditional Guelph links with the French. Conversely many Whites had dealings with Ghibelline Pisa and with certain Ghibelline towns in the Romagna, to the north-east of Tuscany. So it comes as no surprise that White policy favoured a distancing from Angevin interests.

The importance of the House of Anjou in late thirteenth-century Italy was considerable. It was Angevin power that filled the vacuum left after the defeat of the Hohenstaufen in the 1260s. Even after the famous 1282 uprising known as the Sicilian Vespers, which resulted in the expulsion from Sicily of the Angevins, they were still very much a power to be reckoned with, their influence extending well beyond the Kingdom of Naples itself. The stance taken by a particular city-state towards this French dynasty was frequently crucial for its overall diplomatic and economic policy. Although traditional Guelphism favoured the House of Anjou and the papacy, it must not be thought that the interests of these two entities always coincided. Certain popes were closely bound up with the Angevin interest, others markedly less so. Good examples of the former are Urban IV (1261–64) and Martin IV (1281–85), both Frenchmen. As early as 1262, Urban had presumed to offer the throne of Sicily to Charles I of Anjou, and during Martin's pontificate, papal policy was deliberately geared to serving King Charles' interests. Examples of popes with a different stance are two of the intervening pontiffs, Gregory X (1271–76) and Nicholas III (1277–80), both Italians, the latter being a member of the Orsini, the powerful Roman patrician family. Whilst both men welcomed the traditional support of Guelph cities and factions against the Ghibelline opponents of papal power, both were anxious to contain the potentially destabilizing ambitions of Anjou. Nicholas was able to take certain practical steps to check Charles; these included his suppression of the extremist Guelph Society of the Cross in Bologna. The conflict between Black and White Guelphs in Florence has to be seen not only in terms of clan rivalry, but against this broader historical background. The Blacks' policy was one of traditional Guelphism, trenchantly anti-Imperial and favourable to the ascendancy of Anjou; the Whites, on the other hand, pursued a line that would have secured the approval of Gregory X and Nicholas III, had they lived to see it. The pope reigning when the split within Florence's *Parte Guelfa* became apparent was Boniface VIII. He sided wholeheartedly with the Blacks, as we shall shortly see.

At first Dante was not overtly linked to either the Donati/Blacks or the Cerchi/Whites. He was connected to the former through his wife Gemma Donati, and of course he was a close friend of Corso Donati's brother Forese. At the outset of his political career his formal relations with Corso would seem to have been neutral and distant. His other great friend was Cavalcanti, an ardent partisan of the Cerchi. Although by 1300 Dante was clearly identified as siding with the Cerchi/Whites, this had not always been so.

## (v) Dante in the Jubilee Year

The year 1300 is famous in Italian history as the year of Pope Boniface's Jubilee. This was the first Jubilee of the Catholic Church, and was officially inaugurated in a Papal Bull (or Letter) of February 1300 (though in fact the Jubilee year had begun on Christmas Day 1299). In short, this was a year in which pilgrims were encouraged to come to Rome (and they did so, in very large numbers). The Pope granted them a plenary indulgence (i.e. full remission of their sins) if they confessed and repented of these, and if they visited the churches of St Peter and St Paul a specified number of times. It has long been suggested by Dante scholars that our poet may have been among the pilgrims early on in 1300, and perhaps about the time of Holy Week, precisely the time at which the action of the *Divine Comedy* is set. Several passages in the *Comedy* allude to the Jubilee, and the one from the *Inferno* reads like an eyewitness account.[11] But we know for certain that Dante was in Rome in 1301, and he could well have heard detailed accounts of the previous year's spectacular events then. His 1300 pilgrimage must remain a matter of conjecture.

It is time to focus on Dante's political career in the Jubilee year, when he attained his highest political office. The year began for Florence on a note of relative calm. Corso Donati had been exiled at the end of 1299, because he was implicated in a major financial scandal centring on the misdeeds of Monfiorito di Coderta, who had been *podestà* for the first half of that year. Corso's banishment mitigated his direct influence on Florentine politics—he was not to return in person until the November of 1301. But he was still active in promoting the Black cause. Scarcely had he been banished when Pope Boniface offered him protection, making him *podestà* of Orvieto (a town in papal territory, to the north of Rome). From there, and a little later from a small town near Urbino, he exerted his fractious influence on the affairs of Florence. Black-White strife in the city was soon to become exacerbated, and the Pope to become increasingly involved in it. The government was now in the hands of the Whites, and on 18 April the priors took action against three

Florentine businessmen, residents of the papal court, who were alleged to have conspired against their native city. It will come as no great surprise to learn that they were allies of Corso. They were sentenced, in their absence, to heavy fines and to have their tongues cut out. Later in the year Dante, on becoming a prior himself, had to—or was quite happy to—ratify this sentence. Boniface, now openly supporting the Blacks, reacted swiftly: within a matter of days he tried via the Bishop of Florence to have the sentence annulled, but in vain.

Very shortly thereafter, there was a major incident involving young supporters of the White and Black factions in the Piazza Santa Trinita, on the eve of May Day. There is some evidence that the disturbance was not fortuitous, but the work of Corso, busily fomenting discord at a distance. A few weeks after the incident the Blacks organized a provocative rally in the Church of Santa Trinita. Tension was mounting.

Dante, in this same month of May, was entrusted by the priors, his immediate predecessors in office, with a diplomatic mission: he was sent on 7 May to nearby San Gimignano, in a move designed to secure the participation of that commune in the forthcoming election for a new *capitano* of the Tuscan Guelphs. Dante was successful: San Gimignano did send delegates to a convention in Castelfiorentino, in late June. Not a momentous mission, perhaps; but it was part of a series of embassies then taking place which the White Guelph rulers of Florence had authorized, to try to secure the support, or at least the co-operation, of their most immediate neighbours. In any event, it shows the confidence the Florentine commune now had in Dante.

The priors who sent him to San Gimignano did something else, which was to have rather more dramatic repercussions: they sentenced Corso Donati to death and ordered the destruction of his property. Whites and Blacks seemed now to be on an unavoidable collision course. Boniface again intervened in the affairs of Florence: on 23 May (almost a month after he had attempted to annul the sentence passed on his three Florentine protégés) he appointed Cardinal Matthew of Aquasparta, a Franciscan and notable theologian, as Papal Legate and 'Peacemaker' in Tuscany, the Romagna and elsewhere. As far as Florence itself was concerned, the Cardinal's ostensible brief was to pacify the factions, but it is tolerably clear that Boniface wanted him to promote Black interests. After a very brief stay in the Romagna, the Cardinal arrived in Florence early in June with a proposal for electoral reform, designed (allegedly) to defuse the situation by making it easier for the Blacks to participate in government. By now the Whites had an effective monopoly of the priorate, and the proposal met with no success.

Very soon after Cardinal Matthew's arrival, the priors who had so incensed Boniface came to the end of their term of office. Elections were held on 13 June and Dante emerged as one of their six successors for the customary two-month period. The new priors began their sequestration in the Torre della Castagna two days later. Because of the gap in the official records we cannot be sure of Dante's precise role during the tenure of his highest office. But there is no doubt that the decisions taken during those crucial months sufficed, as things were to turn out, to seal his fate. If Bruni's testimony is reliable, Dante in the now-lost letter related all his sub-sequent misfortunes to his priorate.[12] A mere eight days after the new priors assumed office there occurred an event to which they responded with great vigour. 23 June was the eve of the Feast of St John the Baptist, and sadly it was the occasion of yet another civic disturbance. Although this was essentially a manifestation of inter-class hatred rather than of rivalry between the two Guelph factions, its aftermath was to drive Blacks and Whites still further apart. As was traditional on St John's Eve, officials of the guilds processed with offerings to the Church of the city's patron saint (the present-day baptistery). But on this occasion the procession was physically assaulted by various *grandi* who, it seems, took the opportunity to remind the merchants, with blows as well as words, that it was they, the *grandi*, who had won the victory at Campaldino, and it was they, the *grandi*, who had been excluded from office four years thereafter.

Dante and his fellow priors took a dim view of this latest dis-turbance and their response was swift. Having taken advice from a number of leading citizens (including Compagni, one of our chief sources for the events of these months), they decided to banish a number of *grandi*, both Black and White, together with their families and retainers. Seven White leaders were exiled to Sarzana, near the Ligurian coast in Lunigiana, to the north-west of Florence. Eight Blacks were sent a roughly similar distance in roughly the opposite direction, to Castel della Pieve in Umbria. The White leaders agreed to leave at once, among them Guido Cavalcanti, Dante's great friend. Whatever personal distress this may have caused Dante, there is no reason to doubt that he was in agreement with the other five priors in taking resolute action to defuse the mounting tension. But whereas the White leaders co-operated with the priors in leaving for Lunigiana, the Blacks refused for several weeks to go to Umbria. In these circumstances the priors offered Cardinal Matthew certain powers of intervention in Florence's affairs. But instead of using these to attempt to make the Blacks comply with the exile order, he took the provocative step of requesting military aid from nearby Lucca in order to impose his own personal rule on the city by force. The priors immediately warned the Lucchesi of the danger to them of any military confrontation with Florence, and nothing came of the Cardinal's request. Relations between the papal 'Peacemaker' and the priors continued to be strained throughout July, not least after a Florentine *popolano* had made an attempt on his life around the middle of the month. The priors tried, somewhat unsubtly, to assuage the Cardinal's anger by offering him a silver cup filled with 2,000 gold florins. He refused to accept it. But at some point in late July the eight Black leaders did finally agree to leave for Umbria.

On 14 August Dante and his colleagues left the Torre della Castagna. One of the very first things their successors did was bound to be, and perhaps was intended to be, seen as a snub to the Cardinal, and thus to Boniface himself. They revoked the sentence of banishment passed on the Whites, but did no such thing in the case of the Blacks. This was blatantly partisan, and was to prove a bad political mistake. It is true that while at Sarzana Cavalcanti had fallen ill with malaria—he was in fact to die (back in Florence) in late August. But even if the new priors' decision had been affected by humanitarian considerations, it did nothing whatever to improve relations between them and Rome. Cardinal Matthew, having abandoned all efforts to pacify the Florentine factions, finally left at the very end of September, not omitting to excommunicate all the city's rulers.

The Whites were now hopelessly at odds with Rome, and Boniface was to have his revenge before long. Meanwhile Corso Donati bided his time.

# 5

# Boniface VIII and the Black Coup
## (1300–1302)

To call Pope Boniface VIII Dante's *bête noire* would be an under-statement. When in his exile the poet came to write the *Divine Comedy*, he especially reserved a place in Hell for this pope, who is variously denounced by characters in the poem (sinners and saints alike) as an avaricious Simoniac; the 'Prince of the New Pharisees'; a plotter; and a usurper. This last accusation comes from the soul of St Peter himself, the first pope, in one of the highest heavens of the *Paradiso*. The Apostle vehemently attacks his medieval successor, a man who is usurping *his* throne: 'Quelli ch'usurpa in terra il luogo mio' (*Par.* XXVII, 22). Dante regarded Boniface as a key protagonist in his exile from Florence, and his harsh judgement can scarcely be considered impartial. But in any case, this strong-minded, dynamic and sometimes intemperate pontiff was a highly controversial figure in his own lifetime, widely criticized on a number of grounds. Although this chapter will give some account of his general character and career, its chief focus will be on the events leading to Dante's banishment early in 1302, events in which Boniface was closely involved.

## (i) Dante's Last Months in Florence

After Dante's term as prior came to an end in August 1300, there is no further mention of him in public documents until eight months later. There exists a private document from March 1301, but this has simply to do with a loan for which he and his brother Francesco acted as guarantors.[1] On 14 April 1301, Dante is known to have made two speeches in the *Consiglio delle Capitudini*. This body had been convened to discuss (again) procedures for electing the priors, and Dante appears on this occasion as a 'wise man', just as he had, in connection with this very same matter, back in December 1295. Dante supported the more 'democratic' of two alternative proposals, namely selection by lot from four, rather than two, nominees for each *sesto*, or electoral ward.[2]

Far more momentous, not least for his own political future, was Dante's involvement in the deliberations of the Council of One Hundred, on 19 June.[3] On that day this body met twice, to consider a request by Matthew of Acquasparta, on behalf of Boniface. The Pope was conducting a military campaign in the Maremma region against the redoubtable Margherita Aldobrandeschi, the much-married 'Red Countess'. He had already been granted the assistance of a hundred Florentine knights, and now he was seeking to retain their services. In the first session of the Council, four opinions were expressed. Two speakers were for acceding to Boniface's request, and one proposed delay. The fourth speaker was Dante, and he alone was for refusing the Pope, in blunt terms to judge from the minutes: 'Dante Alagherii consuluit quod de servitio faciendo d[omino] pape nichil fiat' ('Dante Alighieri advised that, as to assisting the Pope, nothing should be done'). When the Council reconvened in more restricted session the question was again raised, and Dante re-affirmed his position. But when it came to a vote, the view of an opposing speaker prevailed, by forty-nine votes to thirty-two. Boniface was to have his cavalry then, but the day's proceedings show that the Whites were by no means unanimous in their policy towards him. The majority favoured caution; Dante was an outspoken member of a defiant, even intransigent, minority.

Dante again spoke in the Council of One Hundred on three occasions in September 1301. On the last of these (28 September) he supported eight proposals, the sixth of which may well have had a bearing on his forthcoming banishment: together with Albizzo Corbinelli, a judge, Dante himself proposed an amnesty for Neri Diodati, whose father Gherardino had been one of Dante's immediate predecessors as a prior.[4] This Neri had been wrongly condemned to death by Cante de' Gabrielli during his first term as *podestà* in 1298, and he had fled the city. The amnesty proposal was overwhelmingly carried. But very soon, in just over a month, Cante de' Gabrielli was to return to Florence in some splendour and to be re-appointed *podestà*. He it was who condemned Dante and other leading Whites, including Gherardino, Neri's father. By his action on 28 September Dante may well have made another enemy. Very shortly afterwards he embarked on his last diplomatic mission for Florence, a vain attempt to prevent the *coup d'état* referred to in the title of this chapter. The mission was sent to Boniface.

## (ii) Boniface and Celestine

Benedetto Caetani was born around 1235, almost certainly at Anagni to the east of Rome, where his family (minor aristocrats) had property and land. Some sixty years later he was to be elected pope, taking the name of Boniface. His pontificate lasted less than a decade, but it was one of the most eventful of the Middle Ages. Boniface VIII has sometimes been called 'the last medieval pope', and this is true in the sense that he was the last great upholder of papal power both in the temporal and spiritual spheres, something characteristic of several outstanding popes during the later Middle Ages. Though his reign ended in humiliation at the hands of Philip IV of France, he was a trenchant and eloquent champion of the papacy, a worthy successor to Gregory VII (the great Hildebrand) in the eleventh century, Alexander III in the twelfth and Innocent III at the beginning of the thirteenth. Readers of Dante who are not specialists in medieval history tend to form a thoroughly negative view of Boniface. It is true that he was aggressive, waged a relentless crusade against the powerful Colonna family and undoubtedly abused his position to advance his relatives and other supporters within the Church. He also had territorial designs on Tuscany. But judged as a leader of the Church he was resourceful, dynamic and until the very end bold-spirited. His only English biographer called him 'great of heart'.[5]

Some of the problems of his troubled reign stemmed from the strange circumstances of his election. His immediate predecessor, who was as unlike Boniface as could be imagined, had taken the unprecedented step of abdicating. This was Pope Celestine V, a most improbable pontiff. He had succeeded Nicholas IV, but only after a prolonged interval. Nicholas had died in 1292 and there had followed an interregnum of nearly two years, during which time the cardinals failed to agree upon a new pope. This was largely the result of a series of impasses caused by rivalry between the Colonna and Orsini factions. But in mid-1294 Cardinal Latino Malabranca apparently received a letter from an evangelical hermit (the founder of a new religious order), threatening divine punishment if the cardinals did not come to a decision. Surprisingly they did; meeting at Perugia in July 1294 they elected the letter-writing hermit himself, Peter Morrone, a southern Italian then almost eighty years old. His piety was undisputed, but he was a man of little education, quite unworldly and hopelessly unsuited to lead a complex organization like the late-medieval Church. At no stage did he come to Rome; he chose to be crowned at Aquila (29 August) and spent the few months of his reign in Neapolitan territory, from October residing in Naples itself. He seems to have been from the first very much under the influence of King Charles II of Naples. Indeed, of the twelve new cardinals he created, 'many of them men whose names were completely unknown to him', all but three were 'very clearly nominations made by Charles'.[6] (All his appointments and decrees were later annulled by Boniface, apparently with Celestine's consent.) Many in the curia were soon appalled and exasperated by the new Pope's unsophisticated incompetence. It was clear that a mistake had been made; Celestine desperately wanted to return to his simple hermit's life and it needed little pressure to make him resign. Having consulted various cardinals (Caetani included) as to the legality of such a step, he did so in Naples on 13 December. This time there was no lengthy conclave: on Christmas Eve the cardinals chose Benedetto Caetani as his successor.

Boniface's reign had begun. From the outset he was worried about Celestine, or rather Peter Morrone. Aware of the hermit's considerable popular following (there had been mass protests by the common people of Naples after his abdication), he feared an outbreak of discontent if Peter returned to his hermitage. Indeed, Boniface already had numerous opponents and rivals who might exploit the old man's simplicity. At first he ordered Peter to be brought to Rome, but he escaped from his escort and had to be recaptured after remote mountain wanderings and an abortive attempt to sail to Greece. In the end Boniface had him confined in a castle near Anagni, where he died in May 1296. In 1313 he was canonized (unlike Boniface!) by Pope Clement V as St Peter Morrone, not St Celestine V.

Despite this canonization, Dante probably classed Celestine among those neutral or uncommitted souls whom he confines in the vestibule of Hell, unworthy, so to speak, to enter the realm of the truly damned. Certainly the earliest among the fourteenth-century commentators on Dante took the view that the cryptic expression 'colui/che fece per viltade il gran rifiuto' ('he who out of cowardice made the great refusal'—*Inf*. III, 59–60) does indeed refer to the hapless Celestine.[7] It would be typical of Dante to scorn as weak-mindedness what others might see as meekness. However, it is also true that Dante subscribed to the widespread view that Boniface had somehow tricked Celestine into resigning; this is one of the sins the poet accuses him of in the famous Canto of the Damned Popes, where the word 'inganno' ('deceit') is expressly used (*Inf*. XIX, 56). What precise form such deception may have taken is unclear, but almost from the moment of Boniface's election, rumours began to circulate about Celestine's resignation. The most bizarre story was to make its first appearance in a Florentine chronicle, completed in 1303, to the effect that Cardinal Caetani had secretly gone to Celestine's cell at night and addressed him through a speaking-tube (*tromba*), claiming to be an angel sent from God and unsubtly indicating that failure to give up would seriously damage his spiritual health. This particular tale soon became widespread; it was used against Boniface in his posthumous 'trial' mounted by Philip IV in 1310–11 and reappears in numerous later chronicles, and even in a fifteenth-century Icelandic saga.[8] But it seems a little crude for Boniface. An outstanding expert in canon law, he is much more likely to have concentrated on quelling the simple hermit's doubts as to the legality of his abdication. Whatever the truth of the matter, Boniface throughout his reign and after his death was to be accused of coming to power by suspect means. And the darkest mutterings of all surrounded Peter Morrone's death. Although there is no evidence whatever that Boniface did murder him, this was already being openly asserted by members of the Colonna family in a manifesto of 1297, at the height of their bitter feud with the Pope.[9]

One of the most dramatic moments in this feud was the surrender the following year of Palestrina, where the Colonna had their most secure fortress. Though the Colonna themselves never accused the Pope of treacherously making a false promise in order to induce them to surrender, Dante most vigorously did, in another famous *Inferno* episode: Canto XXVII, 85–111, where he encounters the fraudulent Guido da Montefeltro, the warrior turned friar.

## (iii) Boniface, Charles de Valois and Florence

Boniface's belligerent struggles with the Colonna, his two major confrontations with Philip of France and his complex rapports with Naples and Sicily lie largely outside our scope, fascinating as they are. It is time to consider his relations with Florence. He was by no means the first pope to have designs on what was after all the dominant city-state of Tuscany. Were that province to come under papal control, the Holy See's territory would extend right up to the southern border of Lombardy. Boniface was well aware of the financial and commercial importance of Florence—his family included merchants in Pisa who had close contacts with the Florentine Spini bankers. He was equally aware of the convoluted politics of the city, and here he made his own position quite clear in the very first year of his reign. He had no time for Giano della Bella and his *Ordinamenti di Giustizia*. To his autocratic mind these were, in Boase's words, 'a challenge to sound government'.[10] Already in 1295 Boniface's policy was to influence Florentine affairs through the disaffected *grandi*. (Five years later, in the year or so leading up to Dante's exile, this amounted to backing the Blacks.) 1295 saw a mitigation of the *Ordinamenti*, and this change had the Pope's support. But by January 1296 supporters of Giano were encouraging him to return from exile in France, and now Boniface intervened: he issued a bull denouncing Giano in typically violent language and threatening the Florentines with excommunication if they dared to welcome him back. By this time Boniface was on cordial terms with Corso Donati, and in May 1297 he granted him a dispensation recognizing the validity of his second marriage, which had been questioned on grounds of consanguinity. As we have seen, when in late 1299 Corso was banished from Florence, he went directly to Rome where he was well received by the Pope and installed in Orvieto as *podestà*. Throughout 1300 and 1301 he was a frequent visitor at the papal court.

Relations between the Florentine Whites and Boniface had become particularly strained during 1300, culminating in Matthew of Acquasparta's sentence of excommunication. Shortly after the Cardinal's departure the Whites, in a sort of damage-limitation exercise, sent an embassy to Boniface attempting to placate him. This was led by Vieri de' Cerchi, and it is just possible (as Petrocchi has tentatively suggested[11]) that Dante took part, though the general scholarly opinion is that he was involved not in this but in the far more desperate and dramatic mission a year later. The White emissaries were received by Boniface on 11 November 1300.

Although he agreed to revoke the sentence of excommunication, the mission did nothing to mitigate the Pope's support for the Blacks (his official policy, of course, was to pacify both factions). Already the days of White power were numbered. Less than a fortnight after the audience with the Whites, Boniface sent a letter to the clergy of France, urging them to support him in a move to involve the French prince Charles de Valois in the affairs of Italy. Charles was to be the means whereby the Blacks regained power, though Boniface also had larger-scale schemes in mind for him.

Charles de Valois (1270–1325) was the younger brother of Philip IV of France (with whom Boniface was to quarrel so bitterly) and the second cousin of Dante's friend Charles Martel. He was intimately connected with the ruling French dynasty and though his elder son was to become Philip VI of France (the first in the great line of Valois monarchs), Charles himself never became king of France, or anywhere else. He had in fact aspired unsuccessfully to the thrones of Aragon and Sicily, not to mention the Imperial crowns of Constantinople and the (Western) Holy Roman Empire. After his brief and abortive Sicilian campaign in 1302 he was popularly referred to in Italy as 'Carlo Senzaterra'[12] (i.e. 'Lackland', the nickname given a century before to King John of England prior to his succeeding Richard the Lionheart). So at first sight 'his career may have some appearance of frustration', as Boase puts it.[13] Yet for all the unfavourable turn of events, Charles was widely admired as a dynamic and capable young man, brave and resourceful. Certainly Boniface held him in high esteem, and in 1300 formally invited him to come to Italy. There were two chief aims behind this invitation. The grander (though as it proved, unsuccessful) design was that Charles should assist Charles II of Naples in his Sicilian war against Frederick II of Aragon. Since the Sicilian rising of 1282 the island had been ruled by Aragon; the former Kingdom of Naples and Sicily was now divided. As far as Tuscany was concerned, Boniface intended to use Charles de Valois as yet another 'peacemaker'.

Charles agreed to the papal proposal and finally arrived on Italian soil, with around 500 knights and his pregnant wife Margaret of Anjou, on 11 July 1301 (very shortly after Dante's defiant anti-papal remarks in the Council of One Hundred). The White leaders were understandably alarmed; not only had their relations with Rome been very strained, but in May they had actively helped their fellow Whites in nearby Pistoia to expel the Blacks from that city. There were now plenty of Tuscan Blacks seeking revenge, and military intervention involving outside forces seemed a real danger.

Throughout the summer Charles progressed steadily down from northern Italy. At Parma, in Lombardy, he was lavishly entertained by Azzo VIII d'Este, who lent him 10,000 florins. He went next, at the beginning of August, to Bologna, whose leaders assured him of their devotion to the Holy See and declared that their recent treaty with Florence had been 'to the honour, praise and reverence of the most Holy Father, Boniface VIII and of Cardinal Matthew of Acquasparta'.[14] During Charles' stay in Bologna the Florentine Blacks sent an embassy to him; according to Compagni (one of our most important and reliable sources for these events) they declared themselves true Guelphs, faithful to the Royal House of France, and implored the Prince's protection since, as they put it, their city was in the hands of 'Ghibellines' (a typical smear against the White Guelph rulers). The Whites also sent their own emissaries to Bologna, but the Blacks had preceded them and, it would seem, had been more favourably received.[15] The remainder of August saw Charles ominously (for the Whites, at least) skirting the confines of Florentine territory, passing successively through the Tuscan cities of Lucca, San Gimignano and Siena. He was *en route* to the Pope, and from 3 September he is known to have been at Anagni— Boniface tended to stay there until very late every summer (in 1301 he did not in fact return to Rome until 2 October). Charles was splendidly received, the occasion being characterised *inter alia* by falcons and (more) florins. The former were presented to him by Charles II of Naples, and their number is not known. But the florins amounted to 200,000 and Boniface was the donor. The Pope did not merely bestow money, however; it was at Anagni on 5 September that Charles' brief in Italy was officially confirmed. This seems to have occasioned a typically lively scene. Boniface conferred upon him the titles of Duke of Spoleto, Rector of the Romagna and the Marche, and Peacemaker in Tuscany. As to this last, 'I will not call you vicar,' said Boniface, 'else the Florentines will say that I am seizing rights over Tuscany.' He added with characteristic vehemence, 'I know their rights well enough, for they are usurers, and their lives are at the Church's disposal'.[16]

Charles left the papal presence by 19 September at the latest, and set out on his Tuscan mission. By mid-October he was again in Siena. Here he received two rather different gifts. His wife gave birth to a daughter; Corso Donati gave him money. The Blacks had been fund raising in earnest, and 'Il gran barone', as Corso was popularly known, arrived with yet more florins—70,000, no less. The Blacks and their friendly 'peacemaker' were now poised for action. But before the November coup, the Whites were to make one final diplomatic effort.

Probably at the very end of September a small delegation had been despatched to Rome. Compagni names just three ambassadors, though it is possible there may have been more; there is also the possibility that the Florentines were joined by emissaries from Bologna, anxious to promote peace in their allied city. The three named ambassadors were Maso Minerbetti, Corazza da Signa and Dante.[17] It is not certain whether the Pope received them in Rome or whether they arrived in time to catch him at Anagni, proceeding from there to the Holy City. But this is a minor point; what matters is Boniface's treatment of them. This was typically haughty; he was not interested in concessions, but in obedience. The audience, which Compagni claims was reported to him verbatim, seems to have been curt in the extreme. The Pope addressed the ambassadors in camera thus: 'Why are you so stubborn? Humble yourselves before me; and I tell you in truth that my only intention is for your city to be at peace. Two of you will go back [to Florence]; and may they have my blessing if they can ensure that my will is obeyed.'[18] The two emissaries who returned with this uncompromising message were Minerbetti and Corazza; Dante alone remained at the papal court. No doubt Boniface thought it wiser to keep him away from Florence until his pro-Black schemes had been put into action. The outspoken and eloquent poet might well have galvanized his fellow citizens into tiresome resistance, whereas there was little to fear on that front by sending back the other two, who were scarcely of the same calibre. Compagni had a poor opinion of Minerbetti, at any rate.[19] Unfortunately we do not know when Dante left Rome. He would have heard of the disastrous turn of events in Florence by the end of the first week in November. At this point he may well have left, since he could no longer hope to achieve anything in Rome. It is just possible that he then returned to Florence, still hoping to escape the consequences of the *coup d'état*, only to flee shortly afterwards. This however seems improbable, and it has been traditionally held that Dante was absent during the tumult preceding his downfall. But there is no firm evidence on these points. It is a pity that we cannot know just when, and in what circumstances, Europe's most famous literary exile since Ovid last looked upon his native city.

### (iv) The Coup and its Aftermath

Let us now turn to the rapid sequence of events in Florence. From Siena, in late October, Charles de Valois sent two emissaries to the city. They were deferentially received; even at this late stage the Florentine government still hoped to avoid having united against it two such powerful (and commercially important) entities as the papacy and France. They in return sent ambassadors to Siena, beseeching Charles to guarantee the security of their city. This he did, and on that basis was invited to come to Florence, but solely as peacemaker, and not with a view to claiming any jurisdiction over the city, or to changing any of its laws. Compagni tells us that Charles' chancellor (Guillaume de la Perche, one of the two emissaries, who had remained in Florence) was specifically asked to ensure that his master did not arrive in the city on All Saints' Day, since on that day (1 November) there was always a *festa* featuring wine from the new harvest, and the common people were liable to get out of hand![20] But the Blacks were pressing Charles to leave for Florence as soon as possible. This he did, stopping at the castle of Staggia near Poggibonsi, some miles to the south of Florence. This castle belonged to a firm friend of the French monarchy— Musciatto Francesi, one of Philip IV's financial advisers. A native of Florentine territory, he had made a fortune in France as a usurer. Eventually he managed to get himself ennobled, and had returned to Italy as part of Charles' entourage in July. He is a classic example of the parvenu Dante so despised.

From Staggia Charles proceeded to Florence, entering on All Saints' Day after all (despite the threat of drunken disturbances). As well as his own entourage, various other contingents arrived, all ostensibly coming to honour the great Prince. According to Compagni there were 200 knights from Perugia, others from Lucca, and Cante de' Gabrielli, the former *podestà*, with a substantial body of cavalry from Siena. Individuals such as the renowned commander Mainardo Pagano da Susinana (who managed to be

Ghibelline when in the Romagna but Guelph in Tuscany) also arrived on the scene. Charles may have been able to count on the support of no less than 1,200 knights.[21] From the Whites' point of view the situation now rapidly deteriorated. On 4 November Corso Donati and the exiled Blacks entered the city, in contravention of the banishment order still in force against them. They opened the prisons, and large-scale disturbances ensued. For five consecutive days the Whites' property was pillaged and burnt, the Casa Alighieri being among the houses attacked. Throughout this time Charles, the so-called peacemaker, did nothing to intervene. Dante quite clearly regarded him as treacherously siding with the Blacks: in the *Purgatorio* he will be described as armed with 'la lancia/con la qual giostrò Giuda' ('the lance that Judas jousted with'—*Purg.* XX, 73–74). Rapid changes in the government itself followed. The priors who had taken office on 15 October (including our chronicler Compagni) tried to salvage the situation by standing down prematurely, though this contravened the *Ordinamenti di Giustizia*, and proposing a new ruling group of three Whites and three Blacks. But this was not enough for the triumphant Blacks. The legitimate government was deposed, and on 7 November a new *Signoria* (i.e. the six priors plus the *Gonfaloniere di Giustizia*) took power; they were all Blacks. The following day a new *podestà* was elected— none other than Cante de' Gabrielli. Just over a fortnight later the new rulers issued an elaborate edict seeking to give *de jure* status to what was now the situation *de facto*. What had happened was nothing short of a *coup d'état*.

In December the Pope once again despatched Matthew of Acquasparta to Florence as papal legate. Notwithstanding the usual peacemaking brief, it would seem that Boniface wanted a papal presence in the city as a counterweight to any excessive upsurge in Black Guelph/French ascendancy: he wanted his protégés to be sufficiently powerful to implement his designs but not so strong as to be able to act independently of him. The Cardinal arrived on 15 December to find a far from peaceful city. Destruction and murder continued. Christmas Day itself saw no respite: there were reciprocal killings by the Donati and Cerchi families, one of the assassins—subsequently a victim himself—being Simone Donati, Corso's youngest son. It seems most improbable that Dante was still in Florence by this time (if indeed he had ever returned from Rome). What is certain is that he was not there on 27 January 1302, for on that day he was condemned *in absentia*, along with four others. Cante de' Gabrielli issued a juridical proclamation falling into two parts; the first condemned Gherardino Diodati and the second Dante, together with three others. They all stood accused of *baractaria* (that is 'barratry', or financial corruption whilst in public office—the secular equivalent of simony), of opposing requests for aid from Charles II of Naples and from Boniface, and furthermore of having connived at the expulsion of the Pistoian Blacks (who are described as 'loyal devotees of the Holy Roman Church'—'expulsionem ... eorum qui dicuntur Nigri, fidelium devotorum sancte Romane ecclesie')[22]. Although there is no evidence that Dante—or any of the others, indeed—was guilty of corruption, we have seen how in 1300 he had defiantly rejected Boniface's military requests, and there can be no doubt of the involvement of leading Florentine Whites in the events at Pistoia. Cante's sentence prohibited the five condemned men from ever again holding public office in Florence, fined them each 5,000 florins and banished them from Florentine territory for two years. They were further required to appear before him within three days to justify themselves, if they could, and to pay the fine; otherwise their property would be destroyed. They all failed to do so. It might be naive to wonder how they were supposed to have been informed of the sentence.

Charles de Valois, having more or less accomplished the Pope's wishes by masterly non-intervention, left Florence on 13 February for Rome, where he spent just over a month. Relations between him and Boniface seem now to have become somewhat frosty; in particular, the Pope appears to have thought he had given him quite enough money and every opportunity to have acquired more elsewhere. Charles returned to Florence on 18 March, but for barely a fortnight. Early in April, with the Blacks now firmly in charge, he left the city for ever, bound for Naples where he was to launch his ill-fated Sicilian campaign. During Charles' visit to Rome a second, far harsher sentence was issued against Dante and fourteen others by the *podestà*, on 10 March. Cante now extended the banishment order in perpetuity, and decreed that if any of these men should ever return to Florentine territory he would be burnt to death ('talis perveniens ingne [*sic*] comburatur sic quod moriatur').[23] Dante of course never did so, even when invited to many years later, on terms quite unacceptable to him. But he and his fourteen fellow victims of the 10 March sentence were by no means the only ones banished. The revenge of the victorious Blacks was wide ranging; on 9 June they decreed that the wives of those condemned, together with their sons and descendants in the male line (upon reaching the age of fourteen) should also be expelled. By the end of 1302, Compagni tells us, upwards of 600 Florentines had been forced from their homeland, wandering some here, some there.[24] And in the *De Vulgari Eloquentia* (II, vi, 4) Dante was to write of the many who could now revisit their city only in dreams.

If this chapter has not discussed Dante's writings, it is because nothing of his literary output can be assigned with certainty to 1300 or 1301. Perhaps that is not surprising. It is to the bitter yet fruitful leisure of the long years ahead that we must now turn.

# 6
# Early Exile
## (1302–1304)

### (i) Dante in Tuscany, Forlì and Verona

Tu lascerai ogne cosa diletta
più caramente; e questo è quello strale
che l'arco de lo essilio pria saetta.
Tu proverai sì come sa di sale
lo pane altrui, e come è duro calle
lo scendere e 'l salir per l'altrui scale.

You will leave behind all that you have loved/most dearly, and this
is the arrow/the bow of exile shoots first./You will find out how
salty/someone else's bread tastes, and how hard is the way/up and
down another's stairs.

These famous words are spoken in the *Paradiso* (XVII, 55–60) by
Cacciaguida, the twelfth-century crusader who was Dante's great-
great-grandfather. They form part of one of the many 'hindsight
prophecies' in the *Divine Comedy*, and refer of course to the grim
consequences of the events we have just described. The remainder
of this book will be concerned with the historical political and
literary events of an exile that was to last almost twenty years. For
the biographer, this period falls into two rather different halves;
whereas from 1312 until his death in 1321 Dante is known to have
been largely resident in Verona and then Ravenna, his complex
wanderings in the first decade of banishment can by no means be
plotted with certainty. The very first two years of exile, however,
present fewer problems in this respect than those following the rift
(mid-1304) between Dante and the other banished White Guelphs.

At first he stayed in Tuscany with his fellows. We know of two meetings in 1302 between the exiles and various Ghibelline leaders, whose own banishment had lasted ever since their momentous defeat at Benevento back in 1266. The Whites were not prepared to accept the consequences of the Black Coup lying down, and the Ghibellines were very willing to ally with them in military preparations for a comeback. The first meeting, which may well have been relatively informal, probably took place early in 1302 at Gargonza. Petrocchi, along with Pampaloni, believes it to have been as early as February, that is between Cante de' Gabrielli's first condemnation and the passing of the death sentences.[1] Indeed Petrocchi specifically infers that the latter were a direct result of the new White Guelph/Ghibelline threat to the recently established power of the Florentine Blacks. It is generally held that Dante was present at Gargonza, and of his involvement in the second, better-attested meeting there is no doubt. This took place early in June at San Godenzo in the Mugello region, about twenty miles to the north-east of Florence. On this occasion Dante and sixteen other Florentines undertook to recompense the Ubaldini, a powerful Ghibelline family, for any loss or harm that might come to them in a proposed war against Black Florence.[2] Vieri de' Cerchi was present at San Godenzo and, as Petrocchi puts it, the *stato maggiore* (the 'General Staff') of the Whites were all assembled there: it was a fully-fledged convention. The great Ghibelline clan of the Uberti were soon to be involved in the preparations for conflict: Lapo degli Uberti arrived. He was the son (or possibly the nephew) of the famous commander Farinata, the Ghibelline victor of Montaperti (1260), whose soul Dante is to meet in one of the *Inferno's* most dramatic encounters (X, 22–120). Although the joint White/Ghibelline campaign was to end in failure, there may well have been hopes among certain of the exiles that Montaperti would be repeated, after more than forty years.

This was not to be. There was sporadic military action on a relatively small scale during the second half of 1302, but the White successes were very limited. In fact it was not a bad year for the Tuscan Blacks generally. In May the Florentine Blacks, together with the Lucchesi, had captured Serravalle from the ruling Whites of Pistoia. And in July the Florentine Whites lost the castle of Piantravigne in the Valdarno. This was being held for them by Carlino de' Pazzi, but he treacherously betrayed it to the Blacks for a bribe; in fact he struck a deal with Gherardino da Gambara, the new *podestà* of Florence. It will come as no surprise that Carlino has a place reserved for him in the *Inferno*. In the lowest depths of Hell, the region reserved for traitors, Dante meets Camicion de' Pazzi (XXXII, 52–69), a relative of the betrayer of Piantravigne, who tells him he is awaiting the arrival of the damned soul of Carlino, beside whose sin his own will pale into insignificance (Camicion had merely murdered one of his relations). Since at Easter 1300—the date when Dante's journey into the afterlife is set—Carlino was still alive, he cannot appear as a character in the *Inferno*. So Dante damns him in advance, just as he does in the case of Boniface VIII, who was not to die until 1303.

There was further but inconclusive fighting in the Mugello until late in 1302, when military operations were postponed because of the approaching winter. It does not appear that Dante was personally involved in any of these conflicts, though he was active on his fellows' behalf in another way. In the autumn he left for Forlì in the Romagna, roughly twenty miles north-east of San Godenzo. Here he was to spend the first protracted period outside Tuscany of his banishment. His host was Scarpetta Ordelaffi, head of a long-established Ghibelline family, who was quite ready to help the exiled Whites; they were in fact to nominate him as their military commander. It would seem that Dante's role at Scarpetta's court was to advance preparations for a renewed campaign against Black Florence the following spring. It also appears that very early in 1303 he carried out certain official tasks on behalf of the Chancery of Forlì. (During his exile he was frequently to act in administrative and diplomatic capacities for the various noblemen at whose courts he resided.)

Warfare was resumed in spring 1303, but the Whites were again unsuccessful. Whether Dante himself was present in the theatre of war (the Mugello area once more) is not clear, but Petrocchi has shown that in May or June he left for Verona, another Ghibelline city.[3] Here he stayed until the following spring; whether as part of a White embassy or simply as a political refugee is unclear. (It is not surprising that the Whites should have turned to Verona for support; many of them had trading links there, as they did with Ghibelline towns in the Romagna.) At any event the interlude in Verona, away from troubled Tuscany, seems to have been a relatively peaceful time for Dante. His noble host was Bartolommeo della Scala, who appears to have befriended him. In the *Paradiso*

(XVII, 70–71) Cacciaguida speaks of Verona as Dante's 'first refuge and lodging' ('Lo primo tuo rifugio, il primo ostello')—this need not conflict with the previous mission to Forlì—thanks to the courtesy of Bartolommeo, the 'great Lombard' ('la cortesia del gran Lombardo'). It is highly probable that Dante's literary output increased markedly at Verona, and this chapter will return to his writings, which we have not discussed directly since Chapter 3. Certainly two very important post-exilic *canzoni* can be dated to the years 1302–4, and may well have been written in Verona. The *De Vulgari Eloquentia* was completed at the latest by the beginning of 1305, by which time the *Convivio* had also been begun. And Dante's earliest two surviving letters date from 1304, almost immediately after his departure from Verona. The precise location, both in a temporal and geographical sense, of these works cannot be determined, and many may question the order in which they are discussed here. But I shall begin with the *De Vulgari* and the two *canzoni* before once again turning to political events, which constitute the background, or rather the foreground, of the two letters. The *Convivio* is considered in the next chapter.

## (ii) The *De Vulgari Eloquentia*

This is a treatise in Latin on the vernacular language (or congeries of dialects) spoken and written in the Italian peninsula. Much attention, often of a highly technical kind, is paid to Italian poetry, and Book II is a sort of *ars poetica*. Although at least four books were originally planned, the treatise is incomplete, breaking off abruptly in the fourteenth chapter of Book II. It does not appear to have attracted much attention prior to the sixteenth century, when it was first printed; indeed its full importance has been appreciated only in modern times. It offers a pioneering attempt at a classification of languages; a subtle probing of the art, or artifice, of the poetic craftsman; and, not least, it is a great work of literary criticism. For all its technicalities, the *De Vulgari* is no abstract, let alone arid disquisition. It is a lively, passionate, at times piquant text. Its appeal is by no means confined to linguistic specialists or to historians of Italian literature; all those enquiring into Dante will find the *De Vulgari Eloquentia* of great interest, not least because it also has a moral and political dimension, never far away in Dante, whatever his theme.

As ever, Dante is acutely conscious of the originality and importance of what he is writing. The very first words of the treatise assert
that no one before has ever written about the vernacular. In a trivial
sense this is incorrect, for there were practical manuals of Provençal
verse composition, widely circulated in thirteenth-century Italy as
well as in southern France. But the aim of these works is essentially
practical and technical only; the *De Vulgari* has a far loftier perspective on language as a crucial component of human culture.
Dante will not attempt his task unaided, however; he will make use
of learned authorities who have preceded him, and—more strikingly—what he has to say will be said with the inspirational help
of the Heavenly Word, the word *par excellence* ('Verbo aspirante
de celis'). Dante begins by defining a vernacular as that speech
which we acquire as infants, not by learning any rules, but simply
by imitating our nurses. It is to be distinguished from 'secondary'
languages ('locutio secundaria'), such as Latin and Greek,
languages which only a few, after long and patient study, can
acquire. The vernacular must be considered nobler than the
scholarly ancient tongues, and for three reasons: the tongue first
used by the human race was a vernacular; all peoples speak a vernacular (even though languages differ in grammar and vocabulary);
finally, our vernacular speech is natural to us, Latin and Greek
being more a question of art.

Dante goes on to emphasize the essentially, and peculiarly,
human nature of language. Angels, those beings immediately above
us in the scale of creation, communicate by direct intuition, and
thus have no need of language. Nor do animals, who rank immediately below us, since they communicate by instinct. But we, being
rational creatures endowed with mortal flesh, need a 'rational and
sensible sign' ('rationale signum et sensuale'—I, iii, 2), that is,
something which is based on the senses (since it involves speaking
and hearing) yet which can convey the contents of one mind to
another. That something is language.

Chapter iv sees Dante probing the origin of human language. He
sets out, somewhat ambitiously, to determine who it was who first
spoke, what that person said, to whom, where and when it was
said, and which tongue was being spoken. All this on the basis of
the Bible, with not a little of Dante's own conjecture. The Book of
Genesis tells us, says Dante, that the first person to speak was presumptuous Eve ('presumptuosissima Eva') when she replied to the

serpent's question (Genesis 3. 2–3). But Genesis 2. 19–20 has already related how Adam gave names to all the animals, before Eve had been created. In saying that according to the Bible Eve was the first to speak, Dante may perhaps mean that she was the first to have a 'conversation'.[4] Or he may have mis-remembered the text of Genesis. In any case, he now asserts that Adam was the first to give utterance, not Eve. Language being so elevated a function of mankind, it seems simply inappropriate to Dante that the first human to speak should have been a female! He supposes (without any sanction in Scripture) that Adam, immediately after the moment of his creation, uttered the first word ever spoken, as an expression of joyous gratitude to his maker. That word was 'El'— simply the name of God Himself. What else could the first man's first utterance have been?

Thus Dante has boldly answered all but one of the questions posed at the beginning of Chapter iv. Chapter vi deals with the remaining one: here we are told that Adam's language was Hebrew, as was that of all his descendants (i.e. all mankind) until the building of the tower of Babel (Genesis 11.4).[5] This Dante regarded as a historical event, and the origin of linguistic diversity; the futile, presumptuous tower, a vain attempt by sinful men to scale the heights of heaven, was a tower of confusion ('turris confusionis'), and more precisely of confusion in the matter of language. Yet the Hebrews, as distinct from the other races engaged in building the tower, preserved Adam's original God-given tongue. Indeed, Hebrew, by contrast with other languages, was to remain in an unchanged, uncorrupted state till the coming of the Redeemer, so that He would find for His use not a language of confusion but one 'of grace' ('non lingua confusionis, sed gratie'—I, vi, 6). Dante would not have known that Jesus of Nazareth spoke Aramaic, rather than Hebrew.

After further reflections upon man's sinful pride, and the dire consequences of Babel, Dante in Chapter viii sketches out the fragmentation of human language, in terms of the migrations of three ethnic groups within Europe and the surrounding areas. In the north there are the Teutons, Slavs and Hungarians (all grouped together!); in the south there are the Romance peoples; in the (south-) east the Greeks (by which Dante means the inhabitants of the Balkan region in general, and of Asia Minor).[6] The linguistic and anthropological shortcomings of this scheme (not at all unusual in a western medieval context) need not concern us. The classification is merely a prelude to the chief aim of *De Vulgari*, Book I: a comparative examination of the dialects of Italy, and the hunt for an 'illustrious' Italian vernacular.

Chapters ix and x narrow the focus to the Romance tongues, with which Dante was of course far better acquainted than with those of his other two groups. He makes the conventional tripartite division into (northern) French, Provençal and Italian, where the words for 'yes' are respectively *oïl*, *oc* and *sì*. All three have some claim to literary and intrinsic merit, but Dante asserts for 'Italian' pre-eminence over the other two, first because certain of its poets have written more 'sweetly and subtly' than those of the other vernaculars, and second because it is closer to Latin. As examples of sweet and subtle poets Dante adduces just two, Cino da Pistoia and 'his friend' ('Cynus Pistoriensis et amicus eius'—I, x, 2). The friend is Dante himself. But literary questions are not pursued further at this point in the treatise. Dante now emphasizes the marked linguistic diversity within the Italian peninsula: he distinguishes at least fourteen dialects. Chapter xi opens with a hunting call; we are to set out in pursuit of the most decorous and illustrious of Italy's vernaculars. The chase that now ensues occasions some of the most memorable and lively, not to say vehement, writing in the *De Vulgari*. Notwithstanding the claim, so recently made, to the literary superiority of 'Italian' over its Romance sisters, we now have a relentless onslaught upon all its *spoken* dialects (and on much of its literary output as well). Dante begins by dismissing the dialect of Rome: since the (contemporary) Romans in their presumption like to come first, let them have the dubious honour of being the first to be 'weeded out'. And this they fully deserve, for their dialect is the ugliest of all: an uncouth 'tristiloquium'. Nor is this surprising, given the Romans' exceptionally repulsive customs! The dialects of Ancona, Spoleto and, in the north and north-east, Milan, Bergamo, Aquileia and Istria are all bluntly discarded: let us extirpate them ('eruncemus'), says Dante. Casentino (just south-east of the Mugello region) and Fratta (the present-day Umbertide, on the Tiber) fare no better. The last to be condemned in this vituperative eleventh chapter are the poor Sardinians, who are in fact trying to speak Latin (*sic*), but with as much success as monkeys imitating humans.

Chapter xii is a very important one: here the political undercurrents in the *De Vulgari* surface. Dante turns now to the written vernacular, to Sicily and the achievements of the *Scuola Siciliana* poets, whom he regarded as the forerunners of his own *Dolce Stil Novo*. Indeed, he says, in honour of those early masters, all Italian poetry may be called 'Sicilian'. Might our elusive quarry, the *volgare illustre*,[7] have been found in Sicily, then? Yes, for a time, and precisely at the court of the great Hohenstaufen monarchs Frederick II and his son Manfred. To Dante it was entirely natural that such a noble environment should produce such artistic achievement. As Took says, 'literary excellence … is bound up in his mind with political excellence, with the notion of government by men of moral and intellectual virtue'.[8] As long as Fortune permitted (i.e. until the triumph of Anjou), those illustrious heroes 'Fredericus Cesar' and Manfred, a son worthy of him (though illegitimate), showed the nobility and righteousness of their souls. They lived like true men, not brute beasts (a very strongly implied contrast here with the Italian princes of Dante's own day). No wonder talented men of great spirit flourished under such majestic princes. But Dante straight away turns to the present-day rulers, and these lofty sentiments give way to the most virulent sarcasm. 'Racha, racha' ('Curse them!'),[9] scorns Dante: what of the new Frederick, King of Aragon and Sicily, what of Charles II of Naples, and (so as not to leave out northern Italy) what of John I of Montferrat, what of Azzo d'Este? The only message their trumpets proclaim is: 'This way, murderers, traitors and misers!' Such rulers are unlikely to cherish the *volgare illustre*, implies Dante. Clearly there could be no greater contrast than that between the political and cultural highpoint of the Hohenstaufen court and the degeneracy of these latter-day princes. (They must be taken as typical of the times, though not universally typical; no doubt Dante would have exempted from censure, among others, that 'great Lombard' Bartolommeo of Verona, at whose court he may well have written these lines.) So after its brief early flowering in Sicily the *volgare illustre*, we can infer, now lacks a base, and wanders here and there (an idea made explicit in Chapter xviii).

It might be thought that in Dante's view Tuscany, whose literary achievements he has already praised (but whose spoken dialect still awaits discussion) could provide an approximation to the *volgare illustre*. But Chapter xiii gives the lie to this. Dante roundly condemns his fellow Tuscans for presuming to arrogate the honour of having the most illustrious language in the peninsula. This foolish opinion is not confined to the masses; noted poets have been similarly deluded. As his first example of the latter Dante has Guittone d'Arezzo, who never strove for that vernacular which is *curiale*. Here Dante has expanded his 'identikit-picture' of the elusive *volgare*: it is now called 'curial', meaning normative, i.e. setting a standard against which other language may be matched and measured. (*Curia*, besides its ecclesiastical meaning of a papal or episcopal court, meant more generally any court of law or tribunal.) Not only Guittone but his follower Bonagiunta of Lucca, together with Gallo of Pisa and even Dante's mentor Brunetto Latini (not primarily a lyric poet), are similarly relegated to the status of 'municipal', not 'curial' writers. Dante now adds five examples of *spoken* Tuscan which are hopelessly municipal, hopelessly local. First the Florentines themselves are examined, and found wanting; the same verdict awaits the inhabitants of Pisa, Lucca, Siena and Arezzo. There is now a southward glance at Perugia, Orvieto, Viterbo and Civita Castellana, all of which Dante declines even to consider, as being far too close to Rome and Spoleto to escape contagion. He returns instead (briefly) to Tuscany; although most Tuscans remain steeped in their foul idiom ('in suo turpiloquio') a few—but only a few—have recognized what excellence in the vernacular entails and demands. Step forward the *stilnovisti*. This group was never exactly numerous, and here Dante names just four of them: Calvalcanti, Lapo Gianni and 'one other Florentine', together with Cino da Pistoia. The expression *unum alium* ('one other') refers undoubtedly to Dante himself, and recalls the reticence of Chapter x where he is called simply 'Cino's friend'. With Dante modesty is often a literary convention rather than a moral virtue. A few Tuscans, then, have achieved literary excellence, so does this not say something for the qualities of the Tuscan tongue? Not really. For the point Dante now insists upon is that these achievements were the result of a conscious distancing from the spoken idiom; the *stilnovisti* wrote well in spite of, not because of, their (spoken) linguistic environment. Chapter xiii ends with wry mockery of Genoa's dialect: such is the prevalence there of the harsh letter 'Z' that were the Genoese by some lapse of memory to forget it, they would be rendered quite dumb, unless they devised a new language!

Mentally crossing the Apennines, Dante comes to those regions as yet undiscussed: the Romagna, and then Lombardy and the

Veneto. By the time the *De Vulgari* was written Dante would have had first-hand—or rather 'first-ear'—experience of the speech of (at least) Forlì and Verona, respectively in the Romagna and Lombardy. Both linguistic areas are judged inadequate (though not in the harsh terms meted out to the Romans, Sardinians and Genoese); the dialects of the Romagna are too soft and effeminate, whereas those of Lombardy and Venetia err in the opposite direction, being too harsh and crude. Chapter xv turns the spotlight on Bologna, which has produced notable poets (chiefly Guinizelli); Dante is prepared to consider sympathetically the view that Bologna's dialect has some claim to be the most beautiful. It offers a harmonius blending of its Lombard and Romagnol neighbours' acoustic extravagances. Yet for all the good verse written by its poets (and here Dante mentions specifically Guinizelli, Onesto degli Onesti and two far more obscure names), the Bolognese dialect must remain 'municipal'; it is not in any absolute sense ('simpliciter') superior to all the others (I, xv, 6). More precisely, it is not to be equated with the illustrious *volgare*, to which Dante now attaches the further epithet *aulicum* ('courtly'). So no one city or region, it seems, possesses that linguistic excellence which is being sought.

The final chapters of Book I abandon any geographically empirical search. Chapter xvi begins with a vivid confirmation that we are still on a hunting trip, but have not yet found our 'panther': though its scent is detectable, it remains unseen.[10] So Dante now turns to a definition of his ideal *volgare*. Adding the final epithet *cardinale*, he explains (Chapters xvii–xviii) just why his quarry is to be called illustrious, cardinal (i.e. like a hinge, that upon which the rest turns), courtly and curial. With the third of these epithets the *De Vulgari*'s political dimension comes once again to the fore: the Hohenstaufen dynasty is gone, and lacking a great court, how can the illustrious, *courtly* tongue flourish? It cannot, and so is forced to wander like a refugee, seeking humble asylum (I, xviii, 3; the analogy here with Dante's personal predicament hardly needs stating). Book I's final chapter is a visionary assertion of the truly Italian quality of the *volgare illustre*: such a tongue would transcend all the narrow municipalism of the Italian states. This language had not (quite) come into being when Dante wrote the *De Vulgari*; but by the time he had finished the *Convivio*, not to speak of the *Comedy*, it had.

For our purposes, the (unfinished) second book of the *De Vulgari* need not be discussed in much detail; in particular, the technical portion on poetics (from Chapter v on) lies somewhat outside our scope. This second book begins with a discussion of the use to which the *volgare illustre* should be put. Although both prose-writers and poets may use it, it is poets with whom Dante is concerned. The point is forcefully made that the *illustre* is not for all; such is its excellence that only poets with the loftiest themes should use it. It would be ridiculous to suppose that intrinsic excellence of language could compensate for poverty or banality of content. Outward formal elegance by itself is not enough for true art. But which elevated themes does Dante have in mind? Only three are worthy of the *volgare illustre*: war, love and virtue (or righteousness), and Dante gives examples of poetic excellence in these areas. Among the Provençal troubadours we have Bertran de Born (war), Arnaut Daniel (love) and Giraut de Bornelh (righteousness). But their Italian counterparts have not yet treated the theme of arms. They have however sung of love and virtue, and here Dante's examples are Cino da Pistoia and 'his friend' (i.e. Dante himself), respectively. In fact Dante mentions as a specific instance of his own treatment of righteousness (*rectitudo*) the *canzone* 'Doglia mi reca', which we shall discuss shortly. It is significant that at this stage in his career Dante is happy to relinquish the palm in the field of amorous verse to Cino (since Cavalcanti's death the foremost Italian poet after Dante). Evidently he now sees himself as above all an ethical poet.

Having established that the *canzone* is the most exalted vernacular lyric form (a form which by now he had thoroughly mastered and raised to unprecedented heights) Dante sets out in Chapter iv his basic understanding of what it is to make poetry. The essential point here is the supreme importance of craft, or technique, allied to caution and discretion. Lyric poetry cannot be written casually ('casualiter'); if it is to be any good, the discipline of the craft must be mastered. Great mental striving and assiduous attention to technique, as well as learning, are required. In a famous passage (II, iv, 11) Dante scorns the presumptuous folly ('stultitia') of those who would sing of the highest things in the highest of styles, trusting only to inspiration ('de solo ingenio confidentes'): this will not do in the absence of skill and learning ('arte scientiaque immunes'). Artifice, then, is central to art.

The remainder of the treatise is of a technical nature, often highly so; but Chapter vi provides an unexpected reminder that Dante is writing the *De Vulgari* in exile and that his sad circumstances are much in his mind. Here he is concerned with the syntactical construction of certain types of sentence, and two of the examples he makes up are telling. The first is a general statement (though put into the first person): 'I, more than anyone else, grieve for all those who, languishing away in exile, see their homeland only in dreams'. The second example is far more pointed: 'Having cast out from your bosom, O Florence, the finest of your flowers, the second Totila went in vain to Trinacria [i.e. Sicily] (II, vi, 4–5)'. The 'second Totila' clearly refers to Charles de Valois. There was some confusion for Dante and his contemporaries between Totila, the sixth-century Ostrogothic king, and Attila, King of the Huns in the previous century, who was mistakenly believed to have destroyed Florence. But the point is that Dante, even when writing as a technician of rhetoric, cannot help thinking about the dire political events of 1301–2. These references in Book II, vi look back to the *De Vulgari*'s most striking comment on its author's exile: in the corresponding chapter of Book I Dante describes himself as now a citizen of the world, just like a fish in the ocean. Though nurtured in and by Florence, he has been unjustly cast out by her, and precisely because he loved her so much (I, vi, 3). The key word here is, of course, *iniuste* ('unjustly'), analogous to phrases such as *exul immeritus* ('undeserving exile'), soon to be prominent in the letters.

## (iii) The Poems of Righteousness

Justice, or rather the lack of it, is the concern of one of the two great *canzoni* of Dante's early exile—'Tre donne intorno al cor' ('Three ladies have surrounded my heart'). And the other, 'Doglia mi reca' ('Grief makes my heart bold'), is related to it thematically in so far as it laments the absence of another virtue: liberality. If Dante had in fact completed both these poems before the *De Vulgari*—or at any rate before Book II, ii—they would have amply justified his self-description as a 'poet of righteousness'. (But in any case his important ethical *canzoni* 'Le dolci rime d'amor' and 'Poscia ch'amor' had already been written.) For Foster and Boyde 'Tre donne' is 'the fullest expression outside the *Comedy* of Dante's reflections on his exile'.[11] In the first part of the *canzone*—a general

75

and public lamentation of the absence of justice in our world—Dante does not speak directly: the interlocutors are Love, dwelling in the poet's heart, and the three ladies of the title, who surround it. These ladies personify aspects of Justice, the precise identification of which dates back to the exegesis of Pietro Alighieri, Dante's son.[12] *Drittura*, the first of the trio (and the only lady explicitly given a name), tells Love how she and her companions were born in the Garden of Eden. They dwelt there with our first parents—an all-too-brief encounter, at least on the view that Dante had adopted by the time he wrote *Paradiso* XXVI (139–42), namely that initial innocence was followed by expulsion from the Garden after just six hours. Ever since, Justice in all her aspects has been neglected and spurned by mankind, so that she wanders the world disconsolately seeking a place of refuge. This general lament for the world's injustice (and the *canzone*'s tone is one of grief, rather than reproof) switches dramatically to Dante's own sad lot. 'E io …', he begins, powerfully personalizing the poem's theme; as Took so eloquently puts it, now exploring Justice 'from the point of view of one who has himself lived out the complex psychology of exile, its alternating courage and despair'.[13] For while at first (ll. 73–80) Dante is boldly determined to endure his fate in the company of Justice, so illustrious a fellow exile, the mood soon shifts to nostalgia for the city that has rejected him. And the poem ends with two separate *congedi* (in which Dante bids farewell to his *canzone*); the second of these surprisingly holds out some hope of reconciliation with the Blacks. They could still make their peace with him, had they a mind to. These closing lines can be linked to the end of the fifth stanza, where Dante appears to be repenting of some undefined fault.[14] There are implications here for the poem's chronology, but all that can be definitely asserted is that it was written in exile and that the second *congedo* (though not necessarily the whole of 'Tre donne') dates from 1304, perhaps as late as the end of that year.

'Doglia mi reca' was written at much the same time, and it too is one of Dante's greatest works; to quote Foster and Boyde once more, it represents together with 'Tre donne' 'the summit of Dante's achievement in ethical poetry prior to the *Comedy*'.[15] The first line ends with the word *ardire* ('boldness'), and the *canzone*'s predominant tone is one of bold vehemence: Dante is determined to be a friend to truth, even if this means speaking out against virtually everyone. Justice is not in any strict sense his theme here, but liberality and avarice (its opposite) are. For, like 'Tre donne' this is an 'absence poem', the absentee being this time liberality, or generosity. In fact the poem's most striking feature, thematically, is its attack on avarice (though the general clash of vice and virtue is also prominent). After the psychology of exile, that of avarice. The gentle grieving of 'Tre donne' is replaced by an outburst of exasperated contempt, directed against greed. What Dante stresses above all is not just the futility, but the sheer insanity of avarice. The miser inevitably becomes a slave, his mind blinded; wealth is a tyrannical force. These sentiments look forward to many later analyses and invectives on this topic in the *Convivio* and the *Comedy*, all of them utterly typical of Dante. Had the *Convivio* been complete, it may well have included a discussion of these *canzoni*, for Dante tells us that Books XIV and XV were to be devoted respectively to Justice and Liberality. This would involve a commentary on two *canzoni*, in all probability 'Tre donne' and 'Doglia mi reca'. But in any case the *Convivio's* fourth book has much to say—and all of it negative—about material riches.

## (iv) Boniface and Philip IV

It is time to turn from these remarkable poems of righteousness and catch up with political events. What had occurred since Cante de' Gabrielli's pronouncements gave Dante scant confidence in human justice, and here one must take a look at a wider European scene, beyond the misfortunes of a few hundred Tuscan exiles. Dante would not have been long at Bartolommeo's court in Verona when news arrived of the death of Boniface VIII. He might be supposed to have been relieved, overjoyed even; yet the events leading up to the Pope's death in October 1303 were to wound the poet's sense of justice deeply, moving him to moral outrage. Here some measure of historical 'background' is again indispensable.

From the very outset of his embattled pontificate Boniface was a staunch promoter and defender of the rights and jurisdiction of the Church (and more specifically the Papacy). Simoniac and nepotist he undoubtedly was; indeed his local policy—his 'micro-politics'— seems highly questionable, and not just morally. But on this point it may be said in his defence that he abused his power in order to protect his family from the fierce foes they certainly had. On a wider 'macro-political' front, he has to be recorded as a great champion of the institution at whose head he found himself in 1294. Dante detested him, but never sought to belittle his talents. An outstanding lawyer, and benefactor of higher education, he was probably the most intelligent pope—and actively, vigorously so—since Innocent III, who had died in 1216. We have already seen his early interventions in Florentine matters in 1296. Later that year he promulgated the bull *Clericis laicos*, directed against Philip IV of France (and Edward I of England). The issue was clerical taxation, only too familiar to every medieval historian. The European kings were in constant need of fiscal revenue, most notably of course to wage war. Boniface insisted that lay rulers had no right to tax the Church without his permission. Although the terms of *Clericis laicos* were soon modified (in 1297), the Pope was to remain at loggerheads with the French King (and his team of ingenious lawyers).

Boniface's collaboration with Charles de Valois in 1300–2 did nothing to reconcile him with Philip. In fact the last and most bitter conflict between King and Pope was to begin in October 1301, with Charles in Siena, *en route* to Florence (and Dante at the papal court). Philip ordered the arrest and trial of Bernard Saisset, Bishop of Pamiers in the Languedoc. This was all to further the King's aim of asserting his power over the Church in all parts of his kingdom; the Bishop's trials appear to have been a mockery of justice and the string of charges against him a fabrication—the work of Guillaume de Nogaret, the lawyer who before long would become Philip's chief adviser.[16] Boniface reacted with characteristic vigour; in December he issued a flurry of bulls, proclamations and invitations. He demanded that Saisset should be freed immediately and sent to Rome; the bull *Salvator mundi* revoked all the concessionary modifications to *Clericis laicos* made in 1297; and in a further bull beginning with the ostensibly mild words *Ausculta fili* ('Listen, O my son') Boniface warned Philip of grave consequences if he did not cease his open hostility to the Church. Finally Boniface wrote to all the bishops and other leading churchmen in France, inviting them to a special Convocation the following autumn, at which they could 'advise' the Pope as to the best way of dealing with Philip. The war of words quickly intensified in 1302, Philip having no scruples about publishing a forged version of *Ausculta fili*. Boniface's Convocation did in fact take place (beginning on 30 October), but fewer than half the French bishops attended (not least because of threats from Philip) and little was achieved. There was certainly no formal reproof of the King. But on 18 November 1302 Boniface drew up yet another bull, excommunicating anyone who had prevented the clerics from coming to Rome. And on the very same day he issued the most famous of all his documents: *Unam Sanctam*. This great papal bull is a solemn and uncompromising assertion of the absolute supremacy of the spiritual power. Although Philip is not directly mentioned in it, he certainly is in a further document issued less than a week later, in which Boniface listed under twelve heads the Church's grievances against him. This amounted to an ultimatum, and Philip chose the path of defiance rather than submission.

The climax of the struggle came in 1303. In March (not long before Dante left Forlì for Verona) Guillaume de Nogaret publicly denounced Boniface as a heretic and usurper, and urged Philip to convene a General Council of the Church with a view to deposing the Pope. (Letters of invitation to the proposed council were in fact despatched.) In May Nogaret left for Italy, bent on inciting opposition to Boniface. The Pope's next move came in August, from his summer headquarters at Anagni. He drew up a final bull of excommunication against Philip, *Super Petri solio,* threatening to put it into practice if the King did not submit by 8 September. By this time Nogaret was at Musciatto Francesi's castle at Staggia, where Charles de Valois had stayed almost two years before. When news of the excommunication threat arrived he decided to abandon the pen and reach for the sword. Together with Sciarra Colonna, brother and nephew of the two deposed Colonna cardinals, he levied a force of local troops and set out for Anagni. They arrived on 7 September and after two days of chaotic fighting managed to enter the papal chamber. But whilst Sciarra Colonna wanted to kill Boniface there and then, Nogaret favoured forcing him to resign or, failing that, taking him to France for trial. At this point, however, the inhabitants of Anagni came to the Pope's aid and succeeded in forcing the attackers to withdraw from the city. On 16 September Boniface left for Rome, protected by an escort from the powerful Orsini family, implacable enemies of the Colonna. Whether or not he had been physically assaulted, he was tired and broken in spirit. His reign had come to an end, and he died on 12 October—not in the Lateran Palace but in the more secure surroundings of the Vatican.

Dante's initial reaction to these events is not known. However, when he came to write *Purgatorio* XX he condemned the attack on Boniface in a truly remarkable passage. Here he is conversing with the soul of Hugh Capet, the tenth-century founder of the Capetian dynasty, which was to provide all the French kings down to 1328. Hugh looks grimly forward to the accumulated wickedness of his direct descendants. The climax of their crimes was the outrage at Anagni ('Alagna'):

> veggio in Alagna entrar lo fiordaliso,
> e nel Vicario suo Cristo esser catto.
>   Veggiolo un'altra volta esser deriso;
> veggio rinnovellar l'aceto e il fele,
> e tra vivi ladroni esser anciso.
>   Veggio il nuovo Pilato sì crudele ...

I see the fleur-de-lys enter Anagni,/and Christ made captive in the person of His Vicar./I see Him mocked once more,/once more the vinegar and the gall;/I see Him put to death 'twixt two live thieves./I see the new Pilate, so cruel ...

(Purg. XX, 86–91)

So here Philip is cast in the role of Pontius Pilate, and Boniface is compared to the captured, reviled and crucified Christ. No one can fail to be struck by the sheer force of these lines, yet no one need be unduly puzzled. Dante has not 'changed his mind' since writing the equally trenchant *Inferno* XIX, where Boniface is damned to Hell in advance. The key to any apparent contradiction lies in the word *Vicario* (line 87); for all his atrocious sins, Boniface was still as pope the successor of St Peter, the Vicar of Christ, His representative on earth. So what occurred at Anagni was in this sense an affront not just to a mere mortal, but to the Son of God. The distinction between the (unworthy) man and the (sacred) office could not be sharper. Yet this is not some peculiarly Roman Catholic piece of sophistry. No 'visible' Church, no Church with sacraments, could possibly function were the personal shortcomings of its clergy held to hinder its ministry. The Anglican Church's Thirty-Nine Articles make precisely this point—whilst referring of course not to popes, but to bishops and priests.[17]

## (v) Dante's Break with the Whites

Ten days after Boniface's death the Dominican Niccolò Boccasini was elected Pope Benedict XI; there was not to be another Italian pontiff until 1378. Benedict's reign was short (only eight and a half months) and most of it was spent trying to sort out the aftermath of Anagni (he had not himself been directly involved in the struggle between Philip and Boniface). But he also found time for Tuscany, and this is what concerns us. While Dante was still in Verona, on 31 January 1304, the new Pope appointed Cardinal Nicolò da Prato as peacemaker in Tuscany, along with the Romagna, the March of Treviso and adjacent areas. The Cardinal was specifically instructed to reconcile the opposing factions in Florence. For there was now considerable strife *within* the city, indeed among the ruling Blacks themselves, chiefly owing to the increasingly autocratic pretensions of Corso Donati and his rivalry with Rosso della Tosa. The appointment of Cardinal Niccolò would surely have stirred the hopes of the exiled Whites; Benedict had not been associated with his belligerent predecessor's pro-Angevin and pro-Black policies, and this latest peacemaker might turn out to be very different from Matthew of Acquasparta. The exiles looked to him not merely to pacify the Blacks, but to bring about a general reconciliation of all the Guelphs, such that they, the Whites, could return to Florence.

On 17 March the Florentine rulers agreed to accept the Cardinal's jurisdiction—he was now present in the city—and it seems that around this time Dante left Verona. He almost certainly made straight for Arezzo, where the Whites had their headquarters. In fact Leonardo Bruni tells us Dante was now one of twelve White councillors.[18] He may have had an additional reason for leaving Verona. On 7 March Bartolommeo della Scala had died, being succeeded by his younger brother Alboino, of whom Dante later wrote disparagingly in the *Convivio* (IV, xvi, 6) and who may not have continued Bartolommeo's patronage. In any case Dante was certainly involved in the peace process. In mid-April, at the same time as a delegation of Whites (not including Dante himself) plus a few Ghibellines arrived in Florence from Arezzo, he wrote a letter to the Cardinal (Letter I). It should perhaps be pointed out that all Dante's extant letters are essentially public documents (even though some have much to say about his personal circumstances), and this one is no exception. Dante addresses Pope Benedict's peacemaker in grandiloquent language on behalf of Alessandro da Romena, whom the Whites had chosen as their captain, and of the 'Council and General Body' of the Whites ('Consilium et Universitas Partis Alborum'). The substance of the letter proper is preceded by a surprising quotation: 'Preceptis salutaribus moniti', part of the very phrase which in the Mass comes immediately before the Lord's Prayer. Here these words, aptly translated by Toynbee as 'In submission to salutary admonishment', refer to a letter from the Cardinal to the exiles.[19] Dante then acknowledges their receipt of this and expresses their gratitude for his role as peacemaker. He declares that the sole reason they ever engaged in armed conflict was precisely the restoration of peace to their city; but now they will submit entirely to his judgement and suspend all warfare, as his letter has enjoined them to do.

So at this stage the exiles, through their distinguished spokesman, profess confidence in arbitration, eschewing (for the moment) the military option. What precisely transpired at the diplomatic level during May is unclear (though little progress can have been made), but there is a strong indication that by the middle of that month Dante *was* already present in Arezzo: on 13 May Francesco Alighieri, the poet's half-brother, undertook in that city to repay a loan of twelve florins. Despite all the political upheavals, Francesco's business activities in Florence were flourishing; if he took out a loan in Arezzo it could only have been for the benefit of someone else there—very probably Dante,[20] who alludes, precisely at this time, to his poverty. He does so in the second of his letters, addressed to the brothers Guido and Uberto da Romena. This letter is one of condolence on the death of their uncle Alessandro (the Whites' captain). When he died is unknown, but it was certainly before the White débâcle at Lastra late in July—no chronicler mentions him in connection with that enterprise. In all probability it was no later than the end of June, for Dante's letter regrets the blow to the Whites' hopes that the death of their commander represented; but by early July he had almost certainly distanced himself from his comrades' military schemes. Not only does this letter praise the deceased Alessandro's prowess in the highest terms; it is also of special interest in that it sounds an altogether more private note than its predecessor. Here we have for the first time the expression 'exul inmeritus' ('an undeserving exile') which Dante applies to himself in the titles of four subsequent letters (III, V, VI and VII).

Furthermore this letter to the Romena brothers ends with an apology for the writer's absence from their uncle's funeral; this is due not to negligence or ingratitude but to the unexpected poverty that exile has brought him.

In Florence things were not going well. The Cardinal seems to have achieved little, and on 8 June he advised the Whites and Ghibellines who had been there since April to leave, presumably for their own safety. On 10 June the Blacks burnt a number of houses, and that same day the Cardinal left, having (as was becoming almost traditional) placed the city and its inhabitants under sentence of interdict and excommunication. Not long after this—on 7 July—Pope Benedict died. The Whites' position was now very delicate. The papal peacemaker's efforts had failed signally and there was no knowing what might be the stance of Benedict's successor. The majority of the Whites favoured a fresh military initiative, but it is practically certain that Dante did not agree. As Petrocchi convincingly suggests, the experience of exile, of milieux outside Florence (and outside the Guelph party) had already brought about a greater political maturity and wisdom in the poet.[21] The outspokenly defiant figure of 1300–1 was no more. At any event, Dante now broke with his fellow Whites, certainly prior to the Lastra escapade. This was an abortive and premature attack launched against Florence from Lastra (very near Fiesole, just to the north of the city). It was wholly unsuccessful, and as many as 400 Whites and Ghibellines lost their lives.

How much longer Dante stayed in Arezzo we do not know.[22] But he cannot have hoped to achieve anything more by remaining with the substantial White community there, and soon he set out northward once again, a more isolated figure than ever.

# 7

# A One-Man Party
## (1304–1308)

The previous chapter began with a quotation from Cacciaguida's great speech in the *Paradiso*. Here is how the crusader continues:

> E quel che più ti graverà le spalle,
> sarà la compagnia malvagia e scempia …
> … che tutta ingrata, tutta matta ed empia
> si farà contr'a te; …
> … sì ch'a te fia bello
> averti fatta parte per te stesso.

> And what will weigh most heavily on your shoulders/will be your wicked and foolish companions …/they will be utterly ungrateful, mad and evil/towards you; …/so you will have done well/in becoming a party by yourself.
>
> (*Par*. XVII, 61–62; 64–65; 68–69)

This is just what Dante did. The lonely wanderings of the next few years (until the end of 1308, roughly) will be our concern in this chapter. Although Dante did continue to take part in sporadic political activity, these are above all years of great literary achievement: there was more outstanding lyric poetry, the four books of the *Convivio* were completed, a start had been made on the *Inferno* itself, and Dante's increasingly personal and idiosyncratic political philosophy was steadily taking shape. Where exactly he did his thinking and writing is often very difficult to determine (this is true particularly of the two years following his departure from Arezzo). Early in the *Convivio* (I, iii, 4), having lamented the unjust penalty of exile and poverty inflicted upon him, he says he has wandered, virtually like a beggar, almost everywhere the Italian language is spoken ('per le parti quasi tutte a le quali questa lingua si stende, peregrino, quasi mendicando ...'). This is probably an exaggeration, for there is no hard evidence linking Dante with anywhere south of Rome. Unfortunately we have to wait until October 1306 for irrefutable confirmation of his whereabouts, and the time between summer 1304 and then is something of a lacuna. But Petrocchi, pointing out the unlikelihood of Dante's returning to Verona after Arezzo, given his adverse remarks about Alboino della Scala, very plausibly conjectures that Dante may now have spent an extensive period in the Veneto, and more precisely as the guest of Gherardo da Camino.[1] He was the ruler of Treviso, to the north of Venice, and Dante praises his nobility and virtue in the highest terms both in the *Convivio* (IV, xiv, 12) and in the *Purgatorio* (XVI, 124), where he is simply 'il buon Gherardo'. The evidence linking Dante with the Veneto region is indirect but nonetheless very persuasive: the sheer number and nature of his allusions to it (in the *Inferno* especially) suggest first-hand acquaintance. There are often very precise topographical details, and as we have seen, the *De Vulgari Eloquentia* shows close knowledge of the region's dialects. It is unlikely that Dante remained exclusively in Treviso, and visits to Venice, Padua and other nearby cities are highly probable.[2] In fact Benvenuto da Imola, among the most reliable of all Dante's medieval commentators, says he met Giotto in Padua around this time.[3]

## (i) Cino da Pistoia and the Malaspina

Turning now to Dante's literary output, it should be stressed that any even roughly chronological account of it may give the false impression that he completed this or that work before embarking on the next. In fact he was very likely engaged on several projects at once; indeed the *Convivio* was begun (probably in Verona) before the *De Vulgari* was finished. Although Dante was almost certainly working on the *Convivio* during the obscure period following his breakaway from the other Whites, it will be convenient to postpone discussion of that treatise until after we have considered some distinctive lyric poems—a series of sonnets Dante exchanged with Cino da Pistoia.[4] There are ten in all, five from each poet (though there also survive at least two unanswered sonnets to Dante from Cino). Here Dante is not the ethical poet of the great exilic *canzoni*, but 'reverts' to the Stilnovist debates on the nature of love (which is not to say that ethical aspects of love are absent here). As we have seen, Cino is mentioned in the *De Vulgari* with affection and respect, and these sonnets confirm this, whilst revealing Cino's admiration for Dante, to whom he turns for advice. In fact the exchange is of great interest to literary historians: we are witnessing a dialogue between the two foremost poets then writing in Italian (for after Cavalcanti's death in 1300 they had no serious rivals).

A word may be said here about style. Although Cino proves himself a worthy poetic correspondent, it is Dante's five sonnets that show the greater technical mastery and inventiveness; there is a transparent sense of delight in rising to a challenge, not least a self-imposed one. In all cases the reply sonnet exactly copies the rhymes of its counterpart, and the *order* of the rhyme-sounds, with one exception only, is also identical. This is all part of the challenge. There was no attempt to match each other's rhymes in the earlier exchange between Dante and Forese Donati. But Dante's achievement in these sonnets goes far beyond rhyme-matching, which Cino of course ably does too (though as Foster and Boyde acutely suggest, Dante refrains from taxing his friend unduly in this respect)[5]. Rather, he sets himself special tasks, particularly when he is the respondent. More specifically, he deliberately chooses rare rhyme-words which have to be used figuratively, and this results in very dense imagery. In their technical virtuosity these poems are reminiscent of the *rime petrose* and the legacy of Arnaut Daniel.[6]

Not all the five pairs of sonnets can with certainty be assigned to Dante's exile, though three undoubtedly can. And exile was a fate both men shared, as is emphasized in 'Poi ch'i' fu', Dante, dal mio natal sito' ('Dante, ever since I was [exiled] from my birthplace'), Cino's reply to Dante in the final pair of poems. For Cino was one of the Black Guelphs of Pistoia, who in May 1301 were ousted by their White opponents (not without help from the Florentine Whites, then still in power). The Pistoian Blacks were not to regain control of their city until April 1306 (after which Cino may have returned there, though this is not known for sure). But the manifest friendship and mutual respect between Dante and Cino must have transcended any political differences, and in any case after 1304 Dante had shunned his White comrades. Love though, not exile, is the chief concern of these sonnets, and in the main we see Cino as an inconstant, uncertain and tormented lover, being gently reproved and even warned by the more experienced Dante. Dante's reply to the first sonnet alerts his friend to the peril posed by a mysterious 'green' lady with whom Cino has become infatuated; green is a most dangerous colour when worn by a woman, says Dante—no doubt a general reflection on the fickleness of the young.

There is no space here for a discussion of all ten poems, but the third and fourth pairs are of special interest, for quite different reasons. In 'Dante, quando per caso s'abbandona' ('Dante, when by chance [desire] abandons [hope]'), Cino enquires whether it is possible, having been disappointed in love, to turn to a new affection. Dante's reply begins with a clear reference to the *Vita Nuova*: he has been together with Love since his ninth year and he knows all there is to know about its emotional extremes. The poem then becomes surprisingly fatalistic (surprisingly, in view of Dante's later assertions): it is futile to attempt to resist Love's power, since in amorous circumstances free will never has been free ('liber arbitrio già mai non fu franco'). This emotional determinism is precisely what the adulteress Francesca da Rimini will appeal to by way of (futile) excuse in the *Inferno*; and it is precisely what Dante will vigorously refute, along with all other kinds of determinism, in the *Purgatorio*.[7] For a firm conviction that our wills are essentially free lies at the very heart of the mature Dante's view of human nature. The sonnet ends with an answer for Cino: it is indeed possible for us to turn to a new love-object, and in fact we have no choice in the matter if the previous affection is extinguished. This poem is of further interest in that it is accompanied by a short explanatory Latin letter (Letter III). Cino has asked whether the soul can pass from one passion to another; the attached sonnet, says Dante, will reply in the affirmative, but he is also happy to prove it on the basis of experience, by logical reasoning, and then in typically medieval fashion by appeal to a learned authority (in this case Ovid, in the *Metamorphoses*). The title of the letter does not mention Cino by name, but simply calls him an 'Exile from Pistoia', to whom an undeservedly exiled Florentine ('Florentinus exul inmeritus'—cf. Letters II, V, VI and VII) now writes. And the letter ends with what is surely a further reference to Cino's sufferings in exile: Dante urges him to arm himself with patience against misfortune, to ponder the words of Seneca,[8] and finally not to forget that 'Si de mundo fuissetis, mundus quod suum erat diligeret' ('If you belonged to the world, the world would know you for its own and love you')—Christ's words in John 15.19. The implication of this closing quotation is clearly that the good are cast out by the wicked, just as Christ was (see the whole of verses 18–19 in John 15).

The fourth exchange of sonnets links both poets with the Marquis Moroello Malaspina. In fact Cino's sonnet is addressed not to Dante himself but to the Marquis, on whose behalf Dante then replies. The content of the two poems is not especially remarkable, though it is worth noting that Dante's reply contrasts the excellence of Cino's sweet poetic voice with the capriciousness of his heart. For biographical purposes it is the association of the sonnets with Malaspina that is important. Although Cino's precise connection with him is unclear, we know that Dante was a guest of the Malaspina family, and acted on their behalf in 1306; the exchange of poems in all probability dates from that year. The Malaspina were a powerful aristocratic family of northern Italy, mostly Ghibellines, though Moroello was a vigorous Black Guelph military campaigner. Their possessions were chiefly in the Lunigiana region (the extreme north-west of Tuscany), and for a long time they had been engaged in a tense power struggle with the local bishops of Luni, who were also temporal rulers, with the title of Count. The dispute was finally resolved on 6 October 1306, through the agency of Dante. In a document of that date issued at Sarzana (the very same place to which Cavalcanti and other prominent Whites had been exiled in 1300), Franceschino Malaspina formally invested Dante with full authority to act as procurator and special envoy; his brief was to represent not only Franceschino's interests but those of his cousins Moroello and Curradino as well. Dante successfully brought about an elaborate peace treaty between the Malaspina nobles and Bishop-Count Antonio of Luni; the details are set out in an extensive document also dated 6 October.[9] Although we do not know when Dante arrived in Lunigiana, it is very probable that he had been there for some weeks (or months) prior to his delicate negotiations with the Bishop, long enough to have gained the confidence of all three Malaspina cousins. At any event Dante seems to have enjoyed friendly relations with the family, and in the *Purgatorio* (VIII, 121–32) he was to speak very highly of them.

Dante spent no more than a year in Lunigiana, for in 1307 we find him in eastern Tuscany, after which his next port of call was probably Lucca. But for all the uncertainties as to his precise whereabouts, we do know that throughout this time, and indeed since about 1304, he had been working on the *Convivio*, to which we must now turn.

## (ii) The *Convivio*: Book I

Dante specialists, and medievalists generally, recognize the *Convivio* as among the most significant prose works of its time. Unfortunately it has not been widely appreciated outside these circles, particularly in the English-speaking world; but Christopher Ryan's excellent 1989 version—the first since 1912—will have done much to remedy this.[10] Incomplete though it is, the *Convivio* remains a remarkable work of instruction on a vast range of topics. It is in the broadest sense a philosophical encyclopaedia; moral and political matters are prominent (especially in Book IV), but so are a great many other things, including language, poetics, history, astronomy and theology. And so is Dante, and not just in a few tellingly autobiographical passages. For, as Barbi remarked, the *Convivio*'s ultimate importance lies not so much in its philosophical erudition, but in what it can tell us about Dante as a man.[11] This point is admirably developed by Took, who insists upon the 'confessional' nature of all the 'minor' works, the way in which each of them—no less than the *Comedy* itself—is 'an essay in self-intelligibility'.[12]

After the opening book, the treatise as we have seen takes the form of a commentary on certain of Dante's *canzoni*, but not a narrowly literary one; rather the poems function as a springboard for the most wide-ranging discussions. Some of these might strike the reader as undue digression; yet even a modest acquaintance with medieval didactic literature will show how relatively restrained Dante is in this respect. The title simply means 'Banquet', and Dante explicitly presents his *Convivio* as an invitation to an intellectual feast, a meal for the mind. And for Dante there could be no more appropriate way to begin than with a quotation from the opening words of Aristotle's *Metaphysics*, where *lo Filosofo* ('the Philosopher', *par excellence*) declares that all men naturally desire to know—in the *Inferno* (IV, 131) Dante will refer to Aristotle as 'il maestro di color che sanno' ('the master of those who know'). Dante's praise of knowledge is passionate indeed; he calls it the ultimate perfection of the soul, and the source of our highest happiness. Yet a great many people are cut off from this *nobilissima perfezione*, and for a variety of reasons. Some, through no fault of their own, simply lack the mental equipment. Others are culpably sunk in evil, or in idleness. Dante is not concerned with these. But there is a fourth group, who lack the leisure for serious study, being quite properly involved with family and civic responsibilities ('la cura familiare e civile'—I, i, 4). It is to this group that the *Convivio* is addressed, its exiled author no longer having either kind of distracting burden himself. Dante, then, is writing for busy, intelligent lay people who, moreover, do not necessarily know Latin, hence the very conscious decision to write in Italian. There had of course been works of instruction written in medieval vernaculars; Italian examples include Brunetto Latini's encyclopaedic *Tesoretto* and *La composizione del mondo*, Ristoro d'Arezzo's work on astronomy. But the vast majority of academic writing had been in Latin; Dante's choice of the vernacular, which he confidently feels is now, in *his* hands, mature and versatile enough for the task ahead, is a reaction against a venerable tradition. He generously wants to share his knowledge with as wide an audience as possible, though he recognizes his readers will be few. And although he does not claim to dine at the blessed table where the 'bread of angels'[13] (i.e. knowledge) is consumed, he can at least sit at the feet of the wise, gathering up the scraps they let fall. Sustaining the alimentary imagery, he says that he has already offered his famished readers food, in the form of the *canzoni*; the prose commentary will be the bread, the necessary accompaniment and aid to their digestion. And the Banquet will run to fourteen courses. This initial chapter ends with a word about the function of the commentary, which is to offer an allegorical explanation of the poems, since their surface meaning is not the truer, deeper meaning Dante intended to convey.[14]

The next three chapters reveal a more private purpose behind the treatise. Chapter ii draws attention to two apparent blemishes in the bread of Dante's commentary. The first is that he will speak a good deal of himself; the second is that the commentary, though designed to clarify the poems, itself seems in places obscure. As to the first point, Dante explains that self-preoccupation in a writer can be justified by necessity, and he adduces the examples of Boethius and St Augustine (no less): the first, another undeserving

exile, wrote in order to re-establish his good name, the second so
that his personal experience might serve as an instructive example.
Similarly Dante is impelled to write from a personal standpoint,
both to avoid a bad reputation and to enlighten the reader. The
*infamia* here is one which might arise were the *canzoni* left
unglossed: they could be seen as the product of a personality
enslaved by passion, whereas on the contrary they are the result of
virtue. And the desire to enlighten involves instruction which
Dante, and he alone, is in a position to give. Chapters iii and iv deal
with the potential charge of obscurity, and here not technical
matters of style but private circumstances—misfortunes, in fact—
are more than ever to the fore. Having briefly conceded that the
commentary may be a little hardgoing at times ('un poco duro'),
Dante launches straight into a memorable and passionate depiction
of exile (I, iii, 3–5). He has suffered the unjust penalty of banishment and poverty, since the fair city of Florence has seen fit to cast
him from her bosom; though his most heartfelt wish is still to
return, he has on the contrary been forced to wander here and there.
Striking nautical imagery now takes over: Dante has become a boat
without sail or rudder ('legno sanza vela e sanza governo') driven
from one port or shore to another by the arid wind of hurtful
poverty. He himself has been denigrated, and this has cast a shadow
over his writings too. Personal lament then leads to more general
reflections on good and bad reputation. Now what all this has to
do with the apparent opacity of the *Convivio*'s prose is not yet clear.
The connection is made at the end of Chapter iv: Dante's aim is to
redress the harmful effects of exile through his writing. Exile has
tarnished his reputation, cheapening everything touched by his
hand. He will therefore adopt in the *Convivio* a loftier style ('più
alto stilo') together with a certain weightiness ('gravezza'), which
will lend authority to his words. Hence the difficulty ('fortezza') of
the prose.

The remaining chapters of Book I justify Dante's choice of the
vernacular rather than Latin. A number of arguments (of rather
different kinds) are deployed, but three main points are made. First
there is the question of appropriateness. A commentary is subordinate to what it is interpreting, and so to employ Latin to explain
vernacular *canzoni* would be incongruous; for Latin is intrinsically
superior to the vernacular in nobility, power and beauty.[15] But
secondly Dante's linguistic choice is a matter of generosity ('pronta

liberalitade'); he wants to give something of use to the reader. Here again Latin would not have met the requirements: not only would the gift of Dante's instruction have been confined to a limited audience, it would also have been wasted on those who know Latin but not Italian (I, ix, 1–9). For the *canzoni* must be read and understood in the original, and only a vernacular commentary can draw out their deeper meaning. In the course of this argument from generosity Dante finds space for some scornful words against 'professional' Latinists. The only people who will benefit from the *Convivio* are those with a certain nobility of mind, he says, and there are many more of those among the vernacular-speaking 'laity' than among the 'educated'. Indeed the latter are for the most part prone to avarice, which is inimical to nobility of mind. Such people acquire their learning not for its own sake, but to gain wealth ('denari') or status ('dignitate'). Dante is here inveighing against all those who make learning (or more precisely Latin) pay. Similar statements will occur in Book III (xi, 10) and in the *Paradiso* (XI, 1–6), where doctors and lawyers are expressly mentioned. It might be thought that Dante had a natural affinity with such people, but this is by no means true. Notwithstanding his experiences in the Guild of *Medici e Speziali*, and for all his friendship with Cino (a professional jurist and very important legal commentator, as well as a poet), he did not hold the professions as such in high regard.

Dante has kept until last his most compelling reason for choosing the vernacular. Nothing could be simpler, or more potent: his natural love for his native tongue. This love moves him to praise it, to guard it jealously and to defend it against its detractors—motifs developed in the final four chapters of Book I with exceptional eloquence and passion. In the *Convivio* only love for philosophy itself is expressed more ardently. Chapter x makes very high claims for the vernacular, and in particular for Dante's own Italian, the language of the *Convivio*. Hence the need to guard it jealously; had the commentary on the *canzoni* been in Latin, someone might have had it translated into Italian—and ineptly. That would have damaged the reputation of the vernacular, far too precious a thing to entrust to those who have not mastered it. And Dante, as sublimely confident in this chapter as ever, stresses the immense goodness ('bontade') and power ('vertù') of his tongue. It *can* express the most profound and novel concepts with precision and elegance, very nearly as well as Latin; and this the *Convivio*'s prose will prove. But eulogy now gives way to reproof: so that the disgrace ('infamia') of the vernacular's denigrators may stand out the more clearly, Dante will confound them in a special chapter. And Chapter xi is certainly vituperative. Dante wishes nothing less than ever-lasting shame on those wicked ('malvagi') Italians who despise their own language whilst extolling those of foreigners. The foreign ver-naculars Dante has in mind are northern French and Provençal. His vehemence here stems from the fact that he is championing a language whose literary tradition was still young. What he fears, and what occasions his rage, is that Italians are perversely favouring a fashionable and more venerable Gallic tradition at the expense of their own vernacular: they are holding back its progress.[16]

The closing chapter of Book I is forceful and personal in its thanks for the benefits the vernacular has conferred upon Dante. Not only has it enhanced his well-being; it has contributed to his being, his very existence. For both his parents spoke it, and speaking it brought them together! As for well-being, the vernacular was of great importance in Dante's intellectual development, since through it he first came to Latin, the means to so much learning. The *Convivio*'s first book does not seek to promote the vernacular at the expense of Latin; the two are to be seen as complementary. But the closing sentence does return to the *volgare*'s merits, and in the loftiest terms: it will be a new light, a new sun to illuminate those at present lost in gloom and darkness.

### (iii) *Convivio* II

Here the wealth of Dante's learning—the fruit of some fifteen years' reading and reflection—becomes apparent. This section of the treatise elucidates 'Voi che 'ntendendo il terzo ciel movete', the *canzone* briefly discussed above (p. 30). Dante knows it is a difficult poem; its closing lines admit that few will grasp its meaning fully but the rest can at least admire its beauty.[17] That was the position when Dante wrote the poem in the 1290s, but help is now at hand for that majority of perplexed readers. Dante begins by explaining the difference between the literal and allegorical senses of a text. Following a medieval commonplace, he distinguishes as many as four senses, or layers of meaning. The commentary will deal only occasionally with the moral and anagogical senses; Dante's chief concern will be first the literal and then the allegorical sense, the latter being defined as 'una veritade ascosa sotto bella menzogna' ('truth hidden beneath a beautiful lie'—II, i, 3). The literal sense takes us up to Chapter xii, and Dante's commentary on it, full of explanations, amplifications and digressions (real or apparent) presents a rich panorama of a world now lost: the strange and beautiful world of medieval thought. On the surface, the literal layer, 'Voi che 'ntendendo' is a love poem, about the conflict of two loves: on the one hand the memory of the dead Beatrice, now in celestial glory, and on the other the attractions of a new consoling lady, the same noble lady (Dante now tells us) who made her first appearance towards the end of the *Vita Nuova*. The rival claims of the two beautiful ladies cause Dante bewilderment and anguish, so he turns for consolation to the beings mentioned in the poem's opening line, who move the third heaven by intellection, or understanding.

But who are they? The question will arise not only in the mind of a modern reader, for Dante evidently thought his fourteenth-century audience could do with some help here. The celestial movers who cause the motion of the heavenly spheres are angels, and Dante straight away plunges us into three chapters of cosmology and angelology. Now the very notion of the existence of angels, let alone a branch of learning devoted to them, is remote indeed from modern thinking—the trivialization of the whole subject since the Renaissance is well exemplified in the visual arts. But for Dante, and for all educated people of his age, the angels are no product of sentimental fancy, but a vital component in the divine scheme of creation: the highest-ranking of all creatures, coming immediately between ourselves and God. And for Dante they are not merely messengers and guardians (their Scripturally-revealed role); some of them also have a crucial dynamic and causal function in the cosmos. By moving the heavenly spheres, which contain the planets and stars, they influence material change on earth, for such change—in fact every terrestrial event except freely-willed human choices—is subject to astral forces. In Dante's day the all-pervading influence of the heavens was not something marginal or esoteric but a central element of the generally-accepted world-view. Late medieval thinking on the subject of angels, or 'angelic intelligences', is a prime example of doctrinal synthesis, in this case a fusion of traditional material from the Judaeo-Christian Scriptures with Aristotelian and neo-Platonic thought.

Before directly discussing the nature and function of the angels Dante outlines the structure of the universe (Ch. iii–iv). He recognizes the divergence among the authorities as to the number of heavenly spheres. For Aristotle there were just eight heavens, that of the Fixed Stars being the outermost, with the motionless earth at the centre of the whole scheme. But Ptolemy later posited a ninth heaven, the *Primum Mobile* (or 'first moving thing'), and for medieval Christians there was a tenth, the motionless Empyrean Heaven, the dwelling place of the blessed and in a special sense the abode of God. All the nine mobile heavens have angelic movers, or to use the parlance of scholastic philosophy, 'separated substances', that is immaterial substances, beings devoid of matter. Aristotle thought that the number of these motor substances was limited exactly to the number of movements of the various spheres. But Plato, a quite exceptional man (*uomo eccellentissimo*), thought there were more: for him the immaterial Ideas, or archetypes, were as many as there were particular species of (material) things. Before explaining why they were both wrong, Dante rather surprisingly brings in classical mythology: he asserts that what Plato called Ideas, the ancient pagans conceived as gods and goddesses, building temples to Jupiter, Minerva, Vulcan and so forth. This bold syncretic insight, involving an indirect equation between the classical deities of Olympus and the angels of Christianity, is in all probability original to Dante.[18] But, tantalizingly, he does not now pursue it, returning immediately to the question of how many angels there are. That the ancient philosophers were here mistaken can be shown both by rational argument and by the Scriptures. The latter (from which of course Aristotle and Plato were unable to benefit) make it clear that the angels exist in immense numbers; only a few of them, for Dante, are assigned to moving the heavens. Having enumerated nine different orders of angels, ranging from Seraphim at the top of the scale to Angels (in a restrictive sense of the term) at the bottom, Dante proceeds to link each order with one of the moving heavens. Thus the heaven of the Moon is moved by certain members of the order of Angels, that of Mercury by Archangels, that of Venus by Thrones, and so on. This precise correspondence of the nine angelic orders to the nine moving heavens is not part of official Church doctrine (which has never had much to say formally about angels), and may well be peculiar to Dante. But the main point is that it is the Thrones who move the third heaven, the heaven

95

of Venus, whose influence kindles love in souls on earth. That is why 'Voi che 'ntendendo',on the surface a love poem, is addressed to those particular beings.

So much for the *canzone*'s opening line. Six chapters (vi–xi) are now devoted to the literal exposition of the rest of the poem. Chapter viii is among the most notable; here reflections on Beatrice's blessed state in heaven lead Dante to what he himself calls a *digressione*, in which he discusses—in forceful language—the immortality of the human soul. This is said to be a general belief of philosophers of all schools and people of all creeds, pagans, Christians, Jews, Saracens and Tartars alike. To doubt life after death is bestial (i.e. unworthy of a human being); in fact nothing could be more stupid, ignoble and damaging. Dante argues passionately for our survival beyond the grave on the basis of reason, by reference to the revelatory power of our dreams, and finally because of Christ's promise of hope to His faithful. This above all is why he can be certain of passing into a better life after the present one, where indeed he will rejoin Beatrice.

Book II's final chapters set about decoding the *canzone*. In its true allegorical meaning it turns out to be a love poem, yes, but of a quite different kind from what ostensibly appears. The unnamed and enigmatic noble lady now acquires an identity—she is no earthly woman, but Philosophy itself. The consolation Dante found in his grief after Beatrice's death was an intellectual, not an erotic one, and this is what the poem is really about. The catalysts that stimulated his love affair with philosophy were Boethius and Cicero, after reading whom he began to attend religious centres of learning and philosophical disputations (see above, pp. 22–29). It was not long before all other affections were driven out of his mind, such was the sweetness ('dolcezza') he experienced in philosophical speculation, in his love for that lady whom he now praises as 'figlia di Dio, regina di tutto, nobilissima e bellissima Filosofia' ('daughter of God, queen of all, most noble and beautiful Philosophy'—II, xii, 9).

But it is not just the noble lady who has a hidden, allegorical meaning. The third heaven and its movers also need decoding. In two elaborate chapters (xiii and xiv) Dante sets out, with considerable astronomical knowledge, a series of analogies between the ten heavens and the various branches of learning, as commonly classified in his time. The seven lowest heavens (from the Moon to

Saturn) may, in each case because of some special attribute, be likened to one of the seven Liberal Arts, that is the disciplines of the *trivium* and *quadrivium*—the foundation of medieval instruction. Thus the Moon is like grammar, Mercury like dialectic (i.e. logic) and Venus, our third heaven, like rhetoric, and so on. But there are ten heavens and only seven Liberal Arts, so Dante compares the highest three spheres to more exalted disciplines. The heaven of the Fixed Stars is likened to physics and metaphysics, the *Primum Mobile* to ethics (even loftier, note) and the Empyrean, the highest heaven, is not surprisingly linked with theology, the divine science. The reason for this final comparison is that the highest heaven is motionless, and therefore at peace; theology too is essentially peaceful, in that the certainty of its subject matter (God) precludes the strife that arises from differing opinions (one wonders how many theologians, medieval or modern, would agree). To return to the third heaven. On the allegorical level, then, it is not the heaven of Venus but the art of rhetoric. And as we learn in the rapturous closing chapter of Book II, the movers, when allegorically interpreted, are not angels but those very writers such as Boethius and Cicero who by the power of their sweet words first impelled Dante towards philosophy. The noble lady is lavishly praised, special stress being laid on the beauty of her eyes: these are, allegorically speaking, the explanations or proofs of philosophy. Her looks are unutterably sweet, and they captivate the human mind in an instant ('O dolcissimi e ineffabili sembianti, e rubatori subitani de la mente umana'—II, xv, 4). Philosophy in fact offers bliss and salvation, the latter in both an intellectual and an ethical sense, in that it can save us from the 'death' of ignorance and vice. Yet Dante knows philosophizing can be arduous; the seeker after truth must not shirk hard study and must be prepared to grapple with the doubts and questions that will inevitably arise. But these will fade away like little morning clouds ('nebulette matutine') before the face of the sun, such is the enlightening power of Dante's beloved lady.

## (iv) *Convivio* III

This is a sustained hymn of praise for philosophy. The *canzone* here is one of Dante's very finest, 'Amor che ne la mente mi ragiona' ('Love speaking to me in my mind'). It bears some resemblance to

'Donne ch'avete', the *Vita Nuova*'s greatest praise poem, but here the lady is not Beatrice nor (as it turns out) any earthly woman, but once again Philosophy. Ostensibly, however, this is a love poem about a lady of inexpressible nobility and beauty. Love speaks to Dante's mind about her, but the poet's intellect is overcome; he cannot comprehend all that is said about her, and can convey only part of what he does understand, such are the limitations of human language. The lady is closely associated with the heavens, in both a material and a spiritual sense. The sun, in all the course of its revolutions, sees nothing as noble as she is; all the angelic Intelligences gaze upon her; divine power flows down into her as it does into an angel; her beauty is suggestive of the bliss of Paradise. Moreover she is not only a model of nobility and beauty for all ladies; she also destroys vice and humbles the wicked, whilst herself being an archetype of humility—aesthetic and moral dimensions are intimately linked. For all the hyperbole of the medieval love lyric in general, and of Dante's earlier Beatrician poetry in particular, most readers will have suspected that there is a hidden significance underlying all this. But first Dante expounds the surface meaning, in ten chapters of dense and demanding commentary.

As in Book II, he ranges widely and deeply through the realms of medieval learning; a suitably brief synopsis would be impossible. But highlights include the extraordinary Chapter v, an astronomical *tour de force* sparked off, so to speak, by the line in the *canzone* about the revolving sun; the next chapter, which deals with causality in the universe—the operations of God as first cause and also those of the secondary causes, the angelic Intelligences; and Chapter vii, which outlines the gradations of created being, from angels to minerals, according to the degree of the created thing's reception of divine goodness. All these, and many other ramifications, still fall within the framework of the literal exposition of the *canzone*. But like its Book II counterpart the poem is in fact allegorical, and decoding operations eventually begin in Chapter xi. The bare bones of the hidden meaning are that: the lady signifies Philosophy; Love signifies the study entailed in gaining Philosophy's 'affection'; the sun signifies God.

There are numerous further points in the allegory. However, the chief interest of these final chapters lies not so much in the details of decipherment as in Dante's powerful assertion of the true nature of Philosophy, both in terms of what it is and of what it is not.

Etymologically, it means nothing more than a love of wisdom or knowledge, and in this basic sense everyone could be called a 'philosopher' since the desire to know is common to all. But Dante's notion of philosophy is far more elevated and far more restrictive: mere desire for knowledge is not enough; love of and devotion to wisdom are essential. Yet even these qualities are often only apparent and do not lead to true philosophy. Here a moral consideration comes strongly to the fore: what is the underlying intention of the would-be philosopher? If it is simply pleasure in studying this or that science (the examples given are rhetoric and music), then that is not enough. And what of those whose apparent love of wisdom is in fact study undertaken for gain ('per utilitade')? In this category are included lawyers, doctors and 'almost all' the clergy (III, xi, 10). They do not study in order to acquire wisdom but to gain money or status; if they could get enough of these they would soon stop studying. No, true philosophy arises from integrity ('onestade') alone. In Chapter xii Dante comes to a memorable definition of philosophy, which shows it to be something far more sublime than bare etymology might suggest. We now learn that it is an 'amoroso uso di sapienza' (III, xii, 12), 'a loving use or exercise of wisdom', and that this is to be found above all in God, for in Him wisdom, love and activity exist in the highest degree.[19]

However, although philosophy in this truest sense is supremely in God, it is not exclusively in Him. Some creatures too philosophize—at a secondary level. This is eminently true of the angels, who constantly contemplate God. Demons are debarred; it is precisely because these fallen angels in Hell utterly lack love that they are cut off from philosophy. Moving down the scale of creation, Dante comes to man. The vast majority of people are immediately excluded, not because like the demons they are devoid of love, but because they live sensual rather than rational lives. And even those who for the right motives have attained to a love of wisdom cannot gaze upon the Lady Philosophy continuously; unlike that of the angels, our philosophical contemplation is necessarily sporadic. This may appear disheartening, but Chapter xiv holds up as examples real human philosophers whose lives have shown the power of true philosophy: Democritus, Plato and Aristotle put truth above all merely human conventions, values and concerns, while Zeno, Socrates, Seneca and many others gave up their lives for it. And it is in this chapter, and in the final one of

Book III, that the transcendent, heavenly quality of Dante's philosophy becomes fully apparent. It is something more than human ('più che umana operazione'—III, xiv, 11), and although it enables us to understand rationally much that might otherwise seem a miracle, it also hints at unexplained mysteries beyond our world and actually provides a basis for our believing them.[20] Indeed our religious faith has its origins in such belief, and faith leads to hope, which in turn engenders charity. And through these, the three Christian theological virtues, we may rise up to philosophize in that celestial Athens where Stoics, Peripatetics and Epicureans are all at last united in contemplation of eternal truth! This enraptured vision of a heavenly harmony between the three main philosophical schools of antiquity, a harmony achieved through Faith, Hope and Charity, is remarkable indeed. Whatever its full implications may be, Dante seems here to be claiming for philosophy the power to take us beyond and above the limits of familiar human reasoning. Philosophy is emphatically not mere ratiocination, however subtle; it is of divine origin, and so far from being cut off, let alone divorced, from faith, it can lead us to faith.

Book III ends on an even more transcendent note. Chapter xiv had dealt with love of wisdom, and the power of that love; the final chapter turns to wisdom itself, the 'subject matter' of philosophy, corresponding to the lady's corporeal beauty in the *canzone*. As for the poem's praise of the lady: her eyes are now explained as the demonstrations, or certain proofs of philosophy, while her smile signifies her persuasions, through which the veiled inner light of wisdom is glimpsed. The clear gaze is complemented by the coaxing smile: effective imagery, obviously rooted in human experience. Dante now presents reason as our distinctively human quality: when it is perfected so are we, and precisely as human beings ('l'uomo, in quanto ello è uomo'—III, xv, 4). And such perfection brings happiness. For Dante moreover there seems to be no real distinction between reason and (human) wisdom; philosophical reflections on reason are now fused with a dazzling series of biblical quotations about wisdom, taken appropriately from Proverbs and Wisdom, the sapiential books of the Old Testament which he knew so well. As Solomon (for Dante the author of both books) says: wisdom and learning are essential to happiness; wisdom is 'the brightness of the eternal light and the spotless mirror of God's majesty'; the just man pursues the path of wisdom, and his way is like an increasingly resplendent light. Most powerful of all is the quotation from Proverbs where Wisdom herself declares she was with God from the very beginning of time: 'When God prepared the heavens I was there ... when He laid the foundations of the earth I was with Him, setting all things in order, and delighting day after day.'[21] Wisdom is, pre-eminently and ultimately, the Wisdom of God. So by the end of Book III there is no gulf between sacred and profane: reason has merged with wisdom, and Aristotle with Solomon.

## (v) *Convivio* IV

This is easily the longest book, and for many will be the most accessible—perhaps also the most interesting. Its content is essentially ethical and political. Dante wishes to impart moral teaching of great importance, and such is the urgency of his message that he has abandoned allegory altogether in the *canzone* he is this time explaining. 'Le dolci rime d'amor' is not a love poem, either outwardly or inwardly; its opening lines state that Dante must set aside his sweet poems of love. He may indeed return to amorous poetry (which he did), but for the moment his theme is nobility. *Gentilezza*, that is, nobility—but very much in an ethical sense—is the source of all human virtues, moral and intellectual. Yet what is this nobility? In what does it consist? Dante sets out and refutes the opinions of others, which have resulted in dangerously widespread misconceptions, before stating his own view. His aim is to identify that quality of worth, or excellence, that makes for true nobility, but first he must dispel the popular and pernicious error that sees wealth as nobility's source. The Emperor Frederick II held nobility to be the product of long-established wealth (i.e. material riches) in combination with pleasant manners. Another (unnamed) person, rather less gifted intellectually, left out the manners, and saw the question in crudely economic terms. Dante will devote three chapters to a blistering indictment of riches, but first he has a problem—a very medieval kind of problem—with authority. Is not the Emperor's opinion authoritative, and therefore to be respected? And the fact that so many subscribe to a fallacious notion of nobility raises another difficulty: did not Aristotle, that most authoritative of philosophers, state that what the majority believe cannot be wholly wrong (IV, iii, 6–10)? These difficulties give rise

to a 'digression' in which Dante seeks to establish the basis of the
Emperor's authority and also that of Aristotle. The discussion of
the Empire here is of the greatest interest and looks forward to
Dante's most substantial work on political thought, the *Monarchia*.
The key passages are in Chapters iv and v. Dante begins by arguing
for the necessity of one universal empire in order to promote human
happiness, the goal towards which our earthly lives are directed.
All other political systems frustrate that goal. The fundamental
need for an empire lies in human nature itself, because (as the
Philosopher says) man is a social animal. For his fulfilment the individual needs a family, which in turn needs a neighbourhood, and
this in turn needs a city. Cities moreover, for reasons of commerce
and defence, need to ally with neighbouring cities, and this gives
rise to kingdoms. But human greed being what it is, strife between
kingdoms will break out, and the resulting wars will bring calamity
upon cities, and thus neighbourhoods, families and individuals. But
a single world ruler would possess everything and therefore desire
nothing; he would use his power to confine kings within their
kingdoms, thereby ensuring peace and happiness throughout
human society, right down to the level of the individual.

After this theoretical exposé, Dante turns to the Romans. The
context of the whole discussion, it should be remembered, is the
authority vested in Frederick II, and Dante believed the Holy
Roman Empire to be a direct and legitimate successor to the ancient
one. The right of the ancient Romans to rule is now defended with
quite astonishing conviction. They stemmed from the noble stock
of Troy ('l'alto sangue troiano'—IV, iv, 10) and God Himself chose
them to rule the whole world. Someone might object that they
acquired their empire by force, which seems inimical to reason. But
Dante will have none of that; yes, the Romans did use force but
only incidentally, in the furtherance of God's design for all mankind. Their empire was not opposed to reason but sanctioned by
reason, and divine reason at that. Already the Romans are being
presented as a chosen people through whom God worked—and the
profound implications of this will be elaborated more fully in the
*Monarchia* and the *Comedy*. Chapter v develops the providential
motif further. When it was decreed in Heaven that the Son of God
should come down to earth to fuse a new harmony between human
and divine nature, all the conditions had to be perfect. Not only
were the planets in their optimum conjunction when Christ was

born; the earth too was at its best, being united in peace under one ruler (Augustus). So the Roman Empire was then at its most perfect, and all for the glory of God. Jesus moreover had to be born into a human family of the utmost sanctity: the line of King David, from whom Mary his mother was descended. To link David with the Romans might seem difficult, but Dante manages it: at the very time of David's birth, he asserts, Aeneas the Trojan entered Italy and founded the Roman Empire.[22] This contemporaneity is for Dante of course another remarkable proof of God's intentions. He now launches into a dazzling catalogue of Roman nobility and excellence from the time of Romulus onward, all with the aim of showing that Providence had a hand in the city's growth as well as its birth.

Having thoroughly established the basis of imperial authority, Dante turns to Aristotle (Ch. vi). After considering the various schools of ancient Greek thought he concludes that the Stoics, Epicureans and Academicians were all surpassed, and particularly in moral philosophy, by the exceptional, almost divine intellect of Aristotle. He is the greatest of all philosophers, and he deserves to be trusted and obeyed. Yet his authority in no way detracts from the emperor's; the two ought to work together, argues Dante, for philosophy without the backing of the Empire is weak, and an emperor without the guidance of philosophy dangerous. All rulers, for that matter (Dante implies), should seek wise counsel. But do they? Here is an opportunity for more invective: amongst the contemporary princes who fail to take the advice they should Charles of Naples and Frederick of Sicily are singled out for denunciation. They are not merely usurpers, but enemies of God (IV, vi, 20). This same pair are reviled in the De Vulgari (I, xii, 5).

After a violent attack on the dangerous and stupid view that a nobleman's descendants are necessarily noble (whatever their character), Dante returns in Chapter viii to Aristotle and the Emperor. He has yet to justify his disagreement with these two authorities on the matter of nobility. As far as the Philosopher is concerned, the disagreement is only apparent. For when Aristotle says that what the majority believe cannot be wholly wrong, he is referring to the inner judgement made by reason, not to irrational superficial opinions based on the senses. People's false ideas about nobility are of the latter kind. As for Emperor Frederick II, Dante in dissenting from him has not in fact been irreverent. For no reverence or obedience is due to anyone in authority outside the sphere in which that authority is rightly exercised. Although the Emperor has absolute authority in the matter of (say) laws governing marriage or military service or inheritance, what he may think about nobility is something quite different; for that is a matter of moral philosophy and the Emperor *qua* Emperor is not a moral philosopher. So much for the limitations of authority. But why exactly has Dante dissented from Frederick's view? Because the Emperor's twofold definition is both false and a half-truth. His first criterion, *antica richezza* (long-established wealth) is simply wrong; his second, *belle maniere* (pleasant manners), has some truth in it, provided it is understood that pleasant manners are one of the results of a noble nature, not one of its causes.[23]

Before turning to Dante's indictment of riches, it is worth pausing to consider the long digression on Empire and imperial authority. The imperialist theory sketched out in Chapters iv and v looks powerfully forward to Dante's later work, and can without exaggeration be seen as a dry run for Books I and II of the *Monarchia*. And Chapter vi's vision of the ideal co-operation of emperor and philosopher expresses one half of a formula that will become explicit only in the later treatise. Man's mortal happiness, the felicity attainable in this earthly life, is the proper concern of the philosophically-guided emperor. That is the first half of the formula. The *Monarchia* will reveal the second half: the proper (and only) concern of the pope, the supreme spiritual authority, is to direct man towards happiness in the afterlife. And the two sources of authoritative guidance operate in parallel, but are fundamentally separate—the very cornerstone of Dantean political thought. The *Convivio*'s imperialism marks a striking development in Dante's political thinking since his days as a Guelph politician. The experience of exile, and of political isolation, surely has some connection with the ideas outlined here. Dante dissociated himself not just from his fellow Whites, but from conventional Italian politics altogether. The *Convivio*'s theory of an ideal world empire for the promotion of human happiness is something quite different from and beyond traditional Ghibellinism; it is highly personal and visionary, the product indeed of a 'One-Man Party', to echo Cacciaguida's fully-justified phrase.

To return to the content of Book IV: Dante devotes three chapters (xi–xiii) to a fierce attack on riches (with Dante attacks are usually fierce). Whatever Frederick II may have thought, material wealth is in essence *ignoble*: it is acquired in a morally arbitrary fashion; any increase in it is fraught with danger; the very possession of it is harmful. Dante elaborates on these three charges with a variety of assertions, some of which seem to him self-evident. The main points are as follows. Money can be acquired by pure chance, as in the discovery of hidden treasure, and here fortune favours the wicked more than the just, we are told. Similarly, bequests go more often to the bad than to the good. But wealth may also come by conscious acquisition, either legal (commerce) or illegal (robbery and fraud). Illegally-acquired riches have of course nothing to do with nobility; but it is interesting, though not surprising, that Dante has little time for the commercial sort either. Such riches are rarely gained by the good, for their acquisition requires careful attention, and the good man's attention will be applied to higher things. Once again, the disdain for trade, which we have touched on already. Moreover wealth is always increased in a spiritually dangerous way, for whoever amasses it is always unsatisfied, always greedy for more. Riches treacherously lure the soul into the grave sin of avarice. Finally, even possessing wealth is harmful. For, negatively, the man who retains his wealth is failing to exercise the virtue of generosity. And riches are a positive cause of evil in those who possess them: they become timid and hateful, vigilantly devoting every energy to the protection of their goods. The 'miserable merchants who travel' ('li miseri mercatanti che per lo mondo vanno'), trembling as they do at the rustle of a leaf, know this very well (IV, xiii,11)!

So much for riches. After demolishing the notion that the passage of time is necessary for nobility (Frederick had said '*antica richezza*'), Dante turns at last to his own definition. Nobility is quite simply the perfection of any being according to its own particular nature (IV, xvi, 4–5). In this fundamental sense it may be ascribed to anything in the scale of creation. Thus we can meaningfully speak of the nobility of a stone, or of a falcon. But before focusing on nobility in mankind, Dante makes an excursion into etymology. He reproves those fools who think nobility has to do with renown, with being well-known, deriving *nobile* from *nosco* ('I know'). In fact, says Dante, it comes from *non vile* ('not base'). In fact Dante is wrong here, though it has to be said that etymology is among the shakiest branches of medieval learning.[24] In mankind the results of a noble nature are to be seen especially in the moral and intellectual virtues. This is elaborated in the very important seventeenth chapter, heavily dependent on Aristotle's *Ethics*. Dante lists the eleven moral virtues, each of which is a middle way between two opposite, and reprehensible extremes; thus fortitude (say) is a moderation both of our audacity and our timidity. This is of course Aristotle's celebrated Golden Mean. And what makes us act virtuously, and put the virtues into practice, is a certain habitual right choice ('l'abito de la nostra buona elezione'—IV, xvii, 7). The stress on choice is important; we have to choose to do good for our actions to be good in any meaningful sense. The practice of virtue leads to happiness, and this brings Dante to consider the kinds of happiness attainable on earth. There are two, corresponding to that famous medieval pair the Active and the Contemplative Life. Dante is in no doubt that the latter is the superior way; Aristotle said so and the New Testament confirms it. Although the moral, as distinct from the intellectual virtues have to do with the Active Life, the lesser way, it is these Dante will concentrate on, for instruction in them is more easily imparted and, note, more urgently required. Chapter xix compares nobility to a heaven containing a variety of bright stars, these being not only the different virtues, but also piety and religion, which are good dispositions, together with praiseworthy emotions such as pity and shame. We are now ready for a refinement of the general definition given in Chapter xvi: Dante explains that in man nobility is in fact a divine gift, a seed of happiness infused by God into a soul well disposed to receive it (IV, xx, 9). And, in case there lingers any dynastic conception of nobility, he stresses that this gift is bestowed on individuals, such that no member of (say) the Uberti family, or the Visconti may claim to be noble on account of his birth. The noble individual through his own worth may ennoble his family (in the sense of bringing it honour), but not vice versa. Dante's notion of nobility, then, is eminently moral and personal, not economic or social.

Just how the God-given 'seed of happiness' enters into us is elliptically explained in Chapter xxi, a special ('speziale') chapter and certainly a difficult one, involving a measure of embryology and astrology. The chief point is that God directly infuses into the human foetus the faculty of reason.[25] Human beings receive this rational power to differing degrees, for each soul's disposition, or readiness—in effect capacity—to receive is unique to it, being the complex result of variable factors, material as well as immaterial.

Now nobility presupposes reason, and the degree to which nobility is 'sown' in the individual soul depends on the quality of the rational intellect, itself dependent on the receiving soul's 'purity' ('puritade'). The following chapter returns to the active—contemplative distinction, in terms of two different faculties of the mind, the practical and the speculative. Both can bring happiness (the seed of which, as we have seen, is nobility), but to differing extents. Whilst speculation on the workings of God and nature brings us to a more sublime kind of bliss than does the practice of the moral virtues, this is still earthly happiness and as such imperfect and provisional when compared to the beatitude enjoyed in Heaven. Having said that, the virtuous application of our practical and speculative faculties is the surest way to that beatitude. As Ryan notes, 'the absence of any reference to the theological virtues [i.e. Faith, Hope and Charity] here is remarkable'.[26]

Virtually all the remainder of the *Convivio* is devoted to how nobility shows itself in noble people at the various stages of earthly life (seen as a curve or arch, reaching its high point at the thirty-fifth year, and thereafter declining). There are four stages. In youth (up to the twenty-fifth year) nobility has to do with physical grace and beauty, gentleness, a sense of shame, and reverence for one's elders. In manhood (twenty-five to forty-five) the noble qualities are those of self-control, resoluteness, affection, courtesy and loyalty. Maturity (forty-five to seventy) should involve prudence, justice, affability and generosity, particularly in the sense of sharing one's accumulated wisdom. A noble old age (seventy onwards) means reflecting on past good deeds, but also looking beyond this life and gently preparing for the next with longing. For the life to come is a home-coming, and here Dante uses the beautiful image of the noble soul coming into port after its long sea-voyage. Rushing ahead with full sail is not the right way; rather we should in old age 'lower the sails of our worldly affairs' ('calare le vele de le nostre mondane operazioni'—IV, xxviii, 3), so that we reach our destination in tranquillity and safety. The *Convivio* ends with a gloss on the *congedo*, the closing lines, of 'Le dolci rime d'amor', a gloss which underlines the didactic intent of the whole treatise. In these lines Dante gave his poem the curious title 'Contra-li-erranti' ('against the erring'). Now the gloss specifically says this is modelled on the title of Aquinas' *Summa contra Gentiles*, that great work in which, by *philosophical* arguments, St Thomas seeks to persuade

107

contemporary Jews and Muslims that Christianity is true. Dante's very conscious aim, then, is to enlighten the intellectually and morally wayward, whose error on the question of nobility has so gravely concerned him. And this urgent desire to instruct runs through all four books.

What are the final impressions of this treatise, with its passionate defence of the vernacular in Book I; its elaborate patterns and correspondences (angels, heavens, branches of learning) in Book II; its celebration of philosophy as transcending earthly thought and leading heavenwards (Book III); and Book IV's distinctive and forthright view of human excellence? The unifying factor is delight in the power and potential of the human mind. To philosophize is to exercise reason, a faculty of divine origin. Philosophy is not a body of doctrine, nor a mere process of reasoning—it is more a state of mind. The philosopher is not ethically disinterested, but on the contrary ethically committed. Nor is he dispassionate, for philosophy is a *loving* use of wisdom. For Dante in the *Convivio*, then, our reasoning is inseparably bound up with morality and religion. Yet is there any potential conflict here? It has often been said that the *Convivio* is not merely a celebration of human reason, but that it reflects a stage, in Dante's development, of supreme confidence, even over-confidence, in our rational faculty. The supreme confidence is certainly there; and the charge of *over*-confidence is one Dante himself seems to make in the *Purgatorio* (XXXIII, 82–90). This is not just a matter of the dialectic techniques Dante employs with such enthusiasm. For instance, the firm grounding of nobility, and thus of all the virtues, in reason is an avowedly 'intellectualist' stance. And the *Convivio* is ultimately concerned with the moral potential of rational human beings in their earthly lives. Yet this implies no contradiction with a transcendentally religious outlook—there are many pointers beyond and upwards (and not only in Book III). Reason is not cut off from God, for God is its source—and to its source everything must return. Dante's conception of philosophy is, 'even' in the *Convivio*, not just a moral, but a religious one. (All this is utterly remote from most modern Western ways of thinking; the former close connection between philosophy and religion has more or less disappeared since the eighteenth century, if not earlier.) Having said this, it is true that the *Convivio* in one important sense remains humanistic, 'man-centred'. For, granted that reason comes from God, Dante appears to be saying that it can raise us to astonishing heights even in our earthly lives. After the initial infusion of the rational soul we can, it would seem, 'go it alone'. One does not have to be a Christian theologian to notice the virtual absence of grace in all this. Only in the *Comedy* will Dante tackle the awesome question of man's relation to God in terms of grace.[27]

## (vi) The Casentino: Dante's last *canzone*

When and where Dante ceased writing the *Convivio* we do not know; it may have been as late as 1308, and no longer in Lunigiana with the Malaspina family. What we do know is that after his stay with them he spent some time in the upper valley of the Arno, in the mountainous Casentino region of eastern Tuscany. And it was here, in 1307, that he wrote another Latin letter (Letter IV), which accompanies and introduces his last *canzone*. The letter is addressed to Moroello Malaspina and in it Dante excuses himself for seeming negligence towards him (perhaps simply lack of contact). He presents himself as an affectionate servant who longs to return to Moroello's court, which he has now left. The reason for his neglect is love—a new, human, love; for scarcely had Dante set foot on the banks of the Arno than he was thunderstruck, or rather struck by lightning, at the sight of a beautiful lady ('mulier, ceu fulgur descendens, apparuit'). Love then took full possession of him, just like a tyrant. For Love has now destroyed Dante's very laudable resolve to avoid women (and poems about them!); it has put a stop to his unstinting enquiries into the things of heaven and earth; and worst of all it has enslaved his will. He is no longer his own master—Love is. If Moroello wishes to know more, he should read the accompanying *canzone*.

This great and powerful poem, 'Amor, da che convien pur ch'io mi doglia' ('Love, since after all I must grieve'), is unlike the other exilic *canzoni*. It is not ethical; neither is it an allegorical love poem whose real theme is philosophy. It is a poem of love—and carnal, sensual love at that. And, of course, the love is unrequited. The unnamed cause of Dante's torment is herself impervious to love: her emotional flak-jacket of haughty disdain ('orgoglio') succeeds not just in deflecting Love's arrows, but in blunting them. She is an outlaw from Love's court. The poem's focus, however, is not on her, but on what love for her has done to Dante. It has done him nothing but harm: the bondage of carnal love has led to a disintegration of the personality, to a kind of 'moral death'.[28] The *canzone* begins by emphasizing Dante's grief, and his yearning to express it (though expression in this case is not therapeutic). Dante's love is obsessional: he simply cannot stop his mind conjuring up an image of the cruel and beautiful lady, an image which, as if attracted to its source, compels him to seek her out where she really is, with disastrous results. Despite a show of resistance, against himself as much as anything, Dante yields to this ferocious passion: both his reason and his will are overcome. And in this enslavement his rational soul is cut off from the rest of him—indeed, it is in a state of abeyance, such that he is unknowing and oblivious. He is no longer a whole man, a reasoning man. This sundering, this alienation of the rational faculty is quite different of course from the ecstatic experiences of the *Paradiso*; there the soul will be saturated from above, losing consciousness because over-charged with reality, whereas sensual love here is utterly base, and debasing.[29] The poem's ending is both poignant and political. Dante's closing lines bids farewell to his mountain song ('montanina mia canzon'): it may perhaps get as far as Florence, which (just like the heartless lady) has shut him out, but if it does, the poet himself cannot follow. Even were the Florentines' cruelty to abate, Dante would still be bound by the chains of love—he could not leave the Casentino.

But it would be wrong to read out of 'Amor, da che convien' a passive Dante; for all the yielding to obsession, there is something much more perversely active here than mere wilful compliance. Dante tells us, quite plainly, that his madly impetuous soul has been engineering its own downfall ('L'anima folle, che al suo mal s'ingegna'). And this frankness can help us interpret both the *canzone* and the letter. For although in the final analysis we cannot say whether love in the *montanina* reflects a real experience or is 'merely' literary, there is no reason to doubt the former alternative; Dante's searching self-criticism—Took calls the poem 'self-confrontational'[30]—seems to corroborate this. In any case, to suppose it improbable that this intense intellectual and artist could be violently distracted, in his forties, by really experienced sensual passion is to be strangely ignorant of human nature. Never before in Italian literature had there been so forceful a projection of the terrifying power of sensual love. There is nothing ennobling here—this is an irrational and morally destructive force (very much Cavalcanti's view of love).

## (vii) Lucca

If Dante's presence in the Casentino in 1307 is almost certain, it has to be said that Lucca as a location for 1308 rests on less solid, though most intriguing, evidence. We know from the *Purgatorio* (XXIV, 42–44) that Dante stayed in Lucca: the poet Bonagiunta, in yet another pseudo-prophecy, tells him he will receive kindness there from a certain lady called Gentucca (an unusual name, though highly convenient as a rhyme with Lucca). Many have held that he was there in 1314–15, during the ascendancy of the Ghibelline warlord Uguccione della Faggiuola. But might he also have been there some years earlier, and more precisely in the year following the Casentino visit? The chief clue is a contemporary legal document, unpublished until 1921, which tells us that a certain 'Iohannes f[ilius] Dantis Alagherii de Florentia' ('Giovanni, son of Dante di Alighiero of Florence') was witness to a commercial transaction in Lucca on 21 October 1308.[31] (The document, incidentally, is signed by a notary with the splendid name of Rabbitus Toringhelli.) Dante specialists in Italy have thoroughly debated two distinct questions arising from this: (a) was Giovanni the poet's son, or the son of another Dante Alighieri from Florence (Alighieri, in its various spellings was a not uncommon name)? and (b) if the former is the case, can we infer the presence of other members of the family in Lucca? Neither question has been finally resolved, though many scholars now agree with Barbi, who inclined to the view that this Giovanni was *the* Dante Alighieri's child.[32] The poet would then have had three sons: Pietro, Iacopo and Giovanni, that is, Peter, James and John, the three apostles who witnessed Christ's Transfiguration (Matthew 17. l ff.), and the very same three saints who will question Dante in the *Paradiso* (XXIV–XXVI) on Faith, Hope and Charity. Unfortunately nothing else is known of Giovanni—he did not, for instance, write a commentary on his father's poem, like the other two brothers, not that this is in itself surprising.

But what about Lucca? Why would Giovanni have been there? To start with, by 1308 there may have been a good reason why some or all of the sons could no longer remain in Florence: the banishment order against Dante had been extended in June 1302 to all his descendants in the male line once they reached the age of fourteen. And this edict also included wives of exiles. So at some stage in the first decade of the fourteenth century, Dante's immediate family may have had to leave Florence. (To know the birth-dates of Dante's sons would help.) It might seem unlikely that members of Dante's family should remove to Lucca, a city controlled by Black Guelphs. But until March 1309, when the Lucchese authorities decided Florentine exiles as a whole were unwelcome, there was no formal impediment to their doing so. Indeed the Florentine Blacks would no doubt have preferred the families (at any rate) of exiles to reside in an allied city where they were effectively neutralized, rather than establish themselves in a hostile town such as Arezzo, still an active centre of manoeuvres against the government of Florence.[33] But what of Dante himself? Again, there was no formal bar at this stage to his presence in Lucca. He had long ceased, in any case, to be associated with the White exiles' schemes, and moreover his friend and patron Moroello Malaspina enjoyed great prestige in that city. Nor is there any reason why Dante should not have been in Lucca if his wife Gemma had been there with the children. Although it is frequently asserted that she never joined her husband during his exile, this rests solely on Boccaccio's remark that Dante was careful never to allow her near him then, a remark following immediately after a rhetorical diatribe against marriage and wives. As Barbi suggests, Boccaccio may well have been carried away by his 'misogyny'.[34]

So there is no political, legal or family reason why Dante should not have been in Lucca in 1308. If this is so—and it must remain conjecture—the Black Guelph city may have been where Europe's greatest medieval poem was begun.

# 8

# The Sacred Poem

## A Survey of the *Divine Comedy*
## (1308–1321)

### (i) Preliminaries

A sacred poem that made its author thin! Well, that is precisely
what Dante tells us (*Par.* XXV, 1–3), and we should take his words
literally, not lightly. The effort involved in the conception,
evolution and realization of the *Comedy* must have been colossal;
and the efforts, over six-and-a-half centuries, of thousands of
scholars from many different countries have by no means extracted
all its treasure. Now in a biography some discussion of the *Comedy*
is clearly appropriate; but it has to be stated firmly that although
the completion dates and manuscript dissemination of the three
*cantiche* or canticles (i.e. the *Inferno*, *Purgatorio* and *Paradiso*)
have been roughly established,[1] the precise date and location of the
composition of this or that episode, canto or series of cantos cannot
for the most part be determined at all. Of course the real location
was Dante's own mind, as he drifted in exile from one physical
*locus* to the next. So the present chapter does not slot in chrono-
logically between the previous one and the one following. It is a
freestanding chapter, and in its discussion of the *Paradiso* takes us
almost to the end of Dante's life, whereas the next chapter will begin
with the events of 1308 which were to lead to Henry VII's invasion.
Nevertheless the whole *Comedy* is best considered in one single
chapter.[2]

Of course there are numerous short accounts of the narrative
action of the *Comedy* readily available. To take just two in English:
Bergin has four sections on the *Comedy*, the first of which is a well-
written and skilfully-condensed outline; Anderson's is rather longer
but still admirably concise and informative.[3] To avoid overlapping

unduly with these, this chapter will instead highlight episodes of particular historical, political and moral significance; more strictly literary considerations will be less prominent. Some episodes will be omitted altogether.

## (ii) The Lost People

And so to Hell.[4] This subsection is so entitled because the eternal condition of all those in Hell is to be lost, in that they have lost all hope of salvation. As the stark inscription over the gate of Hell says: 'Lasciate ogne speranza, voi ch'intrate' ('Abandon all hope, ye who enter here'—*Inf.* III, 9). And the expression *la perduta gente* ('the lost people') occurs just six lines earlier, as part of the same inscription. Significantly, it recurs (as *le perdute genti*) in the *Purgatorio* (XXX, 138), where Beatrice dramatically declares that Dante had fallen so low that no other means could have secured his salvation than that of showing him the damned. And of course that strategy worked.

The damned are confined for ever within a series of concentric circles, some with further subdivisions and all steadily narrowing in diameter: for Dante has imagined Hell as a vast funnel beneath the earth's surface, tapering as it goes down to finish at the very centre of the earth, where the gigantic yet impotent figure of Satan is frozen in futile ice. The souls of the damned are tormented in an ingenious variety of ways, their torments being in some sense (not always immediately clear) appropriate to the sins they committed, and did not repent of, whilst alive. And Dante, the protagonist of his own poem, will see many of them, and converse with some, exhibiting a range of reactions to their fate, from compassion to vindictiveness, as he descends from circle to circle. And his guide will be the soul of Virgil, the Roman poet to whom he felt closest. Virgil appears roughly half way through *Inf.* I, in a dark wood in which Dante the protagonist is lost. It is Easter in the year 1300, so Dante is still 35, right in the middle of his life's journey, as he says in the poem's opening line: 'Nel mezzo del cammin di nostra vita.' Perhaps this is the most momentous watershed in all literature. Now the opening canto is unusual for two reasons, no doubt closely related. One is the 'unrealistic' topography: Dante is in a dark wood, yet there is also a sunlit hill, or mountain, which he tries to climb but cannot. There is a dreamlike disorientation here, not at all typical of the rest of the *Inferno*, which is described with considerable attention to concrete physical detail, such that it is indeed possible, and useful, to draw maps of Dante's Hell. And the reason Dante cannot climb the hill (generally interpreted as a symbolic anticipation of Mount Purgatory) is that his way is barred by a fearsome trio of mysterious animals, a leopard, a lion and a she-wolf. These are the second unusual feature of this initial canto. Clearly they symbolize something, and something evil at that. Yet it is not clear just what they do symbolize: critics are still far from unanimous here. It might be that they correspond to the three major moral and geographical divisions of Hell, such that the leopard is associated with the sins of the passions, the lion with those of violence, and the she-wolf with those of deceit. But it seems more plausible to link the lion with pride, and, not least on the basis of other passages in the poem, the wolf would denote avarice or con-cupiscence.[5]

This gives us an early opportunity for a word about allegory and symbolism. A vast amount has been written about both these terms, and the literary techniques they refer to, and these matters really lie outside the scope of this book. But if we take an *allegory* to mean that which is of significance but has no reality outside that signifi-cance; and a *symbol* to mean something independently existent *per se*, but possessing an additional significance beyond (if not always above) itself, then we have a tension between what the two terms refer to. Allegory is, on this definition, typically the allegory of per-sonified abstractions. Symbols however are real.[6] So *Malebouche*, the *Roman de la Rose*'s character who is an allegory of our maligning one another, is different from a lion, which the medieval bestiaries tell us is a symbol of Christ. The point is that lions exist, though for symbolists the symbolic meaning is all-important. Now personification allegory is not used in the Sacred Poem, and symbolism is markedly restrained. Of course, as we have recently seen, Dante wrote allegorical *canzoni* whose surface meaning he expounded in the *Convivio* in terms of a different (allegorical) sense. But this does not happen in the *Comedy*. Whereas Prudentius in the *Psychomachia* (late antiquity), or the *Roman de la Rose*, or Spenser's Elizabethan masterpiece the *Faerie Queene*, or (to take an example still widely read in the English-speaking world) Bunyan's *Pilgrim's Progress*—whereas all these use personification allegory, Dante does not, and clearly has chosen not to. So when he encounters a damned or saved soul, it is first and foremost the soul of a real individual who once did live on earth and in some cases had been personally known to Dante. Not allegories therefore; but symbols? Here again, for all the characters' function as moral *exempla*, for all their symbolic reference or at least resonance in this sense, they are still primarily themselves. This puts the question of symbolism into perspective. And all this applies to Dante the pilgrim too. Yes, he is Everyman, in that his extraordinary experience has a message for us all. But he is still the Dante of 1300. As every reader of the poem will know, there are enormous dramatic possibilities, vigorously exploited, in the contrasts between the protagonist and the poet writing with hindsight.

Dante's message is far too important, and the urgency of its transmission too acute, to leave much room for misunderstanding. That is in my view one reason why allegory and symbolism do not dominate as literary techniques in the poem. Certainly Dante is not in the business of conveying esoteric meanings, or of playing hide-and-seek with the reader, despite numerous unsolved riddles.[7]

To return to the events of the opening canto. Of all the three beasts, the she-wolf has alarmed Dante the most and is driving him back from the sunlit hill to the dark wood. But help is at hand. He sees before him a man, or what appears to be a man. This is of course the soul of Virgil. In a manner very typical of Dante's characters, he does not name himself directly but refers to his birthplace (Mantua) and the time when he lived (the age of Julius Caesar and Augustus). Moreover, he was a poet, who sang of Aeneas—one of Dante the author's more transparent periphrases! Dante the character is astonished and ashamed to be in the presence of his 'master and author' ('lo mio maestro e'l mio autore'—1. 85). But he is still bothered by the wolf, and begs Virgil to save him. Virgil explains that Dante must escape from the dark wood by another path, but before giving some indication of all that will involve, he prophesies that the wolf will be overcome by a greyhound, who will be the saviour of Italy. Another atypical puzzle: but this animal would seem to symbolize a real person, as distinct from a moral category. If this is so, a very probable identification would be with Can Grande della Scala, Dante's most renowned patron during his exile, not least because his name, literally, means 'Great Hound'. Virgil then proposes to guide Dante down through Hell and up the mountain of Purgatory, before handing over to another soul, who will conduct him to Heaven. That soul, we shall later learn, is Beatrice.

There are several reasons for the choice of Virgil as guide. An obvious one is that Book VI of the *Aeneid* recounts the descent of Aeneas, while still alive, into Hades, the classical underworld. Indeed, a great many topographical and other features of the *Inferno* have been adapted from that account: it is not surprising that Virgil (Dante's character) knows his way around Hell, but has to ask directions in the Christian realm of Purgatory. Also the historical Virgil, writing at the very beginning of the Roman Empire, was the great proclaimer of the nobility and supremacy of the Romans, descended as they were from Aeneas and precisely then embarking on their most glorious, Imperial, phase. And he proclaimed all this in very great poetry. Notwithstanding Dante the character's awe in this initial canto, Dante the poet in writing the *Comedy* sought to give to his own age a poem as great as, if not greater than, the *Aeneid*. Moreover, in the Middle Ages it was widely believed that in the fourth of his pastoral Eclogues Virgil had unconsciously prophesied the coming of Christ—this will be the chief theme of *Purg.* XXII. But Virgil remains a virtuous pagan lacking God's grace; indeed he is often presented by critics as representative of what unaided human reason can achieve, and not achieve, without divine revelation. The contrast between Virgil as Reason, and Beatrice as Revelation, is frequently made. But Dante's characters are not symbols in any reductionist sense; the great advantage of his method, as Bergin puts it, is that 'Virgil does not always have to be Human Reason ... Beatrice does not have to be Revelation whenever she speaks'.[8] Let us say that they are characters in the poem, always rooted in the reality of human personhood, though with a frequent symbolic 'over-plus' or 'added value'.

Canto I, the first of *Inferno*'s thirty-four cantos, is thus a genuinely anticipatory prologue. Canto II begins with an invocation for poetic assistance to the Muses, as do *Purg.* I and *Par.* I (the second and third *cantiche* have thirty-three cantos each, making a total of one hundred for the whole poem). But the main theme of this canto is Dante, and the journey before him. He is puzzled and afraid. Aeneas, he says, was granted the privilege of visiting the underworld while still living, but then he was destined by God to be the father of Rome and its Empire. And St Paul made a journey in the opposite direction, for he was caught up into Heaven.[9] But

117

Dante wonders why he should be similarly singled out, exclaiming 'Io non Enëa, io non Paulo sono' ('I am not Aeneas; I am not Paul'— l. 32). Virgil, having charged him with cowardice ('viltade'—l. 45), proceeds to allay his fears with an explanation. It is a remarkable one. The Blessed Virgin herself, moved to pity by Dante's wayward moral and spiritual condition (almost certainly symbolized by the dark wood), has alerted St Lucy (patroness of the weak-sighted) who in her turn has appealed to Beatrice. All this of course is taking place in Heaven: a celestial chain reaction of care and concern. So Beatrice descends from her place in Heaven to Limbo, Virgil's abode, and there bids him go to Dante's aid. It is love that has brought her on this mission, but to Heaven she must return. She only hopes she has come in time. When Virgil has related this to Dante, he urges him to put aside all cowardice and boldly follow him. With the support of a trio of heavenly ladies, and the promise Virgil has already made as to the journey's outcome, what is there to hold him back? Dante now takes heart and sets off with Virgil, whom he calls his leader, lord and master.

With Canto III the action proper of the *Inferno* begins. The first thing the two poets see is the inscription above the gate of Hell. This tells us several very important things about Hell: not only does it entail the loss of all hope, but it will last for ever, and was made by God in his justice. In fact, and significantly, Dante does not write 'God' but states that Hell was made by Power, Wisdom and Love, the traditional attributes of the Father, the Son and the Holy Spirit, respectively.[10] Once through the gate, the poets find themselves in what is often called the vestibule of Hell—here are tormented, in great numbers, the souls of the indifferent, or uncommitted, doomed to go chasing aimlessly after a whirling banner, while wasps and hornets sting them. Although Dante recognizes some (including perhaps Pope Celestine V—see above, pp. 54–55), not a single one is named. They are a wretched, anonymous crowd, and Virgil refuses to talk about them, bidding Dante simply to look and pass on. But it is worth pausing to consider this unusual group of souls. In their earthly lives they had done neither good nor evil, at least nothing so significant as to be worthy either of praise or blame. Indeed, Dante even calls them 'Questi sciaurati, che mai non fur vivi' ('These wretches, who never were alive'—l. 64). For to be truly alive involves making real choices. The uncommitted are confined here on the very outskirts of Hell, as if spurned alike by Heaven and the grim depths below. All this is typical of Dante's zealous scorn for the weak-minded, the morally indecisive. But this is no halfway house: we are already in Hell, on the far side of the gate, and in the region of the damned, of those who have lost 'il ben de l'intelletto' ('the good of the intellect'—l. 18), meaning Divine truth, which alone satisfies the human mind.[11] Curiously, Dante has chosen to mingle these uncommitted human souls with a crowd of neutral angels, those who sided neither with God nor with Lucifer and the rebels in the primordial war in Heaven. Of them Dante explicitly says that they are rejected both by Heaven and 'lo profondo inferno' (deep Hell'—l. 41).[12]

Leaving behind these wretches, Dante and Virgil come to the banks of the Acheron, the first of Hell's four 'rivers' (two of them, Styx and Cocytus, are in fact marsh and lake, respectively).[13] Here they are met by the gruff boatman Charon, the first in a steady succession of figures adapted, like the rivers, from classical mythology, most of them mentioned or described in *Aeneid* VI. On the far side of the Acheron is Limbo (Canto IV), a region much less typical of Hell than was the vestibule. For there are no torments here; indeed in one part there is light, a stream, a meadow and a noble castle. But there are sad sighs, for all those here are suspended in a hopeless desire for what they can never attain. They are not all 'virtuous pagans': in fact Dante's Limbo contains or contained three categories, two of them part of Christian tradition. First, the patriarchs and other virtuous ancient Jews (Abraham, Moses, David and so on): these were liberated by Christ in the 'harrowing' of Hell, and are now in Heaven. Second, the unbaptized infants (the destiny of whom may be the only context in which many modern readers have come across the idea of Limbo). But Dante's third category is very much his own invention: he has taken the audacious step of populating his Limbo with the souls of virtuous men and women, who, living before Christ, were cut off from the true faith, and more precisely from baptism. He even includes three medieval Muslims by name: Saladin (Richard the Lionheart's adversary) and the philosophers Avicenna and Averroes. These, however, are vastly outnumbered by the galaxy of famous names from antiquity, men and women of action and intellect, from Penthesilea to Plato. The key phrase characterizing all the heroes, poets and philosophers is 'li spiriti magni' ('those great in spirit'—l. 119): this contrasts them very clearly with the pusillanimous inhabitants of the previous circle. The most memorable scene is when a coterie of ancient poets, having welcomed Virgil back, allow Dante to join their exalted group. He makes a sixth, the others being Homer, and four Romans: Horace, Ovid, Lucan and Virgil himself—all the Latin poets dearest to Dante (except Statius, who will appear in the *Purgatorio*). Virgil of course will soon be on his way again; but after he has entrusted Dante to Beatrice's care, he will return for ever to Limbo, unable to follow his protégé. And Virgil's condition as a virtuous pagan is surely one of the wellsprings of this canto's poignancy.

Canto V is where the sins really begin. For whereas those in Limbo are marred by a defect, though in themselves virtuous, and the uncommitted have not managed to do anything worth calling wrong, all the souls from now on certainly have. We are now in the second circle,[14] that of the lovers or, less euphemistically, the lustful: those who 'la ragion sommettono al talento' ('subordinate their reason to desire'—l. 39). First the two poets pass the long-tailed monster Minos, the mythical King of Crete, whom Dante has here demonized. Not only is he the guardian of this circle: all the newly-arrived damned must come before him to be 'judged' and despatched to their appropriate part of Hell. Of course the real judgement is God's—Minos is merely an infernal agent. Dante and Virgil then see the lustful souls tossed aloft in a raging whirlwind— an obvious externalization of sexual passion. Virgil points out several to Dante, Semiramis, Dido, Cleopatra and Achilles among them: famous, exotic names, and all but Tristan from antiquity. Dante is almost overcome with pity. But this is far outweighed by the compassion he will feel for Francesca and Paolo, on whom the spotlight now falls.

Here we have two real medieval Italians, as are practically all the souls with whom Dante converses in Hell. Francesca da Rimini was the aunt of Guido Novello da Polenta, at whose court in Ravenna Dante died. For the usual political reasons she was married to Giovanni ('Gianciotto') son of Malatesta, Lord of Rimini. But she became adulterously involved with Paolo, the younger brother of Gianciotto, who, surprising the lovers together, killed them both (probably in 1285). Gianciotto's soul is tormented in the very depths of Hell, his sin being much graver than that of the two lovers. Francesca confides to Dante the details of how their affair began, the French romance of Lancelot apparently acting as a catalyst (*caveat lector*!). But before that she makes some more general observations about the nature of love, couched very much in the language of the *Dolce Stil Novo*. These are in fact an alluring attempt at self-exculpation, and they hinge on the allegedly inexorable power of love. More precisely, Paolo fell in love with her, and so she had no choice but to reciprocate: 'Amor, ch'a nullo amato amar perdona' ('Love, which exonerates no one loved from loving in return'—l. 103). This preposterous statement, apart from being simply untrue, is also incompatible with a belief in free will. Whatever appeal Francesca's predicament and arguments may have had for the thirty-five–year-old Dante-character, her attempt to shift the blame for her adultery can cut no ice in the poet's moral scheme. For the whole *Comedy* is built upon the conviction that our actions are freely willed, and moreover have moral significance and eternal consequences. True, sinful sexual love is considered by Dante to be the least culpable of the evils he describes, for the sins increase in gravity as we descend the funnel of Hell from circle to circle. But Francesca and Paolo are culpable and deserve to be damned; Dante-character's intense compassion for them (he swoons at the end of the canto) is the first major instance of that character-author tension which is among the *Inferno*'s most fascinating features.

After lust comes gluttony. But Canto VI is not really about gluttony at all: it is in fact the first of the *Comedy*'s great political cantos. The gluttonous souls lie in stinking mud, pelted by incessant rain, hail and snow. They are also lacerated by the claws of Cerberus, the ravenous three-headed hound who is the guardian of this third circle. The sin thus punished is merely mentioned, in just one line of this canto (l. 53): there is no discussion as to its nature. Perhaps there is not that much to say about gluttony, by contrast with sex, the subject of the previous circle. The canto is dominated by the dialogue with Ciacco, a Florentine of the generation immediately prior to Dante's. Recognizing Dante, he rears himself up out of the mud, and addresses the visitor. Almost at once he stigmatizes their native city as overflowing with envy. Dante then asks him three questions about Florence. Ciacco's reply begins with the first of the *Comedy*'s hindsight prophecies: the damned, as will later be explained (*Inf.* X, 94–108), have a limited knowledge of the future. He looks ahead (only a few weeks ahead) to the disturbances of May Day 1300, and alludes to the short-lived ascendancy of the

White Guelphs, who within three years will be vanquished by the Blacks, aided by the power of one who is even now plotting—a pretty plain reference to Boniface VIII. Ciacco then informs Dante that there are only two just men in Florence, but no one listens to them. If this is to be taken literally (and by no means all critics have done so), the reference could be to Dante himself and Cavalcanti, or perhaps Dante and Dino Compagni. In answer to Dante's third question, Ciacco asserts that the cause of their city's civil strife is its three prevailing vices: pride, envy and avarice. Dante then enquires about the fate of five distinguished thirteenth-century Florentines; Ciacco tells him that, though their sins differ, they are all in Hell, and among its blackest souls at that. In fact, three are sodomites and one is a factional agitator (crucially involved in the events of 1216 which led to the Guelph-Ghibelline conflicts within Florence); the fifth, however, is not mentioned again in the poem. In short, the sixth canto is a stinging indictment of Florence; this will be a long-running theme throughout the *Comedy,* extending even to the Empyrean, the highest of the *Paradiso*'s ten heavens.

The avaricious and the prodigal (opposite extremes) are jointly punished in the fourth circle (Canto VII), presided over by Pluto, its incoherently gabbling monster-guardian. They unceasingly roll huge rocks against one another, an activity quite as futile as their economic perversions whilst on earth. Like the uncommitted in the vestibule of Hell, they are an anonymous crowd; but though they are not identified as individuals, Virgil stresses that the clergy, popes and cardinals included, are prominently represented here—among the avaricious that is, not the prodigal.

Before the end of Canto VII the poets reach the fifth circle, the marsh of Styx. This is the abode of the angry, who, still furious in the afterlife, bob about in the mire, striking, tearing and biting one another. Phlegyas, the latest in the series of demonized classical figures, ferries Dante and Virgil across. But *en route* a curious incident occurs: a fierce soul, that of a certain Filippo Argenti, emerges from the swamp and, after a brief exchange with Dante, tries to overturn the boat (Canto VIII, 31 ff.). Virgil repulses him and condemns him for his arrogance. Dante-character fervently expresses a wish to see Filippo doused in the mire, whereupon he is violently attacked by his fellow angry spirits, a spectacle for which Dante the poet still gives praise and thanks to God. Now this is something new in the *Inferno*: hitherto Dante-character has reacted to the sinners' torments with horror or pity, even sympathy. But here he is angry, vindictive even. This is certainly unusual, though there are three broadly comparable episodes much further down in Hell.[15] Yet Christianity has always accepted the notion of a righteous or zealous anger, as contrasted with the vicious passion of which Filippo and the others are guilty. It appears he was a Florentine nobleman, a Black Guelph contemporary with Dante, noted for his haughty and disdainful character—he sounds rather like a less intelligent version of Corso Donati. 'Argenti' may in fact have been a nickname, for it was said he shod his horse with silver ('argento' in Italian). He may have been included in the poem as representative of a type of belligerent fellow Florentine particularly abhorrent to Dante. Yet many readers have felt Dante-character's reaction, albeit one of righteous zeal, to be disproportionate. In fact, apart from factional differences, there may well have been an element of family or even personal animosity between Argenti and the poet.

Once over the Styx the poets are confronted by the awesome walls of the city of Dis, a barrier marking one of the major divisions of Hell. So far we have encountered sinners who have indulged their passions, but on the far side of the city walls lie the deeper regions of Hell, wherein graver sins are punished. All of these except heresy come under the broad headings of violence or deceit. But first Dante and Virgil must face a dangerous obstacle. Hitherto the infernal monster-guardians, ignorant of the nature of Dante's journey, have tried to hinder the poets' progress and have had to be rebuked or otherwise overcome by Virgil. Now however, a vast mass of demons and classical monsters, the Furies included, appear swarming on the city ramparts, threatening the visitors. This is the first serious challenge to Virgil's authority during the journey, and only the intervention of a 'heavenly messenger', presumably an angel, assures the poets a safe passage (Canto IX, 64–103).

After this high point of excitement and suspense, Dante and Virgil pass through into the sixth circle, the plain of the heretics. These are imprisoned within a great number of tombs, heated red-hot by flames. Every kind of heresy is punished here, and the tombs are more or less hot, according to the gravity of the error concerned. The Cathars, the most famous medieval heretics, are not explicitly mentioned; in fact the only group pointed out by Virgil are the so-called 'Epicureans', whose heresy was to deny the immortality of the soul, and thus the afterlife.[16] To be kept alive for eternity in a tomb is an especially appropriate torment for them, and the connection between the fire and the typical fate of heretics at the stake is obvious. Canto X is dominated by Dante's unforgettable meeting with two of these 'Epicureans': Farinata and Cavalcante. Like VI, this is another political canto, and again the focus is on Florence. And as in Canto V, the contrasts between Dante-character and the poet are prominent: this is 1300 and the still fairly young Guelph politician becomes involved in a sharp exchange with a Ghibelline opponent. It is not the mature Dante speaking here, the Dante who had come to transcend the factionalism of his city.

Farinata degli Uberti died in 1264, and by then had become the leading Ghibelline in Tuscany. Having been banished in 1258, along with many other Ghibellines, he established himself at Siena, and with the help of King Manfred set about re-organizing the Tuscan Ghibellines in preparation for what was to be their great triumph at the battle of Montaperti (1260). But what of his sin? He and his wife were posthumously condemned for heresy in 1283, but it should not be thought that he belonged to any formal sect of 'Epicureans'. He may well have been simply a materialist free-thinker; in any case Ghibellines were frequently accused of this kind of heresy by their Guelph enemies. Here in the poem he at once appears as imposing and proud: at the sound of Dante's Tuscan voice, he stands fully upright in his burning tomb as if he holds Hell in great contempt ('com' avesse l'inferno a gran dispitto'—l. 36). Having established that Dante is an Alighieri, and thus a member of a Guelph family, he observes that he routed the Florentine Guelphs twice (in 1248, and in 1260, after Montaperti). Dante swiftly retorts that the Guelphs succeeded in returning both times (in 1251, in the aftermath of Frederick II's death and in 1267, following the great Angevin and Guelph victory at Benevento the previous year). But your people, he sarcastically adds, do not seem to have learnt the trick ('arte'—l. 51) of returning. 'Your people' refers not to the Ghibellines in general, but to the Uberti, who together with other prominent families, were never allowed back.

There is then a brief but dramatic interruption. The spirit of Cavalcante de' Cavalcanti, the poet Guido's father, kneels up in the tomb alongside Farinata, and weeping asks for news of his son. He has realized that Dante is still alive, and wonders why his great friend Guido is not with him. Misunderstanding Dante's reply, he thinks Guido is already dead and sinks back into the tomb. Farinata continues his exchange as if nothing had happened. Dante's remarks have stung him to the quick, but he adds a brief prophecy (ll. 79–81) to the effect that within fifty months Dante himself will discover how hard is the trick of returning from exile. This refers to the summer of 1304, by which time Dante had dissociated himself from the other Whites and their abortive comebacks. Here, for the first time, Dante-character learns what lies in store for him— Ciacco's prophecy had not referred to his personal banishment. Farinata then demands the reason behind the Guelphs' unrelenting hostility towards his family. When Dante says this is because of Montaperti, he points out that it was he alone who prevented his fellow victors from razing Florence to the ground (not surprisingly it was the Pisans and Sienese in particular who had urged this course of action). Before Dante takes his leave, Farinata specifically names two fellow 'Epicureans': Cardinal Ottaviano degli Ubaldini, also a prominent Ghibelline, and Frederick II himself, notorious for his unorthodox views.

For all the pathos of Cavalcante's brief appearance, it is Farinata who dominates the scene. It is clear that Dante admires him as a heroic fellow patriot, albeit of the opposing party. Indeed, he calls him 'great of soul' ('magnanimo'—l. 73); we have not heard such language since Limbo, with its *spiriti magni*. A great man, then, with admirable qualities, but guilty of a damnable sin.

With Canto XI we have a pause in the narrative action, whose pace so far has been furious. Virgil orders a rest so that the poets may get used to the stench thrown up from the abyss below them. But time is never wasted in the *Comedy*: even when Dante sleeps, in the *Purgatorio*, he dreams significant dreams. So here, Virgil takes the opportunity to expound the topography, and thus the moral layout, of Hell. This elaborate yet clear account is very important for our understanding of Dante's moral stance. Clearly he thought it important to distinguish hierarchically between different types of sin, and not merely for the architecture of his poem: such a scheme reflects beliefs about human nature and behaviour that he held deeply. Broadly speaking, the scheme can be derived from Aristotle and Cicero, though it should be made clear that these authors were describing and prescribing human conduct, not writing about Hades. Different ethical systems overlap of course, but it is noteworthy that there are only two specifically

Christian categories of sin in the *Inferno*: the unbelief of the pagans and the perverted belief of the heretics. All the rest is wrong behaviour, as distinct from wrong belief. Indeed, as Foster put it, 'most of the people whom Dante represents as damned would be sinners in any world that was human at all'.[17] As Virgil explains, there are just three more circles to be visited, though there are numerous subdivisions (Dante has already departed from the one-to-one correspondence of circle and canto).

Canto XII describes the first of three rings (*gironi*) that make up the seventh circle, that of the violent. Violence is more offensive to God than the sins of the passions, but less so than those of deceit, hence its intermediate position in Dante's scheme. This first ring is the river Phlegethon, a river of boiling blood, wherein are tormented those guilty of violence towards others. They are immersed to varying degrees (cf. the more or less hot tombs of the heretics), but all those seethed here have blood on their hands, whether they are famous tyrants such as Dionysius of Syracuse and Obizzo d'Este, Marquis of Ferrara, or (in two cases) relatively obscure robber-barons from medieval Tuscany. The chief focus of interest is not, however, on the violent spirits, but on the figures from classical mythology: first the Minotaur, who having failed to thwart the poets, dances with mindless rage, and more importantly the centaurs, also hybrid creatures, and also traditionally associated with violent anger, but intelligent and even courteous to the visitors. One of them escorts Dante and Virgil to a ford, and they cross the Phlegethon.

And so to Dante's great encounter with Pier della Vigna, in the weird wood of Canto XIII. This is the second ring, the place of torment for those who have been violent to themselves—notably suicides, but also profligates or spendthrifts, who were similarly bent on a kind of self-destruction. The suicides are transformed into trees, inside which their souls are imprisoned. Once again, this has some relevance to their sin: just as they violently sundered spirit and body, now they are forever condemned to another sort of body, of a lower order than the human one they rejected. Moreover these tree-bodies endure constant pain as their leaves are torn off and eaten by the harpies, repulsive bird-monsters. And they will suffer even more after the Day of Judgement, and the subsequent Resurrection of the Body, for unlike the other damned souls, they will not be re-united with their bodies: these will be draped across

126

their branches, where they will flap, soulless, for ever. The spend-thrifts endure a different punishment: they are pursued and torn apart by ravenous hounds.

Pier della Vigna was born in 1190 and having studied law at Bologna entered the service of Frederick II in 1221. He rapidly rose to prominence, eventually becoming the Emperor's Chancellor. He was his closest adviser during the momentous struggles with the papacy during the 1230s and 1240s. In short he was Frederick's right-hand man, and thus occupied one of the most influential positions in Europe. But in 1248 he was arrested, having been denounced by his envious fellow courtiers for treason; he was blinded and imprisoned, and the following year he took his own life. Not only was he a statesman, but also a vernacular poet, one of the *Scuola Siciliana*, and a famous rhetorician, both as orator and as writer of Latin prose. He had much in common with Dante, whose reaction on hearing Pier's account of his downfall and death is one of intense, disabling pity: he cannot speak, and Virgil has to take over (ll. 82–84). Pier's self-portrait is largely an eloquent protestation of his unswerving loyalty to the Emperor: he even sac-rificed his health for the sake of duty. He swears to Dante his innocence: 'già mai non ruppi fede' ('I was never disloyal'—l. 74). But another aspect of his character also emerges: contempt. Unjustly accused, he smarted under his enemies' scorn and in turn scorned them. He sought in death a release from their contempt, whilst savouring, almost wallowing in, his contempt for them: that is the meaning of the phrase 'per disdegnoso gusto' ('out of taste for scorn'—l. 70). The overall picture we get is of a man utterly devoted to his work, and fatally over-protective towards Frederick. He jealously guarded the keys to the Emperor's heart and kept everyone else at a distance (ll. 58–61): a recipe for disaster in any medieval court, let alone an Imperial one. Pier was just the kind of character who, magnet-like, attracts opprobrium, and more precisely envy. Here in Hell he is still concerned about his reputa-tion on earth, and he asks Dante to clear his name. And that is just what Dante the poet is doing in this canto, for his intention is indeed to set the record straight. Yes, Pier killed himself, and that is why he is where he is in Hell. But no, he did not betray Frederick II, and that is why he is not deep down in the glacial realm of the traitors. This has nothing to do with Dante-character's pity (in which there is not a trace of sympathy for the sin of suicide) but everything to do with Dante the poet's intention. He need not have chosen to place Pier here. Yet he did.

The final ring of violence is a plain of sand, rained down upon by flakes of fire. Sand and fire, not soil and rain: sterility is the keynote, the common feature of all the sins punished here. First, supine on the sand, are blasphemers (violent towards God) and, squatting and squabbling, weighed down by bags of money, are the usurers (violators of human 'art', meaning roughly 'valid industry or endeavour'). Between these two groups are the sodomites (violent against Nature); they are constantly on the move. Cantos XV and XVI are devoted to them, and as in Canto VI, the emphasis is not on the sin, but chiefly on Florence. Canto XV is almost entirely taken up with the dramatic and moving encounter between Dante and Brunetto Latini, of whom some mention has already been made. Dante and Virgil are walking above the level of the sand, on the banks of the Phlegethon, which flows through the plain; they are shielded from the rain of fire by a protective screen of vapour. A group of sodomites comes towards them, walking on the sand, one of whom is Brunetto. He and Dante recognize each another with mutual astonishment, and there ensues an intimate dialogue—of all the *Comedy*'s characters, with the *possible* exception of Beatrice, Brunetto was the one best known to Dante in his lifetime. Brunetto's manner throughout is paternalistic and affectionate: twice he calls him 'figliuol' ('my son'). Dante in turn is affectionate and reverential, always using the *voi* form of address, whereas Brunetto employs the informal *tu*. Brunetto praises Dante for his great promise, which he had already seen in Florence, assuring him that if he follows his 'star' (his intellectual and literary destiny) he will come to a 'glorious haven' (ll. 55–57). But Brunetto is thinking only in terms of earthly fame, whereas Dante is now embarked on a journey towards an everlasting spiritual haven. Had he lived longer, says Brunetto, he would have been able to give Dante further help in his work. This probably does not refer so much to Dante's literary output (when Brunetto died he had already written great poetry) as to his career in public life, an area in which Brunetto's wealth of political and administrative experience would have been a source of sure guidance. Brunetto then turns grimly to what lies ahead: the wicked Florentines, mostly descended from the malign race that came down the hill from Fiesole in ancient times, will persecute Dante precisely because he has done good. They are evidently at the opposite end of the moral spectrum: indeed they are avaricious, envious and proud, just as Ciacco has said. Both Black Guelphs and White will be after his blood. Dante's reply to this prophecy is both a bold assertion that he is ready to face adverse fortune, and a tender tribute to Brunetto, whose dear and kind fatherly image is imprinted on his memory ('la cara e buona imagine paterna'—l. 83). He remembers how Brunetto had often taught him how a man may 'immortalize' himself, in the sense that is, of gaining lasting earthly renown ('come l'uom s'etterna'—l. 85).

Now all this has proved too much for some critics, who have found it difficult to believe Dante could show such affection and admiration for one guilty of (to them) so repugnant a vice. Others, whilst not having this problem, have been puzzled by the canto: *is* it plausible that Brunetto was a sodomite? After all, both the *Tresor* and the *Tesoretto* explicitly condemn sodomy; moreover Brunetto's sin is not attested to by any source independent of the *Inferno*. Both these objections are very weak, the first absurdly so. Nonetheless, there have been erudite and sustained attempts to prove that the Canto XV sinners are not sodomites at all.[18] The consensus, however, remains that they are. Before taking leave of Dante, Brunetto recommends to him his *Tresor*, through which, he says, he still lives. And Brunetto does indeed live on, but chiefly through this fifteenth canto of the *Inferno*.

In Canto XVI the poets encounter more sodomites, three of whom run towards them, having recognized Dante by his style of dress as a fellow Florentine. They were all distinguished noble Guelphs, who lived a generation or two before Dante: Guido Guerra, Tegghiaio Aldobrandi and Iacopo Rusticucci. Despite their repulsive blackened appearance, caused by the flakes of fire, Iacopo hopes that in view of their renown Dante may be prepared to speak to them. He is only too glad to, assuring them that their present condition arouses in him not contempt but grief, adding that he has always heard their honourable names and deeds remembered with affection in Florence. Iacopo is anxious to know whether courtesy and valour (the quintessential knightly virtues) are still to be found in the city, as they once were, in his day presumably. Dante's fierce reply does not answer this question directly, but deplores the arrogance and excess now rife in Florence, the result of the ascendancy of the *nouveaux riches* and their rapid financial gains ('La gente nuova e i sùbiti guadagni'—l. 73). This is the first time in the poem that Florence has been attacked by Dante himself, and the socio-economic slant is characteristic. Iacopo and his companions represent a nobler Florence; not indeed the twelfth-century city of simple, austere righteousness that Cacciaguida will extol in the *Paradiso*, but one which still cherished values that by 1300 were in decline. Yet such values are found here on the burning sand: throughout Dante's encounter with the noble trio, the tone has been one of mutual respect and courtesy.

By contrast, the usurers are gross and ill-mannered. But little attention is paid to them: Canto XVII is dominated by Geryon, another hybrid monster. A hairy-pawed reptile with the face of a just man, he is an obvious embodiment of deceit. And it is to the penultimate circle, that of deceit, that he transports the two poets. Perched on his back they glide down into the abyss: the description of the terrifying descent is a truly powerful piece of writing (ll. 100–36). Geryon is perhaps the most frightening thing Dante's imagination has conjured up so far, not least because, unlike all the other monsters, he is completely silent.

The eighth circle, in which Dante and Virgil now find themselves, consists of ten trenches, the *malebolge* (literally, 'evil pouches'). Here every kind of deceit, with a variety of suitable torments, is to be found: there are seducers, flatterers, fortune-tellers, corrupt officials, hypocrites, forgers, even those who have impersonated others for gain. And that does not exhaust the list. Generally speaking, the mood of the poem now changes: frequently the style is harsh, the language coarse, and the scenes envisaged grotesque, obscene, even scatological. It is in the third *bolgia*, or trench (Canto XIX) that Dante's severe censure of the clergy, only sporadically apparent so far, comes powerfully to the fore: this is the abode of the damned popes. Their presence here may startle many readers, but it need not puzzle them: criticism of church corruption has never been incompatible with religious belief, let alone with piety. In Boccaccio's *Decameron* the clergy *en bloc* are considered fair game, their hypocrisy and foibles vigorously satirized. With Dante the matter is altogether more serious: when it comes to evil clergy, the spotlight is on the prelates, the church leaders, whose venality and political ambition are the curse of Europe. The popes in this trench are Simonists or Simoniacs, named after Simon Magus, who tried to purchase the Apostles' spiritual powers (Acts 8.9–24). Although strictly speaking the sin of simony consists in the buying and selling of church offices and preferments, these popes were also notorious nepotists: Dante's intention is to damn all those who make religion pay, whether for their own direct gain, or for that of their families and protégés.

The rocky floor of the trench is perforated by a great number of holes: each one contains a Simonist, thrust in headfirst, with his lower legs projecting and writhing in torment as the soles of his feet are licked by flames. Just as these sinners had inverted the rightful order of things, setting the material above the spiritual, so now they are physically inverted in Hell. Moreover, the flames are surely a grimly ironic parody of the descent of the Holy Spirit on the heads of the Apostles in the form of tongues of fire (Acts 2.1–3). Also, as is suggested by Pope Nicholas III himself, there is a grotesque appropriateness in that just as the Simonists put their ill-gotten gains into money-pouches, so too they are now thrust into 'pouches' (l. 72). Although corrupt ecclesiastics of many ranks are here, the focus is on the popes, who are all buried in a single papal hole; the most recently dead one is uppermost, and he is pushed down further when a new Simoniac pope arrives. Here in 1300 the one currently uppermost is Nicholas III, of the powerful Orsini family, who reigned from 1277 to 1280.

Before he identifies himself, there is a curious misunderstanding involving Boniface VIII. Many readers will think of this trench as, *inter alia*, the one with Boniface in it, or rather not in it. He is not in fact in the trench, but he is in the canto. Dante was determined to get him into Hell somehow, even though he was not to die till 1303, so he damns him in advance, so to speak. With his knowledge of the future, Nicholas knows that Boniface will take his place in the papal hole, and when he hears Dante addressing him from close by, he assumes his successor has already arrived. Dante forcefully disabuses him, and Nicholas, having admitted his nepotism, prophesies that when Boniface does replace him, he in turn will be succeeded (eleven years later, in fact) by Clement V, whose deeds will be even uglier (see below, pp. 184–85).

Dante-character now launches into almost thirty lines of impassioned invective, his most powerful and sustained speech in the *Inferno*, shot through with hard-hitting biblical allusions. Most memorably, he mordantly contrasts the ecclesiastical greed and corruption of his day with the purity of the apostolic church: after all, did St Peter and the others charge Judas Iscariot's replacement an entry fee (Acts 1.21–26)? Having compared the contemporary popes to the whore of the Apocalypse fornicating with the kings of this world (Apoc. 17.1–3), he ends by deploring the Emperor Constantine's disastrous delegation of temporal power to Pope Sylvester, which marked the beginning of the Church's fatal entanglement with secular politics (for Constantine's 'Donation', see below, p. 203). Dante's words are certainly harsh but, as he says to Nicholas, he would have been even more outspoken were it not for his reverence for the 'supreme keys', for the institution of the papacy, that is ('la reverenza de le somme chiavi'—l. 101). We have already seen this distinction between the sacred office and the unworthy office-holder in Dante's reaction to the physical assault on Boniface at Anagni. Yet for all the element of restraint, this is the most vehement speech by Dante-character in the entire *Comedy*.

At the cost of missing much variety, excitement and superb descriptive writing, we must move on to Canto XXVI, and the eighth trench. Apart from IV, this is the only non-medieval canto in the *Inferno*, and together with XXVII it deals with the most overtly deceitful of all the *malebolge* sinners: those who have given fraudulent advice. They are all invisible, each completely enveloped in a flame. There is a wealth of significance in this particular torment: the early commentators noted, *inter alia*, that flames may look attractive from afar but burn those who come into contact with them; that it is appropriate for those who schemed secretively to be hidden now from view; and, most interestingly, that the flames symbolize deceitful advice. For these sinners, all intellectually gifted, have abused their eloquence, and a well-known biblical passage compares the destructive force of words to that of fire (James 3.5–6). The canto is dominated by the figure of Ulysses, who is shrouded in a single flame with Diomedes, his partner in crime. Virgil specifically mentions three of their deceitful exploits, all connected with the Trojan war: their persuading Achilles to fight, whilst concealing the prophecy of his death; the theft of the Palladium, the Trojans' sacred relic; and that most famous of ruses, the wooden horse, by which the Greeks finally entered Troy.

But the high point of the canto, one of the high points of the poem indeed, is Ulysses' epic account of his final voyage, very largely Dante's own invention. Ulysses does not converse with the poets but delivers a magnificent monologue (ll. 90–142), and only when Virgil has solemnly exhorted him to speak. After escaping from the sorceress Circe, he says, he continued his wanderings, ignoring family duties, and impelled by a burning curiosity to know everything, good and bad. When he and his companions have sailed as far as the Straits of Gibraltar, he urges them, though old and tired, to go on and explore a world unknown. Such is the eloquence of his little speech ('orazion picciola'—l. 122) that they are won over and sail out into the Atlantic. What Ulysses now calls the 'folle volo' (l. 125), 'the rash voyage', takes them into the southern hemisphere, and after five months in the open sea they catch sight of an island, upon which towers the mountain of Purgatory. But a storm wells up and, as was pleasing to God, the ship is wrecked, sinking without trace.

Ulysses is certainly an attractive character: he exudes a heroic dignity, even grandeur, as he calmly recounts his daring but fatal adventure, without a trace of resentment. Yet he also embodies a certain kind of intellectual arrogance, in his all-consuming, morally indiscriminate lust for knowledge and experience. There is a strong element of hubris in the irresponsible voyage, of rebellion against divinely-imposed limits. And the 'orazion picciola' is his final piece of deceitful advice—though not all critics agree.[19] Ulysses may have held a dangerous fascination for Dante, not least because, especially in his dealings with powerful men, he too may have been tempted to misuse his intellectual gifts. Dante-character nearly falls into the trench, and only saves himself by clutching hold of a rock (ll. 43–45); this very probably has a symbolic significance. More importantly, when Dante the poet relives the grief that he experienced there, he has to keep a more than usually tight rein on his intellect, lest it be diverted from the path of virtue (ll. 19–22).

In Canto XXVII we meet a very different deceitful counsellor: the Ghibelline Guido da Montefeltro. Born about 1220, he was a highly successful military leader who inflicted crushing defeats on the Guelphs of the Romagna, his birthplace. He was also briefly prominent in staunchly-Ghibelline Pisa, and in the 1290s, aged over seventy, he made himself lord of Urbino. But in 1296 he repudiated his past sinful life and became a Franciscan. Just when he was set on the path to salvation, he was enticed back into his wicked ways by none other than Boniface VIII, who is at least as important in this canto as Guido himself: Dante found it very difficult to keep Boniface out of Hell. As Guido says to Dante, though a soldier, his methods were those of the cunning fox, not the lion, and for this he was famous (ll. 73–78). That is why Boniface in 1298, at the very end of Guido's life, sought his advice in his struggle with the Colonna family. How best could he destroy Palestrina, their strong-hold? Knowing that Guido's counsel will be sinful, he offers to absolve him in advance, since as Pope, he has power to 'lock and unlock Heaven' (l. 103). Guido's laconic reply advises offering the Colonna an amnesty and then simply renegueing on it: 'lunga promessa con l'attender corto' ('be long on promise, and short on delivery'—l. 110). Guido's presence here in Hell makes it quite plain that he did not repent, and that Boniface's promise of *carte blanche* absolution was worthless, and indeed fraudulent: for without repentance the formulae of absolution are invalid. Guido's tragedy is that he is a deceiver who has himself been deceived, and at the last hurdle, so to speak. His bitterness towards the Pope is pronounced: he curses him (l. 70) and denounces him as the Prince of the new Pharisees, who instead of promoting a crusade against the Saracens, made war on Italian Christians, and who moreover cared nothing for the sanctity of Holy Orders (ll. 85–93). Interestingly, in the *Convivio* Dante had held Guido up as a model of how to end one's days virtuously after a long life (IV, xxviii, 8). But this is no great enigma: there is nothing to prevent our inferring that by the time he wrote this canto Dante had found out more.

The penultimate trench (Canto XXVIII) may not be the most horrifying zone of the *Inferno*, but it is the most gruesome. Here are those responsible for strife or schism, and the social disorder that results from it. They are all horribly mutilated by a sword-wielding demon, the details of their torment being meticulously matched to their particular brand of discord: a typically Dantean touch. The strife is of three kinds: religious, political and family. First Dante sees the Prophet Mohammed, grotesquely cleft from chin to crotch. This may seem very strange to modern readers, but Dante is here following a common medieval interpretation of Islam, which saw it not as a religion in its own right, but as a schismatic deviation from Christianity, an obstacle thwarting the religious unity of mankind. Curiously, Mohammed's son-in-law Ali is also here. Whereas Mohammed's face remains intact, his is split: for Ali was and is regarded by Shi'ite muslims as the source of their legit-imacy—a schism within a schism, in Dante's view. These examples are complemented by a medieval Italian, Fra Dolcino, leader of the so-called Apostolic Brethren. Like Boniface, he is damned in advance: it was not until 1307 that he was captured and burnt alive as a heretic. But he is not with Farinata and the others in the sixth circle, for he and his followers, several thousand strong, caused serious social upheaval, and it is this that Dante is emphasizing. Political strife on a vast scale is recalled by the presence of Curio here; a key figure in the struggle between Julius Caesar and Pompey, it was he who persuaded Caesar to cross the river Rubicon, thus plunging the Roman world into civil war. And of course thirteenth-century Italy is represented here too: there is the relatively obscure Pier da Medicina, and the Ghibelline Mosca de' Lamberti, one of the worthy Florentines about whom Dante had asked Ciacco. Mosca's family were allied to the Amidei, embroiled in a feud with the Buondelmonti over a broken marriage contract. It was Mosca who persuaded his prevaricating faction to kill Buondelmonte de' Buondelmonti. The resulting family strife was to erupt into Guelph-Ghibelline conflict both in Florence and elsewhere in Tuscany, as Mosca here admits. But the Lamberti themselves were in due course all killed or exiled, as Dante pointedly reminds him (l. 109—shades of the exchange with Farinata). Finally, there is the hauntingly macabre figure of Bertran de Born, swinging his decapitated head like a lantern. This famous Provençal troubadour, a literary man of action, is praised in the *De Vulgari* (II, ii, 9) as the greatest vernacular poet of war (of which he had plenty of firsthand experience, all of it quite deliberate). His bizarre torment here reflects his sundering of the bond between a father, the head of the family, and his own son: he incited Henry 'The Young King' to rebel against his father, Henry II of England.

After the *malebolge*, there is another deep drop, and this time the means of transport is a giant, one of several seen or mentioned in the transitional thirty-first canto. All except the biblical Nimrod (*Nembrotto*) are from classical myth, and it is Antaeus who at Virgil's command simply picks up the two poets and sets them down at the edge of the frozen lake of Cocytus. This is the final circle, and the culmination of all Hell's wickedness: for here is punished treachery, laid bare in all its icy-hearted starkness. Worse than mere deceit, this is deceit of one with whom the sinner had a bond of trust. Stuck fast in the ice, in varying postures according to the gravity of their sin, are four types of traitor: those who betrayed their kinsfolk; their country; their guests; and worst of all, their lords. With three vivid exceptions in the final canto, this last group is completely submerged in terrible silence beneath the surface of the ice: the infernal equivalent of absolute zero. Dante's ranking of these sins is characteristic of the Middle Ages, which placed a high value on the duty of hospitality and regarded allegiance as quasi-sacrosanct.

Two striking episodes in Cocytus show Dante-character treating the sinners with cruelty. In the first (Canto XXXII, 73–123) he encounters the soul of Bocca degli Abati, a Florentine who turned traitor during the battle of Montaperti, and cut off the Guelph standard-bearer's hand. Dante savagely threatens to tear out every hair from his head if he does not reveal his identity. He begins to carry out this threat, and only desists when another traitor calls out Bocca's name. In the following canto (ll. 109–50) we meet Frate Alberigo, who poisoned his own guests. He lies in the ice with head tilted back, so that he cannot even weep, for his eyes are blocked with frozen tears. Dante makes an equivocal promise to unplug them if Alberigo will tell his tale. He is taken in by this and talks, but Dante passes on without affording him the meagre relief he craves for: 'e cortesia fu lui esser villano' ('and it was courtesy to be churlish to him'—l. 150). No doubt this duplicity, like the savagery towards Bocca, can be accommodated within the moral framework of righteous anger, but it goes far beyond Dante's conduct in the episode with Filippo Argenti in the Styx.

Between these two passages comes the harrowing tale of Ugolino, with its almost unbearably intense horror and pity (Cantos XXXII, 124–XXXIII, 90). Dante and Virgil come upon two political traitors, one of whom is crouched above the other's open skull, gnawing at his brains. The cannibal is Count Ugolino della Gherardesca, and his victim Archbishop Ruggieri degli Ubaldini. Although none of the traitors wants to be remembered on earth, Ugolino agrees to tell Dante his story in order to defame Ruggieri. The setting is Pisa in the 1280s, with its complex politics. The Ghibelline ascendancy in the city had been weakened following a naval defeat by the Genoese in 1284, and Pisa now faced a powerful Guelph alliance of Genoa, Lucca and Florence. In these circumstances Ugolino, a Guelph though from a Ghibelline family, became *podestà*, and sought to contain the situation by ceding certain castles to Lucca and Florence. But matters were complicated by rivalry between Ugolino and his Guelph grandson Nino. Eventually

Ugolino conspired with the staunchly Ghibelline Archbishop to expel Nino, but by this time (1288) the Ghibellines' fortunes were improving rapidly. This was the moment to re-assert control and eliminate Ugolino. Ruggieri tricked him, and together with two of his sons and two grandsons he was imprisoned in a tower. After some nine months, Ruggieri decided to cut off the food supply and all five starved to death in the spring of 1289.

Those in brief outline are the external facts; but what makes Ugolino's account so moving and powerful is the personal evocation of what went on inside the tiny cell, where the only indication of the passing of time was the alternation of darkness and the feeble light allowed by a narrow vent. When the end approaches and Ugolino hears the doom-laden sound of the outer door being nailed up, his response is stone-like silence. A man of action and violence, he bottles up his emotions to spare the feelings of his little children (in Dante's version there are four small sons). After the first four days without food, one child drops dead, and the three others follow him over the next two days. Only now does Ugolino give vent to his feelings, as, blind from starvation, he gropes over their corpses, calling them by name. The final line (75) of his appalling speech recalls his own death from hunger, and may contain a hint (though this is not certain) that he was reduced to eating his own offspring. Dante-character shows no reaction to Ugolino's account, but Dante the poet does, in an outraged attack on the city of Pisa as a whole, for its shameful cruelty in putting innocent children to such martyrdom, whatever their father's crimes (ll. 79–90).

Two especial points of interest in this tragedy may be noted. First, just as Guido da Montefeltro deceived and was deceived, so Ugolino was a traitor himself betrayed, now forever feeding on the man who once denied him food. Second, he tells Dante what no one else knows, the secret 'underside' of his cruel death: 'quel che non puoi avere inteso' ('what you cannot have heard'—l. 19). There is an obvious parallel here with Ulysses, whose final voyage has remained a secret, locked deep in Hell until Dante's arrival, but also with Pier della Vigna's account of his last moments and indeed with Francesca's revelation of precisely how she came to commit adultery.

The final canto brings us to Giudecca, appropriately named after Judas Iscariot, for here lie the worst traitors of all, those who have betrayed their lords. With the exception of the three arch-traitors, they are all completely immersed beneath the ice, denied all contact, communication or expression of their grief. At the very centre of the frozen lake is the massive figure of Satan, with his six wings and three heads, munching in his three mouths the writhing figures of Brutus, Cassius and Judas. The Roman traitors' torsos protrude from Satan's jaws, but Judas is thrust headfirst into the central mouth—a nice touch. Meanwhile the wings flap unceasingly, keeping the whole of Cocytus frozen. Now in one sense this final episode is an anticlimax. Certainly there is no momentous dramatic challenge to the poets' progress, no evil obstacle to be overcome, no 'George and the Dragon' motif. All is ghastly immobile silence, except for the mechanical chomping and flailing. But in another sense, here is the climax of evil: the ultimate selfish isolation, the soul almost de-personalized, utterly deprived of the creative dynamism of love. And this is pre-eminently true of Satan himself. He is not merely a fallen angel, like the rest of the devils; he was originally the most elevated in rank amongst the Seraphim, the highest of the nine orders of angels. The summit of God's creation, then: 'la creatura ch'ebbe il bel sembiante' ('the creature who was once so fair'—XXXIV, 18). Indeed if he were once as beautiful as he is now hideous, well may all sorrow stem from him (ll. 34–36). A fallen angel then, but also in some sense a failed God: it is widely held that Dante means this three-headed monster to be an absurd blasphemous parody of the Trinity. Each head is of a different colour, though there is no critical consensus as to precisely how this might refer symbolically to the persons of the triune God.[20]

But what of Brutus and Cassius? Some English readers may be surprised to find them so hideously tormented; but Shakespeare's courageous republican statesmen are a far cry from Dante's two traitors, as indeed is Milton's Satan from the monster depicted here. In Dante's view, Brutus and Cassius in murdering Julius Caesar betrayed their rightful lord, and that is why they are in the utmost depths of Hell. But more than that, their assassination of the dictator was a wicked attempt to thwart the establishment of the Roman Empire, and thus frustrate the whole course of human history. Here, in the location of these Roman traitors on either side of Judas, we have another instance of Dante's very distinctive view of the relation between the Graeco-Roman and the Judaeo-Christian worlds—a most striking one too, given the implied parallel between Caesar and Christ. But for Dante all this is not merely a matter of parallels: both worlds are part of the same unified creation, and together they manifest the dual thrust of God's purpose in history.

The action of the *Inferno* concludes with a descent and a climb: Dante and Virgil come right up to Satan and, using his body as a bizarre passive means of transport, clamber down it, clinging to the shaggy tufts that cover his trunk. The midpoint of his body is at the very centre of the earth: on reaching that point the poets twist themselves round and climb up his legs, for they are now (just) in the southern hemisphere. They ascend through a featureless tunnel to emerge on the earth's surface, where they see what Dante so loved, what he had so extensive a knowledge of, and what since his arrival in the dark wood he has not seen: the stars.

## (iii) The Saved Spirits

It is just before dawn when Dante and Virgil finally leave Hell and arrive on the shores of an island, the island-mountain of Purgatory.[21] Here is a new world of light, the light of the stars and the sun; of air, serene and never more than a breeze; of music, sacred and profane, after Hell's cacophony of curses, shrieks and moans. But the most important contrast of all is the dynamic of time: whereas both Hell and Heaven are everlasting and unchanging, Purgatory is a temporary state, a region of constructive change, of purposeful spiritual improvement. All the souls here are *en route* to Heaven: they are already saved. Indeed Virgil addresses some of them as 'già spiriti eletti' ('already-chosen spirits'—III, 73). They are not predestined in any Calvinistic sense: they are here, rather than in Hell, because of a crucial act, or acts, of freely-willed repentance. Sincere repentance, even at the moment of death, is valid and acceptable to God. Purgatory, then, is in no sense a period of probation, a second chance: the only way is up. The processes of purgation involved, though arduous, are quite different from the torments of Hell: the souls here accept them willingly, even joyfully, for they know that their guaranteed goal is salvation. The whole notion of Purgatory, which has no specific sanction in the Bible,[22] is well established in Roman Catholic theology, though it is not accepted by either the Reformed or the Orthodox Churches. Its appeal for many is doubtless cathartic: it gives expression to a deep-seated desire to be cleansed. It also appeals to a sense of justice: is it right that the near saint and the heinous, albeit repentant, sinner should both be straightaway on the same, heavenly, footing? Purgatory ensures that the latter will suffer— but only for a time.

In the opening canto of *Purgatorio* a delighted Dante looks upwards to the sky and sees not only Venus but the four stars of the Southern Cross, visible in the southern hemisphere. These almost certainly have a further symbolic reference to the four 'cardinal' virtues of Prudence, Justice, Temperance and Fortitude. They illuminate the venerable face of Cato, the dominant figure in this first canto. Cato of Utica, renowned in antiquity and the Middle Ages for his moral integrity, was a staunch upholder of the liberties of the Roman Republic, and in 46 BC, after Caesar's defeat of Pompey, took his own life rather than submit to the dictator. Dante portrays him here as an austere, somewhat gruff, character and assigns him the role of guardian of the mountain's first section, generally known as Ante-Purgatory. His presence is certainly problematical, and for two obvious reasons: he is a suicide, and a pagan. As to the first point, it may be that Dante in this matter is judging the pagans according to their own ethical code which, far from damning suicide, exalted it as in some circumstances a noble act. Cato's suicide could be seen as an attempt to affirm his moral liberty, by contrast with Pier della Vigna's wretched abnegation of self. As to the second point, there are in fact pagans in the *Paradiso*; two are explicitly named, and by implication there are more.

Canto II is especially memorable for its sights and sounds. First there is the beautiful description of sunrise, and then the supernaturally rapid approach of a boat, piloted by a creature whose dazzling brilliance is too much for Dante's eyes to bear (a foretaste of the *Paradiso*). This is the first of Purgatory's numerous angels— an obvious contrast with Charon. His cargo of saved souls disembarks, singing. What they sing is significant: it is none other than Psalm 113, 'In exitu Isräel de Aegypto' ('When Israel came out of Egypt'). This is glossed, both in the *Convivio* and the Can Grande Letter, as referring allegorically to the emergence of the soul from the bondage of sin.[23] The new arrivals, having unsuccessfully asked the poets for directions (Virgil has to explain that they too are visitors), cluster round in astonishment when they realize that Dante is not a spirit, but still has his mortal body. The sun is not yet sufficiently risen for Dante's body to cast a shadow, but they *can* see his breath—another deft touch. One of them is Casella, a Florentine musician and close friend of Dante, who now urges him to sing. Casella's song is so beautiful that all present are entranced. All that is, except Cato who brusquely breaks up the party and bids them make haste to the Mountain of Purgation. There is evidently a conflict between the beauty of the song and the duty of not lingering over it. Yet what Casella sings is not some lightweight piece of amorous verse, but one of Dante's own *canzoni*, 'Amor che ne la mente mi ragiona', which is explained allegorically in *Convivio* III as a hymn to Philosophy. It is true that in 1300 Dante had not yet formally allegorized this *canzone*, so it may be that at that stage he still considered it simply as a conventional love poem (though this is far from certain).[24] But to rule out any reference in this episode to the limitations, distractions even, of that philosophy which the *Convivio* promotes and the *Comedy* transcends would be to take Dante's verisimilitude too narrowly. After all, he could have made his character Casella sing one of his other lyrics, one that he did not later allegorize. Either would have sufficed to incense Cato.

King Manfred, son of the Emperor Frederick II, dominates the third canto. His spirit is one of the excommunicated souls, whom Dante and Virgil encounter on the first of Ante-Purgatory's two slopes. They have all died at odds with the Church, denied access to the sacraments, unreconciled with the sacred institution, yet, evidently, reconciled with God. Although they must wait here for a period thirty times the length of their ecclesiastical exile,[25] they are of course all saved. Manfred is vividly portrayed here: he is blond, handsome and of noble appearance, though one eyebrow is gashed, recalling his violent death on the battlefield of Benevento in 1266. Yet this great and powerful man, and his fellow souls, are compared to a flock of timid, demure—and fortunate—sheep (ll. 79–88). Smilingly he tells Dante of his death, of how at the end he surrendered to the embrace of 'Him who willingly forgives' ('a quei che volontier perdona'—l. 120). His earthly enemies had other ideas, though. The victor of Benevento, Charles d'Anjou, refused to allow the King's body to be buried in consecrated ground: instead his troops dropped stones on it as they filed past, thus forming a huge cairn. But this was not enough for the Church: on the orders of Pope Clement IV (another Frenchman) Manfred's remains were exhumed and reburied beyond the borders of what had been his kingdom.

The dramatic, if not the theological, force of Manfred's tale of last-minute repentance is enhanced by the fact that his sins were, in his own words, 'appalling' ('Orribil'—l. 121). Indeed in his lifetime he was accused, not least by the Guelph propaganda-machine, of murdering several close relatives, Frederick himself included.[26] Whether Dante believed any of this is doubtful, but the crucial point is that he presents us with a repentant Manfred—and in the salvific scheme of the *Comedy* repentance is all. For although the Church never went so far as to decree, formally, a causal link between excommunication and damnation, the widespread view and fear in Dante's time was that there was just such a link. The chief purpose of *Purgatorio* III is to refute this. In Manfred's words:

> Per lor maledizion sì non si perde,
> che non possa tornar, l'etterno amore,
> mentre che la speranza ha fior del verde.

> Through their curse [i.e. excommunication] no one is lost/to the extent that eternal love cannot return,/hope still has a little green.
>
> (ll. 133–35)

Dante had high praise for Manfred in the *De Vulgari* (I, xii, 4). There he was described as 'benegenitus' ('well born'); now he is among the 'ben finiti' (l. 73), one of those who have made a good end. In short, the Church could bar him from the altar, but not from Heaven.

Canto IV offers a charming vignette of the indolent Belacqua, a Florentine maker of musical instruments whom Dante had known personally. Languid in posture but sharp in wit, he gently mocks Dante-character's deadly serious astronomical learning; many readers will sympathize. We are now in fact on the second slope of Ante-Purgatory. The souls here have not been excommunicated, but have delayed their repentance until the very end of their lives. With some, such as Belacqua, this was the result of sheer lethargy, but there are other categories. Canto V has three examples of those cut off by violent death, and thus unable to receive absolution from a priest. First there is Iacopo del Cassero, victim of a political murder in the Veneto; and at the end of the canto we meet La Pia, who alludes laconically to her death, apparently on her husband's orders, but not before she has shown a tender concern over how tired Dante will be once returned to earth after his long journey. These two encounters frame the central, and most important episode, that of Bonconte da Montefeltro. Son of Guido, Lord of Montefeltro (already encountered in *Inf.* XXVII), he was killed at Campaldino whilst commanding the Ghibelline forces of Arezzo. (Dante himself was fighting with the Florentines at that battle.) Here in Ante-Purgatory he introduces himself in a significant way: 'Io fui di Montefeltro, io son Bonconte' ('I was of Montefeltro, I am Bonconte'—l. 88). That is, he has put behind him family and title, and is now plain Bonconte. There are various instances of such transcending of earthly rank and status in the *Purgatorio* and *Paradiso*, the most striking of them in *Paradiso* VI (l. 10) where the Emperor Justinian declares that he was 'Cesare' and is now 'Iustinïano'. Bonconte, a classic example of repentance at the very last moment, describes how he fled the battle, unhorsed and fatally wounded in the throat. By now blind, he turned at the end to God, via the Blessed Virgin, and died with 'Maria' on his lips. Hell, however, had evidently been hoping for him: a struggle ensues between a victorious angel and a disappointed demon who ruefully complains that he is being denied his prize because of a 'little tear' ('lacrimetta'—l. 107). There is a close parallel here with the contest between the forces of good and evil for possession of Guido da Montefeltro's soul (*Inf.* XXVII, 112–24). In that case it was St Francis versus one of the 'Black Cherubim'—and the devil won. The difference hinges on repentance: Bonconte did sincerely repent, and is saved, without the aid of a priest, but Boniface's bogus absolution could not save his father.[27]

But though Bonconte's soul was saved, the devil, thwarted, attempted a kind of revenge on his body: it raised a storm, whose torrential rain washed the by now frozen corpse away from Campaldino and eventually down into the river Arno (*Purg.* V, 108–29). He has something in common with Manfred then: in the King's case it was the Church that wrought vengeance on the body; in Bonconte's it was the powers of Hell. But both their souls are saved.

The sixth canto, just like *Inf.* VI, is largely political, but the perspective is no longer narrowly Florentine: the Italian cities as a whole are the target for Dante's violent invective. It is appropriate that in this canto we meet Sordello, himself the author of an important political poem castigating contemporary European rulers: the Lament on the death of Blacatz, a Provençal baron (written around 1237). Sordello was born about 1200, very near Mantua: indeed, here in Ante-Purgatory he affectionately greets Virgil as a fellow-Mantuan (ll. 71–75). He was a courtier and soldier, as well as being the most important of the Northern Italian troubadours, who wrote in Provençal—some forty of his poems survive. His colourful life took him to the courts of Verona, Treviso and Provence, as well as three courts in Spain. As an old man he returned to Italy in the service of Charles d'Anjou, and may have been present at Benevento. His role in the action of the *Purgatorio* will be to guide Dante and Virgil through the Valley of the Princes, where the souls of the spiritually negligent rulers wait. But first comes Dante's vehement attack on the politically negligent. This sustained outburst by the poet, not the character, begins with the arresting line 'Ahi serva Italia, di dolore ostello' ('Alas, enslaved Italy, house of sorrow'—l. 76), and continues till the end of the canto. Italy is compared to a brothel, a ship without a pilot, a riderless horse. The emphasis in this picture of greed and chaos is on negative faults: the pusillanimous shirking of those moral responsibilities that go with political power. Albert of Hapsburg, the absentee emperor, is especially censured for his transalpine negligence: Rome, seat of the Empire, is widowed without him. And the Italian clergy are equally condemned for their interference in temporal affairs. Italy's cities are infested by tyrants and populist upstarts. 'Fiorenza mia' ('My Florence'—l. 127) is singled out for abuse in bitterly sarcastic tones not heard since the opening of *Inf.* XXVI: distinguished as it is for justice, peace, wisdom and a lively sense of civic duty, its legislation would be the envy of Athens and Sparta. The jibe here is directed at the rapid turnover of public officials in Florence, which militated against continuity of policy, as well as the Guelph-Ghibelline cycle of exile and recall (ll. 142–47).

After this pungent anti-Florentine passage, the picture broadens once more in Canto VII as the three poets pass through the exquisitely beautiful Valley (ll. 73–81) where a variety of European rulers, too busy to have repented before the last, are pointed out by Sordello. Some sit in pairs, and here the emphasis, so typical of the *Purgatorio*, is on brotherly reconciliation and transcendence of

144

earthly strife. Thus Emperor Rudolf of Hapsburg sits next to his former foe Ottokar II of Bohemia, and Charles d'Anjou is similarly adjacent to Peter III of Aragon. The Valley is typical of Ante-Purgatory as a whole, a region so different in pace and atmosphere not only from Hell, but from Purgatory proper too. It has a lyrical and peculiarly nostalgic quality, with its patient souls quietly waiting, their often violent and agitated lives behind them. It is more like a departure lounge than an internment camp, but without the uncertainty of either. The journey ahead, however, is arduous, to say the least. Indeed Dante, having described the purgation endured by the proud, will be anxious to reassure us: the last thing he would want is for any of his readers to falter in the task of doing good because of what they will suffer for sins already committed. What matters is not 'la forma del martire' ('the manner of the suffering') but the heavenly reward to come; in any case the pains of Purgatory will not last beyond Judgement Day (X, 109–11).

It is in Canto X that the purgations begin. After further encounters in the Valley and the first of three nights on the mountain, Dante and Virgil have been admitted through the door of Purgatory by its angel-custodian. They emerge on the first of seven terraces, or ledges (*cornici*, in Italian), on each of which is purged one of the Capital Vices, the *vitia capitalia* first enumerated by Pope Gregory the Great in the sixth century. Dante ranks them thus: Pride, Envy, Anger, Sloth, Avarice, Gluttony and at the top, and therefore least blameworthy, Lust. 'Capital Vices' is far less familiar than 'Deadly Sins', but the latter expression is misleading, for the simple reason that no sin is *per se* deadly: if it is repented, the sinner will not be damned. The first things Dante and Virgil see on this first terrace are marble carvings of supernatural quality, utterly surpassing the best efforts of human art, or indeed Nature. They represent outstanding examples of Humility, the virtue opposed to Pride, the vice that is being purged here. The penitent proud must look at them, and then ponder their significance as they stagger round the mountain bowed down to the ground under the slabs of rock they carry—a most appropriate penalty for those whose heads were once held high in scorn of others. They must also trample underfoot depictions of the ruinous punishment consequent upon Pride. This sets a pattern for all seven terraces: all the sinners meditate upon contrasting illustrations of their vice and its opposite (whether visual images, verbal recitations or visions in the mind). The first virtuous example is always from the life of the Blessed Virgin, and the other examples (virtues as well as vices) are drawn in strict alternation from the Bible and from Graeco-Roman sources. This is the clearest instance in the *Comedy* of the parallelism that Dante saw between the two traditions: both furnish us with examples of good and bad conduct, both can teach us moral truths. Thus Canto X's carvings vividly recall the Virgin's humility in the presence of the angel Gabriel; King David's humble barefoot dance before the Ark of the Covenant, the sacred Jewish reliquary; and the kindness of the Emperor Trajan, who at the height of a triumphal ceremony was prepared to listen to a humble widow's plea. In all three cases the power of divine art is stressed, most strikingly in the central episode of David: his dance is accompanied by the singing of seven choirs and the burning of incense. So skilful is the sculpture that Dante's senses are deceived: he seems to be hearing the music and smelling the aroma, though his ears and nose tell him otherwise (ll. 58–63).

All this is intimately linked with the events of Canto XI, where alongside aristocratic pride and political pride we have the pride of the artist, exemplified by the soul of Oderisi da Gubbio. His dialogue with Dante (who knew him personally, it would seem) gives us a glimpse into the highly competitive world of manuscript illumination. A distinguished exponent of that art, he is now, in Purgatory, able to admit that his work is surpassed by that of his rival Franco Bolognese. On earth he would not have been so courteous, because of his powerful wish to excel ('lo gran disio/de l'eccellenza'—ll. 86–87). Of course Dante-character and Dante the poet knew all about that, and the poet at least was conscious of its dangers. It is significant that Oderisi, after a general remark on the vanity and transience of earthly fame, and having observed that Giotto has now supplanted Cimabue as the foremost painter, should turn to poetry. One Guido (Cavalcanti, that is) has taken the palm from another (Guinizelli), but, says Oderisi, there is perhaps already born someone who will 'chase them both from the nest' (ll. 97–99). The most obvious interpretation of this is that Dante, via Oderisi, is indeed referring to himself, here on the terrace of Pride: what could be more exquisite?

The envious (Cantos XIII–XIV) sit in sackcloth, their eyelids sewn up with wire: not prepared to behold the happiness of others while on earth, they are now denied sights which they might enjoy, such as the sunlight or their fellow spirits. One day Dante will be joining them, but not for long, according to his moral self-assessment here. Envy, declares Dante-character, has only been a slight fault in his case, in sharp contrast to Pride: indeed, he can already feel the weight of the heavy slabs (XIII, 133–38)! This self-exoneration (or almost) in respect of Envy could of course be seen as a further act of Pride. The sombre Canto XIV is concerned far more with politics than with Envy. The speaker here is Guido del Duca, an early thirteenth-century Ghibelline from the Romagna. He not only laments the decadence of his native region, but attacks the Tuscans in memorably violent language: tracing the course of the Arno from its source to the sea, he compares those who dwell on its banks to pigs, dogs, wolves and foxes (the rapacious Florentines are the wolves, the cunning Pisans the foxes).

Cantos XV–XVIII, whilst dealing with the terraces of Anger and Sloth, are in fact dominated by five closely-linked didactic speeches on Love and Free Will. Located at the very centre of *Purgatorio*, and thus of the whole *Comedy*, they are central to Dante's view of the nature of human beings: their place in the universe, their relation to God, and their ultimate destiny. Dante's message here may be briefly synthesized and glossed as follows. Love is present in all things, in the Creator and in all His creatures (XVII, 91–93). However, a distinction must be made between 'natural' love (that is, instinctual love, possessed alike by animals and intelligent beings), and love 'of the mind' (something peculiar to humans and angels only). Whereas the former is always morally neutral (XVII, 94; XVIII, 59–60), the latter may be corrupted by misuse of the will (XVII, 95–96; 100–2). More precisely, this conscious love, the 'love of the mind', may err through being directed towards a wrong object, or it may be lukewarm, or it may be excessive love of something which though good in itself should be loved only in moderation. Here, in a nutshell, is the moral basis of Purgatory's seven terraces: Pride, Envy and Anger may be seen as love of something wrong (our neighbour's disadvantage, for instance); Sloth is a defective, lukewarm love; Avarice, Gluttony and Lust involve love of an object not intrinsically bad (food and drink, for example), which however errs by its excess. Indeed, conscious love (to be understood broadly as including all kinds of desire) is the cause of every action, good and bad (XVII, 103–5). And a crucial point is that all such love is freely willed: our actions are not determined by the influence of the stars (XVI, 67–81), nor are we the slaves of our inclinations (XVIII, 61–75).

It is precisely because we do have free will (XVI, 71 and 76; XVIII, 62, 68 and 73–74—the terminology varies) that our choices are *justly* rewarded or punished in the afterlife (XVI, 71–72). The influence of the heavenly bodies merely initiates some of our *inclinations*, but that is all (XVI, 73–76). It is entirely characteristic of Dante's age that a tension should be perceived between the freedom of the human will and astral influence, whereas today the challenge to a belief in free will appears chiefly in terms of social and, increasingly, genetic determinism. The speaker in four of these crucial didactic passages is Virgil, but in Canto XVI it is Marco Lombardo, a somewhat obscure thirteenth-century courtier, probably from the Treviso area. His speech does not stop at a refutation of astral determinism: it goes on to take a sharply political turn. Marco, still rather blunt in manner though now purging his anger, attacks the failure to enforce necessary restraining laws, the fault of the medieval emperors (ll. 94–97), and the usurpation of political power by the popes (ll. 98–114). The links here with Canto VI are close indeed.

The first encounter on the fifth terrace, that of Avarice, is with Pope Adrian V, who reigned in 1276 for little more than a month, as he says (XIX, 103–5). Not all the popes are in Hell then; though it has to be said that of those roughly contemporary with Dante only two are explicitly placed in Purgatory and only one in Heaven (Adrian; Martin IV, one of the penitent gluttons—*Purg.* XXIV, 20–24; and Adrian's immediate successor John XXI, who appears in the Heaven of the Sun—*Par.* XII, 134–35). Dante kneels out of reverence for the Pope; but Adrian at once exhorts him to stand up, for they are now both equal servants of God. Once again, differences of earthly status are transcended. Canto XX is largely devoted to another avaricious spirit, that of Hugh Capet (died 996), founder of the Capetian dynasty of French kings. He delivers a highly charged pseudo-prophecy denouncing the crimes of his descendants, many of them committed in Italy. It is a sustained invective, rounded off with a prayer for divine vengeance, against the ruling house of France, by Dante's time the leading secular power in Europe. In particular Hugh condemns Charles d'Anjou's execution of the young Conradin (1268) and his subsequent murder of St Thomas Aquinas (1274) 'by way of making amends', as he sarcastically puts it (l. 69). Dante seems here to be subscribing to the contemporary rumours (not substantiated by historians) that Aquinas, *en route* to the Council of Lyon, had been poisoned on Charles' orders.[28] The dynasty will be further disgraced by Charles de Valois' treacherous meddling in Florentine affairs, and, worst outrage of all, the assault on Pope Boniface by agents of Philip IV. Finally Hugh looks ahead to Philip's cruel and illegal suppression of the Order of Knights Templar.

Far more important than Pope Adrian or Hugh Capet is Statius, who appears in Canto XXI, having just been released after more than five hundred years' purgation on the fifth terrace. Not that he was guilty of avarice: in fact his vice was its opposite—prodigality. Both however are sins of excess, in that they are a failure to observe due measure in respect of material possessions (cf. *Inf.* VII). Statius (*c*.AD 45–*c*.96) is the fifth in the quintet of great Roman poets who especially influenced Dante, and whom he especially revered. His pagan companions are in Limbo, but Statius is in Purgatory because he converted to Christianity (and of course was repentant). This conversion may well have been an invention on the part of Dante. In any case, it is presented as the climax of what is one of the *Comedy*'s high points: the meeting between Statius and Virgil. Statius acknowledges a triple debt to Virgil: moral, artistic and theological, all of it literary, that is via the older poet's writings. For of course Statius' lifetime did not overlap with Virgil's: indeed, as he says here with technically reprehensible enthusiasm, he would gladly have done an extra year's time in Purgatory to have lived when his hero did (XXI, 100–2). Statius is morally indebted to Virgil in that a phrase in the *Aeneid* convinced him that his prodigality was wrong: had he not repented of it, he would have been condemned to an eternity of rock-rolling in Hell's fourth circle (XXII, 37–42).[29] But Virgil's epic was also the inspiration for his own great achievements in this genre, the *Thebaid* and the *Achilleid* (XXI, 92–99; XXII, 64–65). Most momentous of all though was the theological debt, enshrined together with the artistic one in the magnificent lapidary line 'Per te poeta fui, per te cristiano' ('Through you I was a poet, through you a Christian'—XXII, 73).

The catalyst for Statius' conversion was the fourth Virgilian *Eclogue*. This poem, speaking as it does of a new age of justice, of a virgin and an infant, was widely regarded throughout the Middle Ages and beyond as a remarkable prophecy of the coming of

Christ.[30] Dante's Statius explains that it tallied with the message of the nascent Christianity he saw burgeoning around him to such an extent that he began to frequent the early Christian apostles in Rome and was secretly baptized. But he was no martyr, and during the persecution under Emperor Domitian he kept his new faith hidden, though he did give assistance to his co-religionists. He has purged this timidity during a spell of more than 400 years on the Terrace of Sloth (XXII, 76–93). But the main point is that he repented of this sin, as he did of his prodigality, and as a penitent Christian is now one of the saved. Of course the supreme and excruciatingly poignant irony in all this is that Virgil himself is unable to benefit from the truths miraculously proclaimed in his own poem. Statius expresses this point with a striking simile: Virgil is like someone carrying a lantern at night, but over his shoulder, so that it illuminates the path of those who follow, but not his own (XXII, 67–69). Statius' immense affection for Virgil is fully reciprocated: indeed Virgil has nurtured a love for him for close on 1,200 years, ever since their fellow poet Juvenal (died *c*.140) arrived in Limbo and told him of his admirer and follower. This whole episode is a further outlet for Dante's own great esteem of Virgil, who is now more prominent as a character than at any time since the *Inferno*.

It would be difficult to exaggerate the importance of poets and poetry in this part of the *Purgatorio*. Not only is ancient poetry very much to the fore, as we have just seen: there are also encounters in Cantos XXIV and XXVI with three thirteenth-century poets, two of whom discuss their art. First though comes Dante's reunion with his close friend Forese Donati, on the Terrace of Gluttony.[31] Their encounter involves two exchanges, each intensely personal and each the vehicle for yet another attack on Florence. Forese had died as recently as 1296, and Dante knows his friend quite well enough to be surprised that he is not still lingering among the late repentant in Ante-Purgatory (XXIII, 75–84). Forese explains that his progress up the mountain has been accelerated by the intecessionary prayers of his beloved widow Nella, whom he pointedly contrasts with the general run of shamelessly immodest Florentine womanhood. Dante then ruefully reminds Forese of the kind of sinful life they both have led, and, alluding to the events of *Inf*. I, explains that Virgil has now set him on the right path (ll. 115–30). In the following canto Forese, about to take his leave, affectionately asks Dante when he will see him again; Dante (here as elsewhere seeming in no doubt as to his own salvation) sharply replies that it will not be a moment too soon, such is the ever-increasing wickedness of Florence (XXIV, 75–81)! This leads Forese to lay the principal blame for the city's woes on his elder brother Corso, whose violent death and doom, dragged down towards Hell at a horse's tail, he now foretells (ll. 82–87). In fact Corso Donati, whose arrogance and scheming had finally led him to be condemned by Florence, was pursued and killed by a band of Catalan mercenaries in the employ of the Commune (October 1308).

Dante's conversation with Forese is punctuated by a remarkable encounter with the poet Bonagiunta da Lucca who, quoting Dante's 'Donne ch' avete intelletto d'amore' ('O you ladies who understand love'), wonders whether he is indeed face to face with its author, he who with that poem inaugurated a new kind of love poetry (XXIV, 49–51). Dante's reply characterises the essence of his amatory lyric verse as a faithful response to the inner dictation of the voice of love, involving a scrupulously precise match between language and subject matter. Bonagiunta acknowledges that it was precisely the failure to follow that inner voice closely which was the 'knot', the impediment, holding back Iacopo da Lentini (here standing for the Sicilian School as a whole), Guittone d'Arezzo and him, Bonagiunta, from the 'dolce stil novo' ('sweet new style') which he now hears (ll. 55–57).

Medieval poetry continues to be prominent on the final terrace, that of Lust. By contrast with Hell, both heterosexual and homo-sexual sinners are here found together, albeit segregated into two groups moving round the mountain in opposite directions, enclosed within a wall of purgative, refining fire. One of the souls, anxious like the rest not to lose any of the benefit of his purgation, comes as close to Dante as he can while remaining within the flames. This is Guido Guinizelli of Bologna, presented here as the great pre-cursor of Dante and other unnamed poets (in fact, the Stilnovists): he is indeed their father (XXVI, 97–99). This high praise is rein-forced when Dante tells Guido that the very ink with which his verse was written will be cherished as long as vernacular poetry lasts (ll. 112–14). Guido modestly points out a fellow spirit as being a finer 'fabbro' (literally, 'blacksmith', i.e. craftsman) in his mother tongue. But he also criticizes two inferior poets: the Provençal Giraut de Bornelh and, ironically, Guittone d'Arezzo. Guinizelli's words here are ironic in that on earth he had praised Guittone as 'caro padre meo' ('my dear father'). The finer craftsman turns out to be the great troubadour Arnaut Daniel, who ends this twenty-sixth canto with nine beautifully wistful yet hopeful lines in Provençal, a language in which Dante the poet was evidently quite at ease, and which would have posed no problems for his more educated readers.

Canto XXVII is a true watershed: it marks the transition between the terraces of purgation and the Earthly Paradise, and it is here that Virgil, soon to be superseded as guide by Beatrice, bids Dante farewell. But first the three poets (for Statius is still here) must pass through the wall of fire, which serves not only to purge lust but also as a barrier surrounding the Earthly Paradise. Dante, however, is very much afraid, and all Virgil's efforts to coax him into the flames, including a reminder of how he safely negotiated the terrifying descent to the *malebolge* on Geryon's back, are to no avail. Not without an engaging touch of pique, he now presents the fire as an obstacle between Dante and Beatrice. This works: Dante finally steps forward into almost inconceivably intense heat, such that he would have hurled himself into boiling glass in order to cool down (ll. 49–51). But Virgil talks him through, all the while speaking of Beatrice, her eyes in particular. Indeed, near the end of the canto he imagines her beautiful eyes as 'lieti' ('joyful'—l. 36). Little does he know that Beatrice, when first reunited with Dante, will be unsmiling, to say the least. This is Virgil's final speech in the *Comedy*: he tells Dante he has shown him both the eternal and the temporary fire, and that he can take him no further. Dante's will is now free, upright and made whole. That is, he is now free from sin: for though he will have much to learn in the *Paradiso*, the enlightenment will be intellectual, rather than moral. This sinlessness explains Virgil's closing words, with which he 'crowns and mitres' Dante ('te corono e mitrio'—l. 142): Dante is now independent of emperor and pope alike, and of their institutions. For the Empire and the Papacy presuppose sin; indeed as Dante puts it in the *Monarchia* they are remedies for the sickness of sin: 'remedia contra infirmitatem peccati' (III, iv, 14, ll. 67–71). But Dante-character is now about to enter the Earthly Paradise, the place of man's prelapsarian innocence.

Set at the top of the mountain, Dante's Earthly Paradise is a 'divine forest', an 'ancient wood' (XXVIII, 2; 23). It is clearly derived from and meant to be identified with the Garden of Eden in Genesis; equally clearly, Dante's change from garden to forest makes it the antithesis of the dark wood in *Inf.* I. It is first described in the exquisitely lyrical Canto XXVIII, where we meet an enigmatic fair lady, physically separated from Dante by Lethe, the stream of forgetfulness. She is named, some five and a half cantos later, as 'Matelda' but her identity and function have never been satisfactorily explained. She does seem, however, to be associated with, if not emblematic of, Eve in her primordial innocence before our first parents' sin and fall from grace. (Eve herself, like Adam, will be seen by Dante in the *Paradiso*.)

Purgatory's closing cantos describe a dazzling drama, set in the divine forest, that is quite without parallel in the *Comedy*. It has two obviously distinct aspects which, though, are by no means obviously opposed. Both are nothing short of momentous: the history and prehistory of the Church; and Dante's reunion with Beatrice. The latter is of course personal, yet not private: in the context of the poem's purpose, it is no less public than the former. The two themes alternate, but it will be convenient to discuss each separately here.

The Church is the subject of two remarkable pageants, or masques, in Cantos XXIX and XXXII. They are remarkable not least because they are symbolic; and symbolism of this sustained kind is rarely used in the *Comedy*. Yet here (XXIX, 43–154) we see a highly elaborate procession characterized by light, colour and music, in which seven gold candlesticks signify the gifts of the Holy Spirit and a succession of spirits (probably angels) portrays the twenty-four canonical books of the Old Testament, followed by creatures emblematic of the four Gospels. Then come the seven virtues, and the remaining books of the New Testament, ending with the Apocalypse (or Book of Revelations), very aptly represented by an old man asleep yet with an astute face. The Apocalypse, together with the prophetic book of Ezechiel, is the chief source for the rich biblical imagery deployed in both pageants. The centrepiece of the procession is a vast *carro*, or chariot, representing the Church itself, and drawn by a griffin—a hybrid creature, half lion and half eagle, generally interpreted as signifying the twin-natured Christ. The second pageant has a more sharply historical and political focus. It charts the misfortunes and degeneracy of the Church from its beginnings down to Dante's own day, by which time it had sunk to unprecedented depths of corruption and subservience. This is all symbolized by various mutilations and

153

mutations undergone by the ecclesiastical chariot. First an eagle, the emblem of Rome, swoops violently down upon it: this would seem to signify the persecution of Christians by certain early emperors (XXXII, 108–17). Then it is attacked by a fox, representing various abortive heresies (ll. 118–20). The eagle returns, this time leaving some of its plumage on the chariot: a clear enough reference to Constantine's devolution of temporal power to the papacy (ll. 124–29). It is of course supremely, and tragically, ironic that the reign of the first Christian emperor should mark the beginning of the Church's disastrous involvement with earthly power and politics. The dragon that then attacks and damages the chariot may refer to the rise of Islam, though this is not certain (ll. 130–35). But the seven monstrous horned heads that the chariot sprouts very probably signify the seven Capital Vices, and are most certainly inspired by Apocalypse 17.3: further grist to what is by now one of the poem's most powerful mills, grinding out the message that the medieval Church is grossly depraved and corrupt (ll. 142–47). This motif is made vividly topical in the canto's closing lines: here a semi-clothed harlot appears on the top of the chariot with a giant, and the two repeatedly kiss. Commentators have from the first identified the giant with Philip IV and the harlot with one or more popes of Dante's time, the obvious candidates being Boniface and Clement V. For there is a violent twist to the erotic encounter here: the harlot glances lustfully at Dante (Boniface's territorial designs upon Florence?); the giant beats her from head to foot (surely the attack at Anagni); finally he drags the monster-cum-chariot, the whore still upon it, into the depths of the wood (there could be no plainer allusion to the papacy's decampment to Avignon, that shameful nadir of Clement's reign, in the view of Dante and many others).

Dovetailed between these doctrinal and historical tableaux is the long-awaited reunion of Dante and Beatrice. Ever since *Inf.* II the poem's movement towards her has been like an undercurrent pulsating beneath the narrative surface. When, in stark contrast to the harlot, she appears upon the chariot, clad in white, green and red, the colours of Faith, Hope and Charity, Dante is overwhelmed by all the power of intense deep-rooted love and turns for support to Virgil. But Virgil is not there. He has slipped away, and Dante is distraught: Virgil's name occurs four times in six lines, thrice in a single tercet (XXX, 46–51). But Beatrice, addressing him directly as 'Dante' (the only instance of his name anywhere in the poem)[32] sternly bids him cease weeping over Virgil, for he now has other cause for tears. And so begins the elaborate ritual of accusation and admission, articulated in a number of distinct stages, that forms the chief portion of this dramatic episode. 'Admission' may be an understatement, though: there are strong overtones here of the sacrament of confession, with Beatrice therefore in the role of priest, and Dante in that of penitent. He is indeed now in the place of mankind's primeval innocence, yet he must still formally acknowledge and repent of the error of his ways. This particular cliché seems especially appropriate, given the terms in which Dante couches his self-accusation. For Beatrice charges him with infidelity to what the remembrance of her should have meant and shown: the path to virtue and salvation. Since her death, however, he has fallen prey to the lure of secondary goods. He has trodden an untrue path, following false images of the good, images whose promise is never fulfilled (XXX, 130–32). These words of Beatrice are closely paralleled and confirmed in Dante-character's subsequent confession that the things of the present moment, with their false pleasure, turned his steps aside (XXXI, 34–36). What precisely those things were is largely left unsaid, though the sins of the flesh are surely involved: indeed Beatrice mentions a 'pargoletta' (roughly, 'some young girl or other'—XXXI, 59) and there is no reason at all to take this other than literally. But complementing, and far more interesting than, moral waywardness of this kind is the intellectual's sin of excessive attachment to worldly philosophy. This is what Beatrice finally accuses Dante of as she denigrates the school of thought that he has followed and its teachings: that way of reasoning is as far from God as is the earth from the *Primum Mobile*, the highest corporeal heaven (XXXIII, 85–90). No one particular school or movement, nor any distinct body of doctrine, is being targeted here: rather, Dante is regretting a phase of over-confidence in the power of unaided reason (see above, pp. 108–9).

Apart from these highly significant lines, Purgatory's last canto is important for two other reasons. First, there is Beatrice's prophecy of political renewal, involving what seems to be one of the poem's very rare deliberate puzzles (XXXIII, 37–45). The Empire, she says, will not remain long without an heir: someone sent by God will soon vanquish both the harlot and the giant.

Beatrice refers to this person only as a number: a five hundred, ten and five. Roman numerals give us D, X and V, a simple anagram of *dux*, Latin for 'leader' (the letters 'v' and 'u' being interchangeable). As with the greyhound of *Inf.* I, this saviour's identity has never been securely established, though there are good grounds for thinking Dante means Emperor Henry VII, the subject of our next chapter. Second, it is in this canto that Beatrice confirms her commission to Dante to express his experience in words. Already she has bidden him pay close attention to the second ecclesiastical pageant, and once returned to earth write down what he has seen, for the benefit of a sinful world (XXXII, 103–5). Now she reinforces this with an exhortation to take special note of her prophecy of the *dux*, and of the mysterious tree that he has seen wither and reflower:[33] these things he is to set down for the instruction of the living, those still embarked on the earthly race towards death (XXXIII, 52–57). This sharp reminder of our life's brevity underlines the urgency of the Sacred Poem's salvific message and function, and the whole passage more than hints at the Messianic self-perception of its author. Dante-character has much still to learn, but by the end of this *cantica* of purgation and renewal, he is ready to rise to the stars.

## (iv) The Dancing Lights

Not all the souls in the *Paradiso* dance, but they are all to a greater or lesser extent luminous, and the title of this section, which refers to the measured movement of those in the Heaven of the Sun, seems to typify the harmonious order of the final *cantica*.[34] Indeed order, which for Dante is indissolubly linked with diversity, inequality (*sic*) and justice, is the keynote of Canto I. For as Beatrice explains, every created thing, inanimate as well as animate, stands in an ordered relation to all other things, and some things are closer to their source (God) than others ('più al principio loro e men vicine'— I, 111). Already we have the fundamental idea of a hierarchy of ordered and unequal diversity, a concept implicit in the *Paradiso*'s very first lines:

> La gloria di colui che tutto move
> per l'universo penetra e risplende
> in una parte più e meno altrove.

The glory of Him who moves all things/penetrates throughout the
universe, being reflected/in one part more and in another less.

(I, 1–3)

The full implications of this universal inequality will become
steadily apparent, and some may greatly surprise a modern
reader.

The lines immediately following leap forward, and upward, to
the end of the *Paradiso*, and in a dramatically personal way: 'fu'io'
('*I was*'), says Dante, in that heaven which most receives God's
light—that is, the tenth and final heaven, the Empyrean. His experience there defeats the powers of memory and expression. Not
entirely, though, for he proposes to reveal in the poem such treasure
as he has managed to salvage. But the task will be arduous, hence
Dante's appeal now not just to the Muses (as at the beginning of
the *Inferno* and the *Purgatorio*) but to Apollo himself as well (ll.
13–36). The reader's task also will be arduous: the opening of
Canto II warns that it will be too much for those setting out in only
a modest craft (with limited powers of understanding, that is) to
follow Dante over seas never sailed before. Here is an intensifica-
tion of the sea imagery of *Purgatorio*'s initial tercet, and also of
course a contrastive reminiscence of the Ulysses episode in *Inf.*
XXVI.

The Empyrean Heaven is the climax of the *Paradiso* and thus of
the whole poem, but Dante does not arrive there until Canto XXX.
First there are nine physical, corporeal heavens through which he
and Beatrice ascend. These follow strictly the scheme of the
Aristotelian/Ptolemaic universe of Dante's time. According to this
model, the motionless earth is at the centre, surrounded by a succession of homocentric revolving spheres. The first eight of these
carry a heavenly body or bodies: in order, moving outward, Moon,
Mercury, Venus, Sun, Mars, Jupiter, Saturn and finally the Heaven
of the so-called Fixed Stars. With this eighth heaven Aristotle's
scheme stopped. Ptolemy's however added a ninth, the *Primum
Mobile*, the outermost of the moving spheres, which does not
contain any planet or star. Dante's Christian cosmos has a final
heaven, the motionless Empyrean, which though outside both time
and space is in some sense the 'abode' of God, the angels and the
blessed. It is perhaps curious that the *Paradiso*, which for many
seems less concrete and with fewer clear bearings than the other

two *cantiche*, is the only one whose setting is 'real': there is no reason to suppose that outside the poem Dante believed Hell to be a subterranean funnel or Purgatory a mountain rising from the southern ocean, yet on any clear night he could see, as can we, the planets and the stars (albeit not the *Primum Mobile* or the Empyrean). Now this ten-fold structure is of course a supreme manifestation of order, God's order, yet the hierarchy of the celestial spheres is not a purely physical thing. It is not just a matter of getting higher, further out from the earth: inseparable from that is an increase in spiritual rank and power. For though the heavens are not themselves animate, they are moved by, and derive their power from, the angels, whose hierarchy corresponds exactly, such that (for instance) the *Primum Mobile* is moved by Seraphs, members of the highest-ranking angelic order.

In Canto II Dante and Beatrice arrive in the first heaven, that of the Moon, and it is worth noting that they pass into the Moon, rather than land on it: it is no mere lump of rock.[35] It is here, in the following canto, that Dante has his first encounter with one of the blessed. This is Piccarda Donati, sister of Forese and Corso. As Beatrice explains, she and her companions appear in this lowest heaven because they failed while on earth to be wholly true to vows they had made (III, 30). This may seem curious, to say the least. In fact the souls who appear to Dante in the three lowest heavens (those still 'within the shadow of the earth'—IX, 118–19) are all associated with some imperfection in their earthly lives, even though all sins have by now been repented of, and forgiven. Thus the souls here have been inconstant in respect of solemn promises; those above in Mercury have been preoccupied with worldly power and ambition; those in Venus over-susceptible to earthly love. In Piccarda's case the vow was a religious one. She entered the Franciscan convent of Poor Clares in Florence, but brother Corso had other ideas. At some date in the 1280s he took her by force from her nunnery and, for his own political ends, made her marry Rossellino della Tosa. Soon afterwards she died. She tells Dante her story (without naming Corso) and then points out the soul of Empress Costanza, wife of Henry VI and mother of Frederick II, here referred to as the third and final 'gust' (*vento*) of Swabian, that is Hohenstaufen, power (ll. 118–20). Costanza too, or so it was believed in Dante's time, was forcibly removed from her nunnery and made to marry. Yet in her heart, says Piccarda somewhat mysteriously, Costanza always remained true to the veil (l. 117). Beatrice will elaborate on this later.

These souls in the Moon, then, have a relatively lowly status in Heaven. All distinctions of earthly rank are now transcended, but there is still a hierarchy of bliss. Ordered inequality extends even to the souls of the blessed, and this puzzles Dante-character. He asks Piccarda whether she and her companions, though happy, would not rather be more elevated in the celestial scheme (ll. 64–66). Smiling she explains that were they discontented with their lot, their wills would not be in accord with that of God. Impossible, for a concomitant of their salvation is that they love God and therefore what He desires. This is memorably summed up in the famous eighty-fifth line 'E'n la sua volontade è nostra pace' ('And in His will is our peace', a phrase that was to find its way into many a Victorian sermon).

One of the *Paradiso*'s dynamic principles is the articulation and resolution of a succession of doubts that beset Dante-character. Two of these dominate Canto IV. First, Dante is worried that the assignation of different categories of the blessed to different heavenly spheres might seem to support what Plato teaches, or seems to teach, in his *Timaeus*: that our souls come into being in this or that star, descending thence into our bodies for the duration of their earthly lives, after which they return to their celestial source. Beatrice firmly refutes this: all the blessed dwell in the Empyrean, where however they are still differentiated and unequal (ll. 34–36). The fact that they will appear to Dante in different heavens according to their spiritual rank is a concession to his limited under-standing: as with all mortals, the raw materials for his intellection are sense-data. That indeed is why the Scriptures ascribe anthro-pomorphic attributes to the angels, and to God Himself (ll. 40–49). Dante's second doubt concerns the nuns: if they were forcibly removed from their convents, what sort of justice is it that relegates them to a humble heavenly rank? And has not Piccarda just told him that Costanza, at any rate, stayed deep down true to her vows? Beatrice's answer centres on a distinction between the absolute will and the 'qualified', or 'conditioned', will: whilst the nuns did not absolutely consent to the violation of their vows, they did partially acquiesce, faced with the threat of violence. Beatrice contrasts this with two (male) examples of unflinching steadfastness: St Laurence, who even while being roasted alive refused to reveal the whereabouts of church treasure; and the Roman Gaius Mucius Scaevola, who, also condemned to be burnt, for his unsuccessful attempt to assassinate the Etruscan king, thrust his right hand into the flames and held it there. The nuns' stories are intended to reinforce the importance of Free Will in Dante's scheme: it is because the slightest acquiescence to pressure is still a freely-willed act that it is just for Piccarda and Costanza to be among the least elevated of the blessed. And, Beatrice encouragingly stresses, Dante-character's doubts about the matter are a sign of his faith, not of any wicked heresy (ll. 67–69).

Justice, divine and human, takes on a much broader aspect in Mercury: indeed it is that heaven's chief doctrinal theme. Twice in Canto VI (ll. 88 and 121) the Emperor Justinian calls God 'la viva giustizia' ('living justice'). The sixth canto is a great political one, like the sixth of *Inferno* and *Purgatorio*, and it is Justinian's canto, literally and entirely, for it consists of one uninterrupted speech from him—something unique in the *Comedy*. This great ruler and legislator (who reigned from AD 527 to 565) traces out the way God's justice has been manifested in the history of Rome. He paints on a massive canvas, so to say, the whole sweep of imperial history, from Aeneas to the sad degeneracy of Dante's time. His account is not just historical and political, but eminently theological too. Having extolled the glories of Rome from its foundation down to Titus (died AD 81), Justinian jumps to Charlemagne: this surely reflects Dante's conviction of the continuity between the medieval Holy Roman Empire and the ancient one. Of the many remarkable features in Justinian's monologue, two deserve especial mention. First, the condemnation of the Ghibellines and the Guelphs (the sole occurrence of these terms in the poem): both factions come under the Emperor's prophetic scrutiny, and both are given short shrift. The Guelphs are guilty of backing the interests of the French crown against the legitimate imperial authority; yet the Ghibellines are no better, in that they have misappropriated, and unjustly, the sacred sign of the Eagle for their own narrow partisan ends (ll. 100–8). Second, and far more momentous, are Justinian's earlier comments about the first century, rather than the fourteenth.

All Rome's achievements pale into insignificance, he says, compared with what happened under the third Caesar, Tiberius: the crucifixion of Jesus Christ. God allowed the Romans the glory of avenging His just anger against mankind—for of course in

Christian belief Christ's death is the means of atoning for human sin (ll. 82–90). Yet Justinian adds something remarkable, charging Dante indeed to marvel at his words: this just vengeance was itself later avenged by Titus, a reference to his destruction of the Temple at Jerusalem in AD 70 (ll. 91–93). It falls to Beatrice to explain this, in the next canto. There Dante not unreasonably wonders why a just revenge would need to be avenged (VII, 19–21). Beatrice's answer centres on two dualities: the dual nature of Christ and the dual involvement in His death of the Romans and the Jews. In that He was man, the crucifixion was a supremely just penalty; in that He was God, it was an outrage without parallel. The former was entirely to the credit of the Romans, the latter entirely the fault of the Jews. One and the same death in fact pleased both God and the Jews: 'ch'a Dio e a' Giudei piacque una morte' (l.47). Extraordinary as this may seem it is what Beatrice says and without doubt what Dante believed. There is more to come: Dante further wonders why the cross was God's chosen means of redemption (ll. 55–57). Beatrice replies that because of Adam's primordial sin mankind had fallen so low that nothing any human being could do would have sufficed to make amends. So God Himself, in the person of His only Son, generously did so. He could of course have simply cancelled the debt but that, although merciful, would not have satisfied the demands of justice: by His suffering death in proxy for the whole of the sinful human race, both justice and mercy were combined (ll. 85–120).

Space precludes more than a glance at Venus, where three colourful medieval personalities predominate: Charles Martel, whom Dante had briefly befriended in 1294; Cunizza da Romano, sister of the tyrant Ezzelino, who had four husbands and whose lovers included Sordello; Sordello's fellow troubadour Folquet de Marseille, a hedonistic courtier turned monk, who later became Bishop of Toulouse and vigorously persecuted the Albigensian heretics.

The Heaven of the Sun is an extraordinarily rich and vivid section of the *Paradiso*, noteworthy for the brilliant description of the circles of dancing souls; for the role of Aquinas; for Dante's critique of thirteenth-century Church history; and for illumination concerning the Trinity, the creation and the nature of wisdom. Like the three succeeding heavens (Mars, Jupiter, Saturn) it is distinguished by a remarkable visual spectacle, in this case the three concentric spinning circles. The members of the inner two are named, twenty-four of them in all, some very famous, one or two obscure, but all associated with learning or teaching or wisdom. For this is the heaven that celebrates the achievements of the intellect, in the broadest sense: an impressive panoply stretching in time from Nathan the prophet to intellectuals of the generation immediately prior to Dante. One of the Sun's keynotes is reconciliation between enemies, and courteous praise of rivals. Acrimonious as the world of learning was and is on earth, all rifts are healed here. So when Aquinas, having welcomed Dante, proceeds to identify his companions (X, 82–138), he begins with Albertus Magnus, his own teacher, but ends, having made the full round of the circle, with Siger of Brabant. This Parisian Averroist was Thomas' doctrinal adversary on earth, but here they dance and sing side by side. Similarly in the second circle St Bonaventure will be next to Joachim of Flora, the visionary preacher whose teachings he had once vehemently opposed (XII, 139–41).

Cantos XI and XII form a fine symmetrical diptych devoted to the two great mendicant orders of friars, the Dominicans and the Franciscans. The intense competition between the two, especially in the University of Paris from the 1260s onward, is now transcended in an atmosphere of brotherly courtesy. So the great Dominican Aquinas, having stressed the providential mission of both Dominic and Francis (XI, 28–42, gives a laudatory account of the latter's life (ll. 43–117) before briefly returning to St Dominic and then launching into an attack on the subsequent degeneration of his own order, sunk as it now is in greed and corruption (ll. 118–39). All this is precisely paralleled in the next canto, and here the speaker is Bonaventure, who in 1257 became General of the Franciscans. He reciprocates with a eulogy of Dominic (XII, 37–105), before praising Francis and then turning on his followers for flouting or perverting the founder's intentions (ll. 106–16).

In Canto XIII Aquinas deals with another of Dante's doubts, arising from Thomas' earlier statement that the fifth light in his circle was unparalleled in wisdom (X, 109–14). That light is the soul of King Solomon, son of David. Dante is puzzled by what Aquinas has said: surely Adam (before the Fall) and Christ, in both of whom human nature was perfect, were wiser than Solomon? Aquinas explains that he had not been speaking of wisdom in an absolute sense, but of that practical discernment which enables the wise ruler to judge the people righteously. That is what Solomon asked God for (III Kings 3.5–9), not for the ability to solve problems of metaphysics or logic (XIII, 88–108). And this leads Thomas to warn Dante, in a forceful closing passage, not to rush in, to be sure to make due distinctions, and not to judge by outward appearances—caveats entirely typical of Aquinas' thought and method (ll. 109–42). And the message is reinforced with a down-to-earth metaphor: Thomas' words should be like lead on Dante's feet, saving him from the pitfalls of hasty judgement (ll. 112–14).[36]

In Mars the spectacle is a dazzling cross, formed by the souls themselves, who are even brighter than their star. And not just a cross, but a crucifix: certain souls, brighter still than their companions, flash forth the image of the crucified Christ. For this is the heaven of the holy warriors, some of whom in fact were crusaders. It is the setting for Dante's meeting with his ancestor Cacciaguida, a highpoint of personal drama in the poem, comparable only to the reunion with Beatrice. Cacciaguida's first words to his great-great-grandson are in Latin, three impassioned lines of it (XV, 28–30). Not only does he call Dante 'sanguis meus' ('my blood'—an echo of *Aeneid* VI, 836); he also asks to whom have Heaven's gates been opened twice, as they will have been to Dante—another clear indication of the poet's confidence as to his own eventual salvation. Cacciaguida reinforces the note of kinship by calling Dante his 'seed' ('seme'—l.48) and his 'leaf' ('fronda'—l. 88). Dante's reaction to this is one of profound reverence, not, however, without a touch of family pride: after all, this great Christian soldier, who was knighted by Emperor Conrad III and died in glorious combat against the infidel, is the man whose blood now flows in Dante's veins. But of course such pride is a little out of place in Heaven, and Beatrice, smiling, gently reproves him (XVI, 13–15).[37]

Cacciaguida's speeches in these central cantos of the *Paradiso* look backward (from 1300) as well as forward. He paints an idealized portrait of the twelfth-century Florence where he was brought up, a city markedly different from Dante's, not least in its economic and sexual mores. Politically too it was stable, such that no Florentine lady of that era feared death in exile and a foreign grave. Nor were there any 'business widows', whose husbands were away making money in France. And of course costume, male and female, was simpler in that smaller, more sober city; cosmetics were out of the question (XV, 97–135). Cacciaguida's socio-economic lament continues in Canto XVI with a eulogy of long-established Florentine families, now sadly in decline. But he also introduces a racial slant: the perennial cause of civic malaise, we are told, is adulteration of pure stock by people of inferior blood (XVI, 67–69)— Brunetto has said something very similar about the inhabitants of Fiesole (*Inf.* XV, 67–69). There is no doubt that Cacciaguida counts himself, and therefore Dante too, amongst the unadulterated. In Canto XVII Cacciaguida looks ahead to Dante's exile in a crucial speech which is the culmination and clarification of all that he has so far heard about his future fate. The grim facts of exile, practical and political, are vividly evoked: not just the day-to-day sufferings and humiliation but, worse still, the ungrateful ill-treatment that Dante will receive from the other banished White Guelphs. More positively though, there is lavish praise for Dante's protector Can Grande della Scala. But the climax comes in Cacciaguida's closing speech, a powerful reinforcement of Beatrice's words in *Purgatorio* XXXIII: Dante must make known all that he has seen, not diluting the truth, however unpalatable it may prove to some (ll. 124–29). It would be wrong to take this in too narrowly political a sense: so far from being a fine opportunity for confounding Dante's foes, the poem has a more profound purpose, nothing less than the salvation of its readers' souls. That is what Cacciaguida means by the 'vital nutrimento' ('vital nourishment') of the poem's message (l. 131).

The ascent from Mars to Jupiter, from the red planet to the white one, is evoked with a beautiful and surely unexpected simile: it is like the blush fading from a lady's face (XVIII, 64–66). There follows what is perhaps *Paradiso*'s most astounding spectacle, bar those in the Empyrean. The blessed souls form the letters of the Latin phrase 'Diligite iustitiam qui iudicatis terram' ('Delight in justice, you who rule the earth', the opening words of the Book of Wisdom): Jupiter's focus is partly, though only partly, on just statesmen, with more than a sideswipe at the many unjust ones. The final 'M' of the word *terram* is then transformed by over a thousand souls, likened to a swarm of sparks, who gradually shape it into the dazzling head and neck of an eagle, the symbol *par excellence* of Rome and of justice (ll. 97–108). The myriad souls of the eagle will speak with one voice on some of the most profound questions in the *Comedy*, but first Dante apostrophizes Jupiter and its inhabitants, praising their justice and contrasting it with current papal avarice and abuse of the weapon of excommunication, the target here being the Avignonese Pope John XXII (ll. 115–36).

There has been a good deal about justice in the *Paradiso*, but in Canto XIX it appears in an unprecedentedly acute form, or rather Dante's doubts about it do, deep-seated doubts that must have gone back many years and stretched his religious faith to the limit. This is the gist: how can it be just to deny heavenly beatitude to someone who though morally righteous, in fact sinless in thought, word and deed, is cut off from the saving message of Christ by a mere accident of geography? Someone born on the banks of the river Indus, for example: no missionaries there (ll. 70–78). And of course just such a doubt about justice attaches to the virtuous pagans of ancient times, cut off from Christ by an accident of history. Dante has seen both kinds in Limbo, the apparent tragedy and incomprehensibility of it all being most obvious in the case of Virgil. The eagle in reply rebukes the presumption of Dante's doubt, and stresses the unquestionable justice of all God's decisions, which *ipso facto* are in utter accord with His will and therefore just. It confirms that faith in Christ is essential to salvation, including anticipatory faith (that of the virtuous ancient Jews, with their belief in a future Messiah). This seems uncompromising, but it is immediately qualified: many will call on the name of Christ who at the Last Judgement will be much farther from God than some who never knew Him (cf. Matthew 7.21ff.); more strikingly the Ethiopian (like the Indian simply an instance of someone remote from Christendom) will be able to condemn such people when it comes to the separation of sheep from goats (ll. 106–11). The eagle then attacks a variety of unjust medieval princes, including Albert of Hapsburg, Philip IV, Edward I of England and his Scottish opponent Wallace, Ferdinand IV of Castile, Wenceslas of Bohemia, and so on.

This critique of the medieval political order is implicitly reinforced in Canto XX. Here the eagle bids Dante gaze upon its eye, and then names the eminently just souls (all rulers, bar one) who form the pupil and eyebrow. The pupil itself is King David; the others are David's son Hezekiah, the Emperors Trajan and Constantine, William II of Sicily and Naples, and the Trojan Rhipheus. It is sharply significant that William (1154–89) is the sole representative of the Middle Ages. But the most remarkable feature of the canto is the presence here in Heaven, as opposed to Limbo, of two apparent pagans, Trajan and Rhipheus. Dante-character is so amazed that an astonished cry breaks from his lips (l. 82), to the great delight of the souls, who respond with a joyous scintillation of sparks. The eagle proceeds to explain, and Dante humbly accepts the explanation even though he does not understand it. Trajan has been saved through the fervent intercession of Pope Gregory the Great, which miraculously restored him to life, whereupon he was converted and died again, a virtuous Christian this time, rather than a virtuous pagan. As for Rhipheus, his exemplary righteousness sufficed to save him: God granted to him through grace the knowledge of our redemption to come, such that he was inwardly 'baptized' by the theological virtues long before the institution of baptism. In the case of Trajan Dante is drawing on a popular legend; the salvation of Rhipheus is however entirely his invention and is based solely on Virgil's description of him as the most just of all the Trojans (*Aeneid* II, 426–27). In this great canto Dante is wrestling with a problem that caused him colossal distress. The final answer involves and demands acquiescence in God's inscrutably just judgement. It *is* just for men as great and virtuous as Virgil to be in Limbo; yet Dante's, and our, difficulties with this may be tempered by the exceptions of Trajan and Rhipheus. Moreover, how exceptional are the exceptions? As the eagle says, even we who see God do not know all He has chosen to save (ll. 133–35).[38]

Saturn surpasses in brilliance anything so far encountered; indeed Beatrice refrains from her usual radiant smile and the spirits are for once silent, lest Dante's sight and hearing be, at this premature juncture, overwhelmed. The spectacle here is that of a golden ladder, stretching high aloft, further than Dante can see and thronged with the souls of monks, those who followed the contemplative way of life. The imagery derives from Jacob's vision of a ladder, upon which a myriad of angels ascend and descend (Genesis 28.12): this biblical episode was widely interpreted in Dante's time as symbolising contemplation. Dante converses with two outstanding Benedictines, members of the greatest and most powerful of the Western monastic orders. Once again the medieval Church is vehemently criticized. Peter Damian (died 1072), a simple (and at his own insistence sinful) monk, reluctantly made a cardinal, lambasts the corruption and greed, not least the sheer gluttony, of his successors in high ecclesiastical office (XXI, 130–35). The assembly of contemplatives applauds this attack with a thunderous roar of righteous indignation. In the following canto it is St Benedict himself, the sixth-century founder of Western monasticism, who speaks. His critique is more narrowly focused than Peter Damian's: it is directed at the very members of the order he founded, those latter-day Benedictines who have gone astray, no longer faithful to his famous Rule, that way of religious living that he laid down and bequeathed to them. The Rule is now a waste of the parchment on which it is written, so bad have things become, with the wealthy monks granting illicit favours not just to their relatives, but even to their concubines! A bitter contrast with the simple poverty of St Peter and St Francis, whose successors, popes and friars, have also become corrupt (XXII, 73–93). The links with the Heaven of the Sun's denunciation of the wicked Dominicans and Franciscans are close indeed.

By Canto XXIII Dante and Beatrice have already ascended to the Heaven of the Fixed Stars, and the particular part of the zodiac where they enter is appropriately the constellation of Gemini, Dante's own star sign. This could well be called a 'transfigurational' canto, for in it Dante sees the brilliant spectacle of the Church Triumphant, more than a thousand of its most illustrious souls, all dazzlingly illuminated by the light of Christ Himself. Dante is privileged to catch a glimpse of Christ (ll. 28–30), and then to behold the Apostles, the Blessed Virgin and an angel (almost certainly Gabriel) who encircles her in the form of a flaming crown (ll. 73–120). The whole episode is a coruscating preview of the Empyrean itself—adumbration would be quite the wrong word! Christ, the Virgin and Gabriel then re-ascend to the Empyrean, leaving the saints to witness a remarkable tripartite intellectual drama, which occupies most of the next three cantos. This is Dante-character's rigorous examination on the virtues of Faith, Hope and Charity, which he compares to the oral exam undertaken at a medieval university by a Bachelor of Arts proceeding to a higher degree (XXIV, 46–51). But what happens here is rather more momentous than the arrangements at Bologna, Paris or Oxford: Dante's examiners are, respectively, Saints Peter, James and John, the very same trio who witnessed Christ's miraculous transfiguration on the high mountain (Matthew 17.1–8). Suffice it to say that Dante passes with flying colours in all three subjects. Noteworthy though is Beatrice's remark in support of him at the start of James' interrogation: among the Church Militant (that is, those Christians still in their earthly lives) there is no one more richly endowed with Hope than Dante. That is precisely why he has been allowed to come from Egypt to Jerusalem (from earth to Heaven, that is) before his life's struggle is over. The hope here is plainly that of salvation, Dante's second and permanent return to 'Ierusalemme' (XXV, 52-57).

Almost immediately after Dante's examination by St John comes his important encounter with Adam. Dante is astounded to be in the presence of the first human being, and burns with curiosity about four questions: the length of time since Adam was created; how long he stayed in the Garden of Eden; the real reason for God's anger against him; and which language he spoke. Adam replies (XXVI, 115-29) that he spent 4,302 years in Limbo, before Christ delivered him, adding that he lived on earth to the age of 930 years. Both periods of time far exceed that of his sojourn in the Garden, which lasted less than seven hours! God's wrath was not a response merely to Adam's disobedient eating of the forbidden fruit, but more profoundly to his going beyond a just limit. The primordial sin then, was one of presumptuous pride, by no means unrelated to that of Ulysses and indeed of Lucifer, who fell from Heaven 'unripe' ('acerbo') because he would not wait for the light God would have given him (*Par.* XIX, 48). As to the language Adam devised and used, it was not Hebrew, but a tongue now unknown, extinct before the time of Nimrod.

St Peter returns to the fore in Canto XXVII, with one of the *Comedy*'s very greatest speeches: a furious antipapal invective, from the mouth of the first pope himself. Blushing dark red with anger and shame he denounces Boniface for usurping his place (the words 'il luogo mio' are immediately repeated twice—ll. 22-23), and for turning Rome, the city of his martyrdom, into a sewer of blood and filth, to the great satisfaction of Satan (ll. 25-27). Moreover Christ's 'bride' (a traditional epithet for the Church) was not nurtured by the blood and tears of the earliest popes only to be used for profit and gain in Dante's day (ll. 40-42). Nor was it Peter's intention that the medieval popes should become embroiled in politics such that Christians are divided into pro- and antipapal camps, or that the sacred emblem of his keys should emblazon military banners (almost certainly a reference to Boniface's campaigns against the Colonna family). He is especially incensed that his image now appears on the papal seal, corruptly used for granting indulgences and revoking excommunications (ll. 52–54). Boniface is bad enough, but Clement V and John XXII are yet to come. Indeed the so-called shepherds of the church are nothing more than rapacious wolves. Although Peter is sure that matters will soon be put to rights, he wonders why God seems to be holding back (l. 57—cf. *Purg.* VI, 118–20; XX, 94–96). He ends with a blunt demand that Dante, once returned to earth, should open his mouth and not hide what he, Peter, has not hidden: a reinforcement of Beatrice and Cacciaguida's exhortations, and coming from the Apostle himself, about as strong an assertion that Dante is to be an instrument of God's will as can be found anywhere in the poem.

Regrettably passing over the *Primum Mobile*, with its major doctrinal passages on angelology and creation and its pungent attack on conceited preachers who put their own ingenuity before God's word (XXIX, 85–126), we must follow Dante and Beatrice to the final heaven. She tells him that they have now passed beyond the nine material heavens to one of pure light, intellectual as distinct from physical light (XXX, 37–40). It is 'here', in this realm beyond all space and time, that Dante experiences his final visions. A key principle here, both theological and structural, is the duality of Heaven's two 'armies' ('l'una e l'altra milizia'—l. 43): the blessed and the angels, armies whose warfare is now accomplished, except for their unrelenting campaign of prayer and intercession on behalf of the souls still on earth and in Purgatory. First Dante beholds them in the astounding spectacle of a river of light flowing between two flowery banks, which are beautifully described as 'painted with a marvellous springtime' (ll. 62–63). Sparks constantly dart out of the river and enter the flowers, just like rubies set in gold, before reimmersing themselves in the flood. These are the angels, administering grace to the souls of the blessed (the flowers). At Beatrice's bidding Dante drinks from the river with the eyes of his mind, and this first spectacle is transmuted into another. With that incisive simplicity that is among his greatest hallmarks, Dante tells us that what had been long now becomes round (ll. 89–90): the river turns into a circular pool of light and the banks become an immense white rose surrounding it, the tiered petals rising up rank after rank. Each petal is a throne for one of the blessed. Beatrice bids Dante consider the vastness of this heavenly city, but also stresses that there are now few seats still to be filled. This is not just because Dante

believed the world to be already in its final age (*Conv.* II, xiv, 13):
it is doubtless also a further indictment of the wickedness of his
times. But before Dante himself joins the heavenly feast (l. 135—
another confirmation that he will be saved), the most illustrious of
the vacant thrones will be occupied, by the soul of Henry VII, who
was to die in 1313. Beatrice immediately offsets her praise of the
Emperor with an attack on blind human greed, and on Clement V
in particular, who will betray Henry. But, she adds—and these are
her very last words in the poem—it will not be long before he is in
Hell, thrusting Boniface deeper down in the papal Simoniacs' pouch
(ll. 145–48)!

The first part of Canto XXXI is taken up by Dante's contemplation of the celestial rose, and in particular the countless mass of
angels flying within it like a swarm of bees (l. 7). His curiosity about
what he sees is as keen as ever, but when he turns aside to question
Beatrice, she is no longer there. Yet she has not vanished, like Virgil;
this parting causes no grief but only momentary puzzlement. For
Beatrice's place has been taken by an old man of kind and fatherly
countenance, who reassures Dante by directing his gaze to her
throne in the rose, where she sits reflecting the radiance of God (ll.
55–72). Dante's final guide is St Bernard of Clairvaux, the great
twelfth-century reforming monk, founder of the Cistercian order.
His intense devotion to the Blessed Virgin was legendary even in
his lifetime and here he simply describes himself as 'il suo fedel
Bernardo' ('Bernard, her devotee'—l. 102). His chief function in
the poem is to plead to Mary, more effectively than anyone else
could, that Dante be granted the Beatific Vision—for the final inter-
mediary between Dante and God will be the Virgin.

The *Comedy*'s penultimate canto sees Bernard naming some of
the rose's inhabitants, identifying their location and therefore their
rank: for hierarchy rules in the rose, as it does throughout Dante's
scheme. All those named are fairly ancient, bar Beatrice and St
Francis. The rose's structure is bipartite, one half being the abode
of the holy ancient Jews, and the other of the Christians. Bernard
specifically points out those enthroned in the segment of petals
topped by the Virgin herself: Eve (immediately below her, now
reconciled in bliss), Rachel, Sarah, Rebecca, Judith and Ruth.
Later, Bernard will locate the souls of Anna (mother of the Virgin)
and St Lucy. Nowhere else in the *Comedy* except Limbo are there
so many female proper names: Dante was clearly impressed by

these Old Testament heroines. When it comes to the men, there are some we have already encountered in the lower heavens, as a concession to Dante-character's understanding, but several new names too: Moses, John the Baptist and, not least, Augustine, that great theologian whose doctrinal power has transcended, in a way surpassed only by Paul's, all denominational divides. This is historical; but there is also a very important theological dimension to this canto, sparked off by Dante-character's last doubt. What worries him arises from the presence in the rose of innocent infants—not the fact of their presence, but their status, for they like the rest are assigned a petal, and all the petals are ranked. Should not these souls be all equal? After all, they never had the chance to make any moral choices (ll. 44–45). Bernard's uncompromising reply centres on God's absolutely free exercise of power and judgement: each little one, at the very moment of conception in the womb, is endowed with its own special degree of grace, so that is why each now has its special place, its special throne, indeed (ll. 52–75).

The final canto opens with Bernard's extensive prayer to the Virgin, backed up by the solidarity of Beatrice and the other blessed souls, that Dante be granted sufficient grace to see God (ll. 1–39).[39] This fervent wish is fulfilled, for Dante's vision grows steadily stronger, though what he is about to see will defeat his memory, let alone his powers of expression (XXXIII, 52–57). Yet he does tell us something of what he saw: three (of course three) final climactic visions, piercing through to the very heart of the Christian faith. Three mysteries, in fact: God, the Trinity, Christ. First he sees the whole of creation in all its multiplicity, conflated in one simple light (God), and also as it were bound up in one sole volume—the imagery of a poet who was a scholar to the last (ll. 76–108). This spectacle gives way to that of three interlinked circles, each of a different colour: two are like mutually reflective rainbows, and the third seems to be a fire breathed forth from the others—the classic Trinitarian theology of the medieval West (ll. 109–26).[40] Then comes the climax to a *Comedy* that is every bit as human as divine: Dante sees within the second circle the image of the incarnate Christ (ll. 127–45). His intellect is overcome and he cannot explain to us his experience; but what he does remember is that his mind was struck by a flash of lightning in which his desire to comprehend this final mystery was in fact fulfilled. His desire and will were now being turned, just like a wheel, by 'l'amor che move il sole e l'altre stelle' ('the love that moves the sun and the other stars'). What could be more typical than this last line of the *Comedy*? How far we are from the arid kinesis of Aristotle's Unmoved Mover! Here the Greek cosmos is Christianized and vivified by Love.

# 9

# Henry VII and Dante's Imperial Dream
## (1308–1313)

### (i) A New Emperor

On 1 May 1308 Albert of Hapsburg was assassinated. His ten years as Holy Roman Emperor had been far from undistinguished, but his administrative, diplomatic and military efforts had been concentrated north of the Alps, on his own German lands as well as on Bohemia and Hungary. Dante, who scornfully refers to him simply as 'Alberto tedesco' ('Albert the German'—*Purg.* VI, 97) did not even acknowledge him as an emperor. This was not just because of his indolence with regard to the Italian states but because he was one of those 'on-paper' emperors—in fact the third in succession—who never underwent the all-important ceremony of papal coronation. Like Adolf and Rudolf before him, he never set foot on Italian soil. His successor was to prove very different indeed. At Frankfurt on 27 November the seven Imperial Electors (all German princes or archbishops) chose the thirty-four-year-old Count of Luxemburg as the next emperor. When he was eventually crowned in Rome as Henry VII nearly a century had elapsed since the last such ceremony (Frederick II had been crowned in 1220). Henry's reign was short—a little under five years—but the last three of them were spent in Italy. During that time Italian politics were dominated by the imperial 'descent' into the peninsula. For Henry did not come to Italy merely to be crowned. He had concrete political and military designs for those Italian states traditionally subject to the Empire, and seriously intended to re-establish imperial power over them. When he finally crossed the Alps late in 1310 he was at the head of an armed expedition, and it was the possibilities of change offered by this fact that so fired Dante's imagination. The first of Dante's three great 'Henrician' political letters, a torrent of impas-

173

sioned adulation, dates from this time.

Preparations for Henry's Italian venture had been prolonged and elaborate. The first formal confirmation of his authority took place in Germany: at Epiphany (6 January) 1309 he was crowned by the Archbishop of Cologne with a silver crown at Aachen (Aix-la-Chapelle). This was the first part of a three-stage process: traditionally an emperor was crowned at Aachen, then with an iron crown at Monza, near Milan, and finally by the pope in Rome, with a crown of gold, as emperor. At the beginning of June 1309 Henry sent an embassy to Pope Clement V, who had recently established the papal court at Avignon. Not long after (on 26 July) the Pope responded with an encyclical letter (*Divine sapientie*), which recognized and confirmed Henry's election as 'King of the Romans'. It also accepted the principle of the separation of the two powers, the spiritual (*sacerdotium*) and the temporal (*imperium*). Although Clement's position vis-à-vis the new Emperor was later to change decisively, at this stage he gave him cautious support. Indeed, he had favoured his candidature the previous autumn, despite pressure from Philip IV, who was backing the claims of his brother Charles de Valois. The encyclical enjoined Henry to steer clear of the papal states in central Italy, whilst confirming his rights elsewhere; in short, it envisaged a degree of power-sharing. Clement also agreed to a coronation in Rome, and even proposed a date—2 February 1312, not exactly imminent. In fact throughout his pontificate, Clement was never to set foot in Rome, or indeed Italy. In August, having received the Pope's letter, Henry inaugurated an imperial diet (or council) at Speyer (Spires), on the Rhine. Here he announced to the assembled German princes that he would mount an expedition to Italy the following autumn (1310). He had no intention of waiting until 1312. His energies were then directed for some months to non-Italian problems, in particular to elaborate dynastic manoeuvres involving Bohemia, which were 'concluded ... with the success that marked most of his efforts north of the Alps'.[1]

In spring 1310 he paved the way for his descent southwards by sending ambassadors to the leading cities of northern Italy and Tuscany. On 10 May two legations left Germany, each consisting of two bishops plus two laymen. Their brief was to announce the Emperor-elect's intention to come in person to Italy to be crowned, and to exact homage from his subjects. He would be arriving no later than Michaelmas (29 September) and expected each city to provide armed escorts and nominate proctors, officials authorized to implement his decrees. He further demanded that all warfare be suspended forthwith and a general truce declared until 1 November. In northern Italy the legation was in general very well received, and not just, as might be expected, by Ghibelline strongholds such as Verona, Mantua and Modena; Guelph Pavia and Piacenza, for instance, were anxious not to alienate Henry, and received his emissaries with great honour. Even at Milan the powerful Guelph leader Guido della Torre, who was hostile, bowed to the more cautious counsels of his allies in Lombardy. Henry's legation had arrived in Milan on 8 June, and the Bishop of Constance, its leader, had read the monarch's requests in the presence of a large crowd of the citizens. He promised that a further coronation, confirming Henry in his title of King of the Romans, would take place in Milanese territory (i.e. not necessarily at Monza—in fact Henry was to be crowned at Milan itself). After a fortnight Guido della Torre replied to the effect that the commune of Milan was prepared to receive and honour the King, and (but?) it had every confidence that he would confirm and maintain all its traditional honours, privileges, immunities, and so forth. There was of course a hint of resistance here, but of all the northern cities, it was only Cremona and Padua (both Guelph) whose response to the legation was significantly less than positive. It should be stressed that Henry's ambassadors presented him as a peacemaker who wished to reconcile Guelphs and Ghibellines, not to take sides, and that too had been Clement's stance in *Divine sapientie*.

Yet how did the envoys fare in Tuscany? Here their first port of call was Pisa (20 June), where they were received with great enthusiasm. Pisa was, along with Arezzo, the chief Ghibelline centre in the region, and its conflict with Florence and the other Tuscan Guelph cities was never-ending. Particularly now that Florence was associating itself with James II of Aragon's plans to conquer Sardinia—the island was of great economic importance—Pisa was anxious for the full support of the new Emperor. Henry was promised a gift of tents for himself and 10,000 followers; this was to be organized by Giovanni de' Cerchi, a Florentine White then in exile at Pisa.[2] Although the Tuscan Guelph cities were nearly all courteous to the envoys, their underlying attitude to Henry was one of misgiving. Florence above all did not want any diminution of its ascendancy over large parts of the region, and its Black rulers certainly did not wish to share power with their White enemies, whom a pacificatory emperor might well seek to reinstall. A new Guelph military alliance had recently been forged (March 1310), involving principally Florence, Lucca, Siena and Bologna. This largely Tuscan league was to be binding for five years and would have the services of some 4,000 cavalry. The timing of this new initiative must certainly be seen in the context of Henry's planned expedition. Yet despite this, the Guelphs did not want military confrontation, or even friction with Henry. At this stage they did not dispute his rights, provided he did not exercise them so as to change things much. In fact the ambassadors were honourably received by members of the alliance. Only at Florence was there any hostility, and this appears to have been not the priors' policy, but the stance of individual prominent citizens (Compagni mentions Betto Brunelleschi by name[3]). On one particular point the ambassadors were simply ignored, however: they had asked Florence to cease hostilities against Arezzo, in accordance with Henry's desire for a general truce, but in fact military operations against the old Ghibelline enemy continued throughout the summer.

### (ii) Henry's Descent and Dante's Fifth Letter

Meanwhile Henry was setting his affairs in order prior to the momentous expedition. He concluded further agreements with Philip IV, and with Pope Clement, and held imperial diets at Frankfurt (July) and Speyer (August–September). These assemblies were designed to secure stability in the German states and in Bohemia during Henry's absence. While the Speyer diet was in progress, Henry received further support: on 1 September Clement V produced another encyclical letter (*Exultet in gloria*). This was addressed to all Italian princes and prelates subject to the Emperor, and commanded them to accept him peacefully as their rightful overlord. The forthcoming expedition was in the interests of peace and justice, stressed Clement, and the Guelph cities could rest assured that they would not be discriminated against: Henry would act impartially. *Exultet in gloria* augured well for Henry's arrival in Italy, and made potential Guelph opposition more difficult. Finally he was ready to leave, and by 10 October reached Lausanne, where he assembled his forces (29 September had proved a little optimistic as an arrival date). The Pisans managed to get an embassy there to greet him, giving him 60,000 florins to help with immediate expenses and promising an equal sum when he reached Pisa. Other Italian cities had despatched embassies, though only the Pisans seem to have got as far as Lake Geneva. On 13 October the imperial party began the journey across the Alps, by the Mont Cénis pass. By 23 October they were at Susa. In military terms Henry's forces were none too impressive—5,000 men, with fewer than 500 horses.[4] Financially, too, the enterprise seems to have been under-funded. However, at first all went well enough. Henry spent the next two months progressing unevenly towards Milan: he stayed a week in Turin; then via Chieri, he came to Asti, where he stayed a whole month; via Vercelli and Novara he arrived at Milan, on 23 December. Numerous oaths of fealty had by now been sworn; exiles (mainly Ghibelline) had been allowed to return; some radical administrative changes had been made—notably at Asti, where the new Emperor had dismissed both *podestà* and *capitano*, showing some insensitivity to, or at any rate ignorance of, how an Italian commune worked.[5]

Before Henry got to Milan, and certainly after Clement's September encyclical, Dante had issued the first of his extraordinary Henrician letters (Letter V). It too is an encyclical, designed to go the rounds: it is addressed to the princes and peoples of Italy, and exhorts them to accept the Emperor-elect, whom Dante, a 'humble Italian and undeserving exile', presents as little short of a new Messiah. There is an urgent sense of the propitiousness of the moment: the letter begins by declaring 'Now is the acceptable time' ('Ecce nunc tempus acceptabile', a direct quotation from St Paul— II Corinthians 6.2). In fact the whole letter is markedly biblical in tone: there are over thirty allusions to or quotations from both Testaments, as against just seven classical references, all to Virgil. A new day of reconciliation is dawning, a new sun of peace has arisen, justice will be restored, a second Moses will come to deliver his people. Italy, currently pitied even by the Saracens, now has great cause for rejoicing, since its new bridegroom, the most merciful and godlike Henry, Augustus and Caesar, is making haste to the wedding feast. This powerful monarch will certainly punish the obdurate who resist his authority, but his mercy too is great, and the virtuous, along with the suitably repentant, have nothing to fear. And so on. Amidst all this passionate declamation, there is room for some political theory too: Dante asserts that each of the twin powers of Peter and Caesar (i.e. Pope and Emperor) derives direct from God, as if bifurcating ('biffurcatur'—§ 17) from a single point. Clement V had indeed accepted the principle of the separation of the two powers in his July 1309 letter, though the theorists of extreme papalism held that the pope's authority alone derived straight from God, the emperor's being devolved to him via the pontiff. Dante is in no doubt that Henry's arrival in Italy is part of God's plan, and the letter ends with a reminder that just as St Peter, the first pope, urged men to honour the king, so Clement his successor is now urging them to do likewise—a clear reference to the 1 September encyclical.

This is Dante's first encomium of Henry VII, the monarch whom years later he was to praise in the *Paradiso* as 'l'alto Arrigo' ('noble Henry'—XVII, 82; XXX, 137). By the time the final cantos of the *Paradiso* were written Henry had been dead some years, his grand design for Italy having failed; but late in 1310 Dante, like a good many others, was still aflame with hope and enthusiasm. We do not know exactly when and where the Letter to the Princes and Peoples was written. It belongs to the earliest stages of Henry's campaign, perhaps even before the crossing of the Alps; almost certainly it can be dated to October or November. It was before Dante met the Emperor in person and did homage to him (probably in Milan), an event recalled in the seventh letter. It seems most unlikely that Henry would previously have known anything about Dante and it may well be, as Petrocchi suggests, that he presented Henry with his fifth letter by way of introducing himself; in any case no previous emperor had ever received such lofty praise from a learned Italian.[6]

Dante's enthusiasm was in marked contrast to the attitude of Florence's rulers, which was rapidly hardening against Henry. No doubt they viewed with dismay his actions at Chieri, Asti and elsewhere—appointing imperial vicars, cashiering communal officials, and so forth. In a letter of 10 November addressed to certain Florentine agents, they set out the conditions under which they would accept the Emperor's authority: in effect that Florence, Lucca and Siena should retain all their lands and possessions exactly as they were.[7] This allowed Henry no effective control whatever. And although there was some debate as to whether the cities of the Guelphic league should send him an embassy they decided in the end not to, thus flouting the injunction given them by his legates in the summer. What they did do was despatch envoys to the Pope, asking for his protection in the event of a conflict. And they also made a number of appeals to the Angevin King Robert of Naples, who had succeeded his father Charles II the previous May. But at this stage Robert was reluctant to oppose Henry directly, and indeed there was still talk of a marriage alliance between the Houses of Luxemburg and Anjou—a scheme promoted by Pope Clement. Meanwhile secular rulers, leading ecclesiastics and communal delegates from many parts of the peninsula were arriving in Milan for the coronation. Even Venice, which had no intention of swearing fealty to Henry, sent an impressive legation. The Lombard region, understandably, was very well represented, by Guelph and Ghibelline cities alike. The two della Scala brothers of Verona, Alboino and Can Grande, were there of course, and some have supposed that Dante (soon to be Can Grande's long-term guest) was with their party. Verona had been anxious from the first to offer Henry its full support, and had in fact sent envoys to his diet at Speyer, even prior to the departure from Germany.

## (iii) The Milan Coronation: Dante's Letters from Poppi

The Christmas period was an intensive one in Milan. Henry managed to effect a temporary reconciliation in the Italian manner between warring interests there (those of Guido della Torre and the Ghibelline Matteo Visconti), and after that all efforts were devoted to the coronation arrangements. The much-heralded ceremony took place on 6 January 1311, in the Church of St Ambrose, two years to the day after Henry's first coronation at Aachen. Milan's Archbishop anointed, consecrated and crowned Henry of Luxemburg as King of the Romans, in the presence of Margaret of Brabant his queen, his court (recently expanded) and the substantial assemblage of Italian dignitaries. These were largely non-Tuscan, for the Guelph cities of Tuscany, and Bologna too, were conspicuously and defiantly absent. And the ceremony was defective in another sense. The revered iron crown of Monza was, it seems, unavailable: according to one account it had been pawned by a hard-up *signore* of Milan. A Sienese goldsmith was therefore commissioned to fashion a replica; but this artefact, for all its jewels, had apart from mere modernity one distinct disadvantage: it did not contain an iron nail from Christ's cross, unlike the Monza original. But nonetheless the coronation was a splendid affair, and was followed by several days of festivity. Henry also took the opportunity to create some 150 new knights; most of these were Ghibellines, but that was not a deliberate policy on the part of the Emperor, who strove to be even-handed with his new subjects. Little more than a month elapsed, however, before Henry was faced with rebellion. The first uprising occurred in Milan itself and was swiftly, and quite mildly, suppressed. But dissatisfaction with the transalpine monarch's rule and reforms led to further unrest in Lombardy. Cremona rebelled on 20 February, and the contemporary chroniclers say that Florence was behind it.[8] Before Henry was able to deal with this, Brescia too rebelled—and that was to prove a far more protracted problem.

Dante's whereabouts in February are once more unclear, but by the end of March he had left Lombardy and was again in peripheral Tuscany, in the Casentino (where he had written the *montanina canzone* and his letter to Moroello). He was now the guest of the Ghibelline Count Guido Novello di Batifolle, and it was from his castle at Poppi (very near the Campaldino battlefield) that on the last day of the month he issued perhaps the most remarkable of his political letters (Letter VI). Anderson has called it 'the most vehement and unbalanced of all Dante's writings', and Anderson was putting it mildly.[9] It is addressed to the iniquitous 'intrinseci' of Florence, those wicked inhabitants still within the city walls, whose failure to honour and obey the Emperor will soon result in the direst consequences. They have defied every law of God and man, they are grossly avaricious, insolent and arrogant, and would set up their own independent 'sovereignty' against the common and universal good. For the Empire has the sanction of the Eternal King, as Scripture and the ancient pagans alike affirm, and Henry is King of the earth and God's own minister: Dante even presents him at one point as a Christ-like figure. Those who defy him will be punished, and quickly: their hurriedly improved fortifications will be shattered by battering rams and set aflame. The populace is already divided: when starvation comes, the mobs will turn on their Black rulers. Most of the city's inhabitants will die or be captured. There will be a few exiles, but they will only know grief. Spurious late repentance without true sorrow will not save the Florentines but only hasten their richly deserved punishment. All this is delivered in language that is highly charged biblically (as with the previous letter). Indeed, Dante specifically casts himself in the role of prophet: these calamities will befall his city, if his prophetic mind does not err ('Et si presaga mens mea non fallitur'—§ 17). It is just as well that Dante was never employed by any of his patrons as a prophet: he would have fared badly under any performance-related scheme of patronage. For Henry never did take Florence, and only besieged it for a few weeks in the autumn of the following year. And Dante's letter certainly fell on deaf ears: the Florentines, now more defiant than ever, soon set about organizing the Tuscan Guelphs into a formal anti-imperial league. In a further development they now refused Henry his due titles: official Florentine documents from April 1311 onwards refer to him simply as 'King of Germany', and in one instance the novel expression 'Emperor of the Germans' is used.[10]

Dante's sustained abuse of the Florentines had by no means exhausted his vehement eloquence. On 17 April, still at Poppi, he addressed a letter to the Emperor himself (Letter VII). Once again the language is highly charged. Henry is the long-awaited Sun, who will bring about a better age in Italy; he is God's minister, the son of the Church, the promoter of Rome's glory. Then a personal note: Dante recalls how he did him homage, rejoicing as he touched and kissed the imperial foot, and saying inwardly 'Ecce Agnus Dei [*sic*] …'—'Behold the Lamb of God, behold Him who taketh away the sins of the world' (John 1.29). Now comes the urgent political message: Henry must attack Florence immediately. He has spent quite long enough in northern Italy, and there is no point in staying because of Cremona. For as soon as rebellion there is crushed, it will merely break out at Pavia, or Vercelli, or Bergamo, or somewhere else. Consider Hercules and the many-headed hydra; as soon as one of the monster's heads was lopped off, two more sprang up, until the hero struck at the throat. So it is now. All the time Henry lingers in the Po valley is time wasted. He should aim for the right river, since the source of the evil lies on the Arno. Yes, it is Florence that has fomented these Lombard uprisings, and Florence—a stinking vixen, treacherous viper, diseased sheep infecting the rest of Henry's flock, and so on—must be overthrown without further delay. The Emperor should rise up like a second David, killing Goliath and liberating his people. Whether Henry ever received this trenchant advice is not known; just two days after the date of Dante's letter he left Milan, but not for Tuscany. He proceeded to attack rebellious Cremona, which he subdued in May, imprisoning its leaders. There was still the problem of Brescia, and on 19 May he began a siege there that was to last a full four months. Meanwhile Dante was still at Poppi, and during April and May he wrote three short Latin letters to the Empress, Margaret of Brabant (Letters VIII–X). He did so on behalf of Countess Gherardesca, the wife of his host Guido Novello. They are skilfully written, but their content is not of great interest: the Countess wishes the Empress and the imperial cause well, and in the third letter (18 May) she rejoices at the latest good news—probably a reference to Henry's success at Cremona, and also perhaps to events at Vicenza, which Can Grande della Scala had taken on the Emperor's behalf. Three years were to elapse before Dante's next letter.

## (iv) Henry's Foes: Florence, Clement and Robert

Henry stayed outside Tuscany during the remainder of 1311. The main task was Brescia, which was well equipped and held out strongly. Late in June its captain, Teobaldo Brusati, was captured during an ill-fated sortie and spectacularly executed in full view of the defenders. Despite this exemplary vengeance, the city did not surrender until September, when Henry razed its fortifications. He then turned his attention to Genoa. Meanwhile, Florence and its allies were consolidating their position, prior to a more overt confrontation with the Emperor. During the summer they recalled their Guelph (though not Ghibelline) exiles, and on 2 September an amnesty was proclaimed, known generally as the Reform of Baldo d'Aguglione.[11] But many exiles were expressly excluded from this, among them Dante (and his sons)—scarcely surprising. His only hope now was that the Emperor would act on the advice given in his letter from Poppi. Certainly the Tuscan Guelphs were becoming more and more intransigent, and armed conflict seemed inevitable. From October onward Florence and Lucca both took steps to secure their frontiers (not just their city walls) against an imperial advance. They blocked passes and roads in Lunigiana, so as to prevent Henry from reaching Pisa. And when in mid-October the Emperor sent two legates to Florence, they were not received; one indeed was nearly murdered. On 20 November the Florentines issued a decree whereby their subjects were given full licence to rob or kill messengers of the 'King of Germany'.[12] On that very day

Henry, now installed in Genoa, accused Florence of high treason on nine principal counts, demanding that it send a delegation to justify itself. Of course the Florentines did no such thing.

December was a very bad month for Henry. First there were more rebellions: Parma on 4 December and Reggio two days later (both with Tuscan Guelph aid). Then there was an outbreak of plague in Genoa, apparently brought from Brescia by the imperial forces; the Empress Margaret herself died on 13 December. And about this time King Robert's brother John, Duke of Gravina, arrived in Rome with a substantial armed force and proceeded to co-ordinate elements hostile to Henry. Brescia again rebelled, though abortively —the intrepid Can Grande soon re-established imperial control there. On Christmas Eve, by now exasperated with Florence, Henry formally banned the city, depriving it of the right to self-government, claiming possession of its *contado* (the territory surrounding the city itself) and declaring the Florentines to be rebels against the Empire. Political exiles such as Dante (though he is not specifically named) were excluded from this sentence.

Further uprisings occurred at the beginning of 1312, first at Cremona (again) and on 15 February at Padua. But by now Henry was determined to proceed to Rome for his third and final coronation, as Emperor. He went first to Pisa, but he could not travel from Genoa overland because of hostile Guelph forces in northern Tuscany. So he went by sea, sailing from Genoa on 16 February. When he arrived in Pisa on 6 March, on Tuscan soil at last, he was rapturously received by the solidly Ghibelline city. The Pisans gave him the 60,000 florins promised at Lausanne, as well as many lavish gifts. Numerous White and Ghibelline exiles arrived, and it has long been thought that Dante was among them. (There is in fact a tradition that Petrarch, then aged seven or eight, saw him there.[13]) Doubtless if Dante gained the Emperor's ear, he would have done his utmost to persuade him to strike at Florence forthwith. It has been objected that Dante would scarcely have been welcome in Pisa after his vitriolic attack on the city in the famous *Inferno* passage (XXXIII, 79–90) where he curses the Pisan rulers' cruelty in starving to death Count Ugolino and his four little sons. But although the *Inferno* was almost certainly completed by now, bar certain crucial revisions, it had not been published, so as Petrocchi observes, the objection loses its force.[14] At any event Henry postponed the showdown with Florence, and towards the end of

April he left for Rome. Already the coronation date originally proposed by Pope Clement had passed. Indeed Clement (not least because of continuing pressure from Philip IV) was already distancing himself from Henry and the imperial cause in Italy; late in March he had been dissuaded from sending letters to John of Gravina, which would have required him to remove his troops from Rome and thus cease trying to obstruct the coronation.

When, early in May, the Emperor reached Rome (via Viterbo) he faced stiff opposition. He entered by force across the Milvian bridge, but only with help from the Ghibelline Colonna clan; typically, their Orsini rivals (Guelphs) had sided with the Angevin forces of Robert and Duke John. And these were now substantially augmented by troops from the Tuscan Guelph alliance. Clearly the aim was to prevent any coronation. Despite some very fierce fighting, notably on 26 May,[15] that aim was strictly speaking unsuccessful: the ceremony—or *a* ceremony—did take place. But when Henry was crowned on 29 June the circumstances were far from ideal. St Peter's and the surrounding area were in Angevin/Orsini hands, so Henry had to be crowned on the other side of the city, in the Archbasilica of St John Lateran. But Clement was still in Avignon, and at no stage had shown signs of moving. He seems not to have sent any clear instructions to Rome, hence a certain amount of prevarication on the part of the local cardinals. In the end it was Niccolò da Prato, Cardinal-Bishop of Ostia, assisted by two others, who placed the crown on Henry's head. It is practically certain that Dante was not present; he was probably now in Verona. By this time Clement's stance had overtly changed: his previous support for Henry had waned, and he began to intervene increasingly on behalf of Robert. Several factors lay behind this, not least the spectre of a new alliance (involving a strategic marriage) between the Emperor and Frederick of Trinacria.[16] Very shortly after the coronation, Clement went so far as to send letters demanding that Henry desist from any attack on the Kingdom of Naples or the forces of Duke John; that he agree to a year-long truce with Robert; and that he leave papal territory forthwith. To Dante all this was no mere policy-shift, but downright betrayal, as the *Divine Comedy* makes abundantly clear.[17] Cacciaguida, in the course of praising the della Scala family, will refer to the Gascon Pope's duplicity: 'ma pria che 'l Guasco l'alto Arrigo inganni' ('but before the Gascon deceives noble Henry'—*Par.* XVII, 82). And Beatrice, in her very last speech in the poem, having pointed out the heavenly throne that awaits 'l'alto Arrigo', refers to the pontiff who will oppose him both openly and covertly—'palese e coverto' (*Par.* XXX, 142–44). Nor should it be forgotten that Clement figures prominently, and infamously, in the Canto of the Damned Popes: Nicholas III says that this 'lawless shepherd' will be guilty of even dirtier work—'più laida opra'—than Boniface himself (*Inf.* XIX, 82–83). Doubtless these lines refer to the events of 1312, and to previous darker manoeuvres.

Not long after the coronation, Henry finally moved against Florence. In August he established himself in Ghibelline Arezzo and made preparations for a siege. This began on 19 September and lasted for six inconclusive weeks. The Florentines were heavily reinforced by their Guelph allies, and Henry's forces never managed to surround the city entirely. However, despite contracting malaria, the Emperor did score a number of military successes locally, and Florence declined to challenge him in the open. But at the end of October Henry lifted the siege (to the immense disappointment of the exiles) and via San Casciano he decamped south to Poggibonsi, where he spent the winter. His military campaign against Florence was petering out, and he never attempted a further siege. In March he returned to Pisa where, after issuing yet another proclamation against Florence, he spent several months preparing to attack King Robert. The preparations were legal as well as military. On 26 April he condemned Robert as a rebel against the Empire: his subjects had two months to sever their relations with him, or face the consequences; all his lands and wealth were to be confiscated; the King himself was condemned to death by beheading. This brought strongly-worded responses from Philip of France, as well as from Robert himself, not to mention an excommunication threat from Clement. Much polemic ensued between jurists on both sides. The Florentines showed the warmth of their relations with Robert by granting him the right to appoint their *podestà*. By August Henry felt able to confront Robert: in addition to his army he now had considerable naval support from Pisa, Genoa (where Uguccione della Faggiuola was imperial vicar) and Sicily—he had made Frederick of Trinacria imperial admiral. Henry began marching southward on 8 August, intending to go first to Rome, and then to launch a combined land and sea assault on the Kingdom of Naples. But he did not have long to live: after a few days he fell fatally ill, probably again with malaria. This was at Montaperti (of all places), the site of the great Ghibelline victory over Florence in 1260. From there he was taken to Buonconvento, where he died on 24 August. His body was returned to Pisa, in whose cathedral he was buried. Pisa and the imperial army were in the deepest mourning, by contrast with the exultation in many Guelph cities. The Florentines lost no time in issuing a jubilant letter (27 August) in which they celebrated the death of a savage tyrant, that Henry whom the Ghibellines (notorious enemies of the Church) chose to call King of the Romans and Emperor of Germany.[18]

## (v) After the Emperor's Death

Henry was dead, and many, though by no means all, of his forces quite soon dispersed. Robert's kingdom remained unmolested. The attempt to re-establish imperial sway in the Italian peninsula had failed, and was never to be repeated, except for Emperor Lewis IV's abortive efforts in the late 1320s. It is easy to dismiss Henry; but only with hindsight do schemes become dreams. In fact his designs ('schemes' is unfair really) stemmed from the highest motives, and had considerable support; his was no more a lone eccentric voice than (at this stage) Dante's was. As Anderson has pointed out, the successes he did achieve were in part due to the continuing esteem attaching to the Empire in early fourteenth-century Italy, even among Guelphs.[19] Henry was the first emperor to have shown any real interest in Italy for over half a century, and if this interest was not matched by an adequate grasp of the peninsula's traditional institutions and political complexities, he is not perhaps to be blamed. But wider factors too were against him: he had to cope not just with the city-states—their internal divisions and elaborate shifting external alliances—but with powerful kingdoms and an unreliable Pope. In Bowsky's words, his expedition 'definitively discredited the medieval imperial solution to Italy's problems'.[20] Whether this would have been Dante's view is quite another matter. His fervent hope that Henry would prevail was of course shattered, but his faith in imperialism, in an Imperial Dream transcending this particular tragedy, certainly remained intact. And in view of Beatrice's closing speech in the Empyrean Heaven (written perhaps in the last two years of Dante's life) it is more than likely that he never abandoned the hope that a future emperor might succeed where Henry had failed. For Beatrice prophesies that Henry will come to set Italy to rights, but at the wrong time—before it is ready: 'a drizzare Italia/verrà in prima ch'ella sia disposta' (*Par.* XXX, 137-38). So a more propitious time might yet come.

What of Dante's whereabouts and writings in 1312 and 1313? We have already conjectured that he might have been in Pisa when Henry first arrived there, in March 1312. But by the summer he was, Petrocchi suggests, at Can Grande's court in Verona.[21] The most famous of all Dante's patrons had by this time been appointed imperial vicar both in Vicenza and Verona, and was now the sole Lord of his native city, his brother Alboino having died in November 1311. If Petrocchi is correct, Dante was to be the guest of this rising star on the political and military scene for some six years. As to his writing: no letters from this period are extant, but he was almost certainly well advanced with the *Purgatorio* and probably already engaged on extensive revision of it. Following Petrocchi again, the second *cantica* would have been finished before Henry's death, though not made public until the autumn of 1315.[22] But what of the *Monarchia*, Dante's most famous political work? The dating of this treatise poses problems of great complexity, which have occasioned rivers of ink; in the history of Dante scholarship of this kind, only the question of the Can Grande Letter's authenticity has proved similarly rebarbative.[23] Many, if not most, have linked the *Monarchia* closely with Henry's expedition, assigning it to the period 1312–14. Nardi, however, thought it was written immediately after the *Convivio*, perhaps in 1308. The *Monarchia* does indeed have close links with the *Convivio*, not merely with the early chapters of Book IV, but also in respect of the view of earthly happiness presented in the two works. Yet there is a serious problem involved in dating it prior to the fifth letter (autumn 1310); for there Dante expresses his view of the relationship between Papacy and Empire in terms of an analogy (that of the 'two luminaries') which is expressly rejected in the *Monarchia* (as indeed it is in the *Comedy*).[24] So Nardi's very early dating seems improbable.

Yet there is another, very serious objection to locating the treatise in the Henrician period. While discussing no less a matter than Free Will, Dante in the *Monarchia* refers back to what he has already said in the *Paradiso*: 'sicut in Paradiso Comedie iam dixi' (*Mon.* I, xii, 6, ll. 26–27—alluding to *Par.* V, 19–22). We can no more be certain about the date of the *Paradiso* than in the case of the two earlier *cantiche*, but it clearly does not belong to the time of Henry's expedition, and it is doubtful whether any of it was begun before 1315. Because of the alleged doctrinal incompatibility between *Monarchia* and *Paradiso*, opponents of the later dating have expended considerable effort in minimizing, marginalizing and, so to speak, criminalizing that awkward phrase in *Monarchia* I, xii. It does not appear in the first printed edition (Basel, 1559), and this has supposedly helped its enemies. There has been much talk of interpolation by a copyist, or even by Dante himself, years after writing the treatise. As with all Dante's writings, no original manuscript in his own hand survives. Yet definitive work on the manuscript tradition of the *Monarchia* now leaves little or no doubt as to the phrase's authenticity.[25] So Petrocchi, accepting this, assigns the work to 1316–18.[26] This does seem more probable than the earlier, and still widely-held view. It should also be pointed out that the *Monarchia* makes no reference to Henry VII, nor to Clement V for that matter; in fact it does not allude to contemporary events and personages at all, a marked contrast with the *De Vulgari* and the *Convivio*. This in itself makes a post-Henrician dating less problematical (though problems remain). Whatever the truth of the matter, the *Monarchia,* like the final parts of the *Purgatorio* and much of the *Paradiso*, belongs to the Verona period, the subject of the chapter that now follows.

# 10

# The Gentleman of Verona
## (1312–1318)

The Ghibelline Can Grande della Scala, Dante's most illustrious patron, was born in 1291 and by his early twenties was well on the way to becoming one of the most powerful figures in northern Italy. An outstanding military commander, he had by the time of his death at the age of thirty-eight brought under his control a number of cities in Lombardy and the north-east: Cremona, Mantua, Vicenza, Padua, Treviso. He did not know the meaning of defeat until August 1320, when the Paduans, his long-standing Guelph enemies, repulsed him from beneath their walls. He was noted by contemporaries for his munificence, and in particular his hospitality towards prominent exiles of all sorts, some of whom set up semi-permanent abode at his court, with, according to an expatriate from Reggio[1], their own apartments, suitably decorated to reflect their particular status or profession. Even Albertino Mussato, the great Paduan patriot, scholar and poet, though critical of Can Grande's impetuous and wilful character, records how well he was treated while a prisoner at Verona.[2] Can Grande's court was even compared by Boccaccio to that of Emperor Frederick II.[3] Dante's own admiration for him was very marked: through the mouth of Cacciaguida, in the Heaven of Mars, he bestows on him some of the highest praise to be found anywhere in the *Comedy* (*Par.* XVII, 76–93). Dante's ancestor hails a fellow warrior whose future deeds will be famous: even before Pope Clement has turned against Henry VII (in 1312) sparks of Can Grande's prowess will be seen. His power will be so great as to change the fortunes of many, from good to ill, and vice versa. He will be indifferent both to riches[4] and to toil, and his generosity will be so apparent that even his enemies will be unable to keep quiet about it. Cacciaguida ends his eulogy by alluding mysteriously to further unspecified marvels, beyond the belief of those who will see them. In short, Can Grande will be a paragon of martial valour and gentlemanly largesse.

Dante's stay with him may have lasted six years, though with intervals elsewhere, including maybe Lucca, when Uguccione della Faggiuola held sway there. The central fact and achievement of this Verona period must be the increasingly intensive work on the *Comedy*, both revision and composition. The revised *Inferno* was probably ready for circulation in late 1314, the *Purgatorio* a year later. And by 1316 Dante would have been actively engaged on the *Paradiso,* roughly half of which he completed before leaving Can Grande's court in 1318. Although no longer personally involved in other than occasional diplomatic activity, Dante had not of course turned his back on the ever-complex world of Italian politics in the years following Henry VII's death. That he did not do so is evident enough from the political discussions and diatribes of the *Purgatorio* and *Paradiso*. But apart from this, two of the three final letters, all of which are of the greatest interest and importance, were written in direct response to political events.

## (i) Dante and the Cardinals: The Eleventh Letter

The first of these letters has to do with Rome and the papacy. Pope Clement V died on 20 April 1314, and there followed an inconclusive and unruly conclave of the cardinals held at Carpentras, near Avignon. It began on 1 May, and of the twenty-four prelates only seven were Italian. The rest were from France, and included an organized group of ten Gascon cardinals—Clement had been busily promoting his fellow countrymen. It was Clement who had allowed the seat of the Church's leadership to move to France, thus inaugurating what was to be dubbed the 'Babylonian Captivity'. Dante was not to know that this regrettable state of affairs was to last some seventy years, and he saw the election of Clement's successor as an opportunity to put matters right. Hence the vigorous intervention of Letter XI, which is addressed to the Italian cardinals, urging them to do their duty and elect an Italian pope, or at any rate one who would end the papacy's shameful exile and restore it to the Eternal City. The letter was a prompt reaction to the news of Clement's death, and was written in May or June (certainly before 14 July, when the conclave was violently disrupted). It has been described as arguably the high point of all

Dante's writing in Latin prose.[5] It opens dramatically with the first verse of Jeremiah's Lamentations, and a rousingly biblical tone is maintained throughout the pages of reproof and exhortation that follow. Dante is utterly unsparing in his attack on the Church's leaders. They are irresponsible, decadent, mercenary and politically devious; they have abandoned Rome, so that it is now doubly destitute, housing neither pope nor emperor. No wonder heathens mock the Church, such is its abject state. Moreover, the cardinals are consumed with avarice instead of charity. They pay attention only to the decretals and canon law, a most lucrative area of study, whilst ignoring the wisdom and true doctrine offered by the Church Fathers: thus Gregory the Great lies festooned in spiders' webs and Ambrose, Augustine, John Damascene and the rest are similarly consigned to oblivion. It is scandalous that the Church should have to be reproved by a private individual, though Dante adds that a great many secretly think or murmur what he is bold enough to cry aloud. Finally, the five native Roman cardinals are addressed, two of them (Napoleone Orsini and Iacopo Stefaneschi) being specifically alluded to. They of all people, they who as children saw the sacred Tiber, must strive to bring back the papacy to its true seat: confound the Gascons!

None of this did any good. The cardinals were at an impasse, no candidate being able to attract the required two-thirds majority. After a few weeks there was fighting in Carpentras between supporters of the rival factions, and on 14 July an armed group of Gascon supporters (led by Bertrand de Got, the late Pope's nephew) burst into the conclave, threatening death to the Italian cardinals. The latter swiftly withdrew. Shortly afterwards most of the Gascon cardinals left Carpentras and returned to Avignon: the conclave was in a state of ignominious collapse. Clement's successor, John XXII, was not in fact chosen for a further two years, and he was another Frenchman: Jacques Duèse from Cahors, the Archbishop of Avignon.

## (ii) Uguccione, Florence and Dante's Twelfth Letter

At just about the time of Dante's fulminating letter, and the cardinals' vacillations, something very decisive occurred: in June 1314 the Ghibelline captain Uguccione della Faggiuola (now effectively Lord of Pisa) took control of Lucca, installing his son Francesco as captain-general and *podestà*. The previously Black Guelph city was now to prove a nightmare to Florence for several years. It is true that in December 1314 Uguccione failed to take Pistoia, but this only led to new military alliances between him and leading northern Ghibellines—the Bonacolsi of Mantua, and Can Grande himself. The Ghibellines were now in the ascendant, threatening the Tuscan Guelphs in a way they had not done for half a century. Uguccione was the undisputed Ghibelline chief in Tuscany, and to an extent may be seen as the heir to Henry VII's aspirations in the region. He certainly inherited more than ideals: after the Emperor's death a substantial body of Germans and other transalpines (including 800 horsemen) had remained in Italy, and had been at Uguccione's disposal since he took control of Pisa—a significant addition to the local Ghibelline forces.

Florence's response to this new threat in Tuscany consisted partly in a series of amnesties. A lot had happened since 1302, and the Florentine rulers thought the time ripe for a recall of exiles. Although Dante and his sons had been excluded from the September 1311 provisions, they were implicitly included in those of 19 May 1315, which were issued against a background of urgent military menace—Uguccione was busily laying siege to San Miniato (midway between Florence and Pisa). The May amnesty proposed a pardon for political 'offenders', but on certain conditions. A fine would have to be paid; anyone not already in prison would have to submit to being technically (re-) incarcerated; and all offenders would have to undergo the degrading ceremony of the *oblatio*, by which common criminals were frequently pardoned. This took place in the city's baptistery and involved being publicly 'offered' to God and John the Baptist by a sponsor. Ordinary criminals had to dress in sackcloth and, wearing a paper mitre and holding a candle, process from prison to the baptistery. Although political offenders appear to have been exempt from the sackcloth and associated paraphernalia, the conditions were still quite humiliating enough. At least Dante thought so, and he made his feelings quite clear in his twelfth letter, a magnificent outpouring of noble scorn.

This letter is certainly a response to the May 1315 amnesty and not, as has been thought, to that of 2 June 1316.[6] It is addressed simply to 'a Florentine friend', evidently a friend resident in Florence. This person seems to have been a priest, and at one time was thought to be Teruccio di Manetto Donati, a brother of

Gemma, though this is no longer accepted.[7] Dante says he has heard about the recent amnesty from several friends, the correspondent included, and also from a nephew. This last was very probably Niccolò di Forese Donati, soon to be fighting for Florence at the battle of Montecatini. Dante's reaction to the news is unequivocal, and splendidly succinct: there was not that much to be said. (The previous letter, to the cardinals, is four times as long.) He simply will not accept the ridiculous terms of the amnesty, a bizarre recompense for a man innocent of every charge laid against him, he a victim of injustice yet always a preacher (note) of justice. Is this the way to treat an indefatigable scholar, an intimate lover of philosophy? The implication is that the years of exile (which Dante rounds up to fifteen) have been years of the utmost intellectual effort and achievement, such that Florence should now recognize the greatness of the exile it has wronged. Yet that is what the terms of the amnesty could never do: so far from giving Dante his due, they would dishonour him. Why should he then demean himself? Were there to be a way of returning to Florence that would not detract from his fame and honour (still a glimmer of hope!), then he would tread that path with alacrity, but if not, then he will never return. After all, he can contemplate the sun and the stars and the sweet truths of the mind anywhere, can he not? The language here is far from fortuitous: astronomy, always a matter of the keenest interest for Dante, must now have been at the centre of his attention, as he completed and revised the *Purgatorio*, and as the *Paradiso*, that stellar masterpiece, was already perhaps taking shape. No, Dante firmly turns his back on Florence with the laconic dignity of the letter's closing words: 'Quippe nec panis deficiet' ('Rest assured, I shall not want for bread').

Soon after the twelfth letter Florence and the other Tuscan Guelph cities suffered a massive military defeat at the hands of Uguccione and his combined forces from Pisa and Lucca. At the battle of Montecatini (midway between Lucca and Pistoia), on 29 August, as many as 10,000 may have been killed, including two Angevin princes (a brother and a nephew of King Robert) along with many prominent Guelphs, and on the Ghibelline side Uguccione's son Francesco. The catastrophe has been not unreasonably compared to the battle of Montaperti in 1260, but although it marked a high point in the Tuscan Ghibelline revival Uguccione did not go on to besiege Florence itself. The city remained under Guelph control and its vigorous commercial life does not seem to have been significantly impaired.[8] But the Florentines were certainly not disposed at this time to make any more offers or concessions to their White Guelph and Ghibelline exiles. On 15 October Ranieri di Zaccaria, King Robert's vicar in Tuscany, condemned to death by beheading a number of 'Ghibellines and rebels against the commune and people of Florence'; their property also was to be confiscated or destroyed.[9] Among those named were Dante and his sons. True, the sentence included a 'let-out clause' but a wholly unrealistic one: the accused might be spared if they appeared in person to justify themselves 'today and for the whole of tomorrow' ('hodie et cras per totam diem'). Ranieri confirmed the death sentence in a further decree of 6 November, in which Dante and his sons again appear among those to be decapitated at the place of public execution ('locus iustitie').[10] Moreover anyone now had *carte blanche* to attack or steal from those condemned with impunity. This sentence was not revoked during Dante's lifetime, and seems to have marked a veritable point of no return; although further amnesties (at least three in 1316) were offered to individuals, Dante was never included. The commune did not try to make amends until after 1321, which was too late. Despite this, Dante did not despair entirely of an honourable reconciliation and return. Indeed the poignant opening of *Paradiso* XXV (written at least three years after Ranieri's sentence) holds out the hope that the Sacred Poem itself might overcome the cruelty that still shuts him out from the sheepfold where once he slept as a lamb ('del bello ovile ov'io dormi' agnello'—*Par.* XXV, 5).

Where Dante was at the time of his penultimate letter and the subsequent events of 1315 we do not know, but if he was at Lucca and in some way associated with Uguccione (who is never once mentioned in his writings, however) he is unlikely to have remained there long. For in April 1316 Uguccione was expelled from Lucca and Pisa, as a result of an internal rebellion against his autocratic ruthlessness. Not that this was to prove any great comfort to the Florentines, for he was succeeded in Lucca by another Ghibelline, Castruccio Castracani, who continued to menace Florence for several years more. The elderly Uguccione (now well over sixty) took refuge at Can Grande's court in Verona, though not as some idle exile: on the contrary, he played a leading role in his host's many vigorous military campaigns. Perhaps Dante too returned to Verona about this time, in which case he may even have had the Letter to Can Grande and the first canto (at least) of the *Paradiso* with him.

## (iii) The Can Grande Letter

A very probable date for Dante's thirteenth and last letter is 1316. It is the lengthy Epistle to Can Grande, which dedicates the *Paradiso*, the 'sublime' final *cantica* of the *Divine Comedy*, to his friend and patron. The text certainly does not imply that the *Paradiso* had already been completed, hence a dating as early as 1316 causes no problem in that respect. Mazzoni assigns it to the period 1315–17, and Petrocchi opts for 1316. Though there has been considerable discussion as to the letter's date, this has been far outweighed by the vast scholarly attention paid to the question of its authenticity, first doubted in 1819. The debates over this remarkable text have been astonishingly exhaustive, impassioned and at times vitriolic. Nearly all Dante scholars continue to think that the question of authorship is an important one, since the letter has a good deal to say about how the *Comedy* should be interpreted. If Dante is the author, then this is an auto-critical document of the utmost interest. But even if (and the debate still seems far from closed) the author turns out to be a contemporary or near-contemporary of the poet, the Letter to Can Grande would still be a highly important and intriguing text. For it displays overtly, as well as more subtly, a considerable knowledge of Dante's writings, not just the *Paradiso*, or indeed the *Comedy*, but the *Convivio* as well; there are even similarities with the *Monarchia*, which may well not yet have been written.

The letter falls into three sections: the first four paragraphs are truly epistolary, but Dante then turns to questions of literary theory in what is generally called the 'doctrinal' or 'methodological' part (paragraphs 5–16), whilst the final portion (paragraphs 17–33) is exegetical, providing a very detailed commentary on the first thirty-six lines of the *Paradiso* and their implications. The grandiloquent opening sentence is addressed to the victorious lord Can Grande della Scala, the Emperor's vicar-general in Verona and Vicenza: his devoted servant Dante Alighieri, a Florentine but only by birth, not in morals ('florentinus natione non moribus') wishes him a long and happy life and ever-increasing renown. Even before visiting Verona Dante had heard reports of Can Grande's greatness; now, with firsthand experience of his splendour and generosity, he knows that such reports were more than justified. Indeed Dante has become Can Grande's friend as well as his servant. The disparity in their social status has proved no obstacle, for men of humble condition but of great virtue have often been intimates of the mighty. Anxious to enrich their friendship by reciprocating Can Grande's munificence, Dante can think of no more fitting gift than the sublime climax of the *Comedy*, the *Paradiso* itself.

Paragraph 4 ends by announcing a switch to the doctrinal section of the letter: Dante now proposes to speak as a commentator ('sub lectoris officio'). There is indeed a marked change hereon, not just in content but in style too: this latter point has led some scholars to conclude (mistakenly, I believe) that only the first four paragraphs are by Dante. This second section of the letter deals with Dante's method and intention in writing the *Comedy*; a number of points are addressed, the most important paragraphs being 7, 8, 10, 15 and 16. The first two of these have to do with allegory. Attention is drawn here to the semantic multivalency of the *Comedy*: it is to be read in more than one sense, for it is 'polysemous' ('polisemos'). By way of analogy, Psalm 113, 'In exitu Israel de Aegypto' is explained in four different (but, it is implied, mutually illuminating) senses. Literally, the psalmist is recalling the Exodus of the Israelites from Egypt; and (not *but*) the text has further, non-literal senses. Allegorically it signifies our redemption through Christ; morally the soul's passage from the grief and wretchedness of sin to a state of grace (in this earthly life); and anagogically the transition from enslavement by a world subject to decay to the freedom of perpetual glory in heaven. Dante's use of this psalm here, implying a special, quasi-biblical, status for his poem—the Sacred Poem—is no cause, I think, for scandal. Nor should it be taken as an injunction to tease out four semantic senses from every single episode, encounter or line of the *Comedy*. Indeed, paragraph 8 simplifies matters: we are now told very plainly that the subject of the *Comedy* is twofold. Literally, it is the state of souls in the afterlife; allegorically (and here the term is used in a generic sense, as against the more restrictive 'allegoricus' and 'ad allegoriam' of the preceding paragraph) the poem deals with the way in which men deserve reward or punishment, according to how they have exercised their free will. Some scholars who favour a 'figural' or 'typological' approach to the *Comedy* have found powerful support in these sections of the Can Grande Letter.[11]

The tenth paragraph explains why the poem is a 'comedy'. Put briefly, the reason is that it has a good, longed-for and welcome conclusion (the *Paradiso*), in contrast with its foul and fearful opening (the *Inferno*). With a tragedy it is the other way round. In medieval literary parlance the terms *Comedy* and *Tragedy* did not have, or no longer had, any specific reference to the theatre. There are considerable problems raised by this section of the letter, though they do not seem to me to invalidate Dante's authorship, *pace* the views of several contemporary specialists.[12]

Paragraphs 15 and 16 briefly set forth the aim and the genre of the *Comedy*; what they have to say could not be more congruent with what we know from the poem itself of Dante's intentions. The aim is frankly didactic, and ethically so: the poem's purpose is to turn its readers aside from misery and lead them to happiness. That is precisely why it is to be categorized as a work of moral philosophy: despite the odd excursion into the speculative realm, the underlying purpose is always practical. The letter is telling us here that the *Comedy*'s concern is not speculation but the promotion of morally and spiritually beneficial action. For Dante is not just a poet but a preacher; and his poem is as practical as any sermon is, or should be. Even though many readers might balk at the notion of Dante's work as Messianic or salvific, many would agree that the Sacred Poem was designed to do far more than astonish and delight aesthetically or instruct intellectually.

The final, exegetical, part of the letter focuses on the very beginning of the *Paradiso*. I do not think it contains anything that would undermine the arguments of those who believe the letter to be genuine. It certainly shows a profound grasp of this portion of the poem. The evident neo-Platonic stamp of the *Paradiso*'s opening canto is fully appreciated and glossed, with apt references to the pseudo-Dionysius and the *Liber de Causis*. And the poet's (apparently) mystical experience in the Empyrean Heaven, tantalizingly pre-announced in *Paradiso* I, is very appropriately addressed, with reference to Augustine, to Bernard of Clairvaux and to his contemporary Richard of St Victor, the twelfth-century mystic *par excellence*. As for the remainder of *Paradiso* I, and indeed the rest of the third *cantica*, this is merely adumbrated in broad outline in the final (thirty-third) paragraph of the letter. For, as Dante has just explained in paragraph 32, he cannot for the moment continue with his exposition because of practical difficulties. He hopes, however, that Can Grande may be so generous as to afford him the opportunity to do so later. This is obviously a request for renewed patronage: the 'practical difficulties' are not defined, but the phrase 'urget enim me rei familiaris angustia' ('for I am hard-pressed by practical difficulties') most likely refers simply to economic circumstances, though Toynbee, following Biagi, was happier to take it as a reference to unspecified family pressures.[13] In fact the very idea that Dante might so demean himself as to mention poverty was anathema to certain critics at the beginning of the last century, notably d'Ovidio, the most trenchant opponent of the letter's authenticity. But this is no more than anachronistic prejudice about how poets (certainly great poets) ought to behave. Besides, we are dealing with a *letter* (paragraph 32 has reverted to the epistolary mode); Dante's second letter, whose authorship is not in dispute, alludes plainly to his poverty (see pp. 82–83). In short this practical, compelling statement of the author's circumstances does not seem to me to suggest the letter is not Dante's. What it does suggest is that it was written outside Verona; if it dates from 1316, this would reflect an interruption in Dante's residence with Can Grande, perhaps the conjectured stay at Lucca, or elsewhere in Tuscany.

Some brief attention will now be paid to the authenticity disputes. D'Ovidio (writing in 1899) could not believe that any part of the Can Grande Letter was Dante's. Moore (1903) set out meticulously and at great length the contrary view.[14] A great many have shared d'Ovidio's doubts, though all but a couple have been prepared to accept the first four (epistolary) paragraphs as genuine, whilst rejecting the rest (the doctrinal and exegetical parts). The debate has at times been immensely complicated, and has involved some of the twentieth century's foremost Dante scholars, not least Mazzoni and Nardi (writing in the 1950s and very early 1960s).[15] Notwithstanding Nardi's learned and characteristically polemical arguments, there was widespread agreement during the 1960s and 1970s that Mazzoni and others had established the case for authenticity. But more recently the controversy has once again erupted: it has been aptly dubbed the 'Vesuvius' of Dante studies.[16] This seems in part to be due to Brugnoli's edition of the letter (finished in 1973, though not published until 1979) which is sceptical (even about the opening paragraphs), and on a number of grounds. The critical debates of the 1980s and early 1990s have been partly stylistic, centring on the use of the *cursus* (the rhythmic cadence character- istic of certain genres of medieval Latin prose) though concern has also been voiced about the letter's content. These matters are acutely surveyed in Hollander's 1993 monograph.[17] This witty, extremely intelligent and well-informed account concentrates on the decade or so after Brugnoli, though it displays an exemplary knowledge too of the earlier debates. Brugnoli's edition is not so much important for textual clarification as for its commentary. This, Hollander shows, is unduly sceptical as to the authenticity question, and, he comes close to saying, disingenuous in its under- representation of Mazzoni's very detailed arguments. Hollander takes to task a formidable array of recent 'Can Grande sceptics': Dronke (1986), Kelly (1989), Hall and Sowell (1989), Barański (1991).[18] He is especially censorious of those who would disprove Dante's authorship of all but the epistolary portion on the grounds that after paragraph 4 the *cursus* is markedly less frequent. Their premises are mistaken, he contends, and their methodology flawed. Despite all this recent work the debate seems set to continue.

### (iv) The *Monarchia*

Apart from work on the *Paradiso*, Dante's principal achievement towards the end of his stay in Verona was the *Monarchia*; with Petrocchi and others, I have opted for the late dating—1317, or even 1318. Almost at the beginning of the treatise Dante gives us a very clear statement of intent (I, ii, 3, ll. 5–10). He proposes to discuss three questions: whether 'monarchy' (i.e. a universal Empire, under one sole ruler) is necessary for the world's well- being; whether the Roman people legitimately took on their historic imperial role; whether the Emperor's authority derives direct from God or is second-hand, deriving from the Pope, God's vicar. These questions will be the subject of the *Monarchia*'s three books. It will be recalled that *Convivio* IV, iv argued for the necessity of a single world ruler in order to secure peace and happiness. This too is the burden of *Monarchia* I, but underpinning the whole argument here is a markedly intellectualist stance. Dante brings in the scope, or end, of mankind as a whole: this, he asserts, is the collective actualization of the human race's capacity for understanding. The full potential cannot of course be realized in any one individual. Mankind collectively must be involved; and since wisdom and knowledge can only be obtained in peace and tranquillity, it is the Emperor's task to ensure these conditions for all. Various supporting arguments follow. The value of unity is stressed: the more society approaches unity, the more it will be stable, well ordered and efficient. There is also the crucial factor of justice: this permits of no dilution or compromise and can therefore truly reside in and be exercised by the universal monarch alone. In the hands of individual rulers, justice is inevitably perverted by greed and lust for power. All political systems other than the monarchical one, whether they be democracies, oligarchies or tyrannies, are twisted systems ('politie oblique'), and promote not freedom but bondage (I, xii, 9, ll. 34–38). Only under a single world ruler, the epitome of justice, will the individual be truly free, able to exercise God's greatest gift to him, as *Paradiso* V has already described Free Will (the famous, or for some infamous, back-reference). Book I ends with a brief confirmation, on historical grounds, of the legitimacy of Empire: the very fact of Christ's incarnation during the reign of a universal monarch sanctioned Augustus' rule.

This leads straight into Book II, an out-and-out *apologia pro Romanis*. It begins, stirringly, with Psalm 2: 'Quare fremuerunt gentes, et populi meditati sunt inania?' ('Why have the nations been convulsed and the people set on vain imaginings?'). The kings and princes of the earth have risen up against the Lord and His anointed one. Whatever the psalmist may have meant by 'Christus eius', Dante's purpose in adapting the psalm here is to refer not to Jesus Christ, but to the Emperor. For, after the theoretical justification of Empire in Book I, Dante now turns to history, as he had done in *Convivio* IV, v. He confesses at once that there had been a time when he doubted the legitimacy of ancient Rome's world dominion, seeing it merely as the result of illicit violence and therefore as usurpation. This was the view expressed most eminently in Augustine's *City of God* (*De civitate Dei*), a view widespread in Dante's time. But further reflection has brought Dante to revise his opinion drastically. He now firmly believes, and will now demonstrate, that everything about Rome's military and political ascendancy bears the mark of God's favour. Consider first the matchless nobility of the Romans, stemming from the exalted Trojan line of

Dardanus, Hector and Aeneas. And what of the miracles that occurred at crucial points in Rome's history? Dante chooses four examples: the rain of shields from the sky in the time of Numa Pompilius; that vigilant goose whose cackling warned that the Gauls were at hand; the timely hailstorm that thwarted Hannibal's forces; and the young girl Clelia's feat in swimming the Tiber and liberating hostages held by Lars Porsenna, the Etruscan King.

Then there are outstanding examples of self-sacrifice in the name of liberty and for the good of the state: Brutus, Mucius Scaevola, the Decii (republican consuls, father, son and grandson, whom Dante here portrays as martyrs: 'ille sacratissime victime'—II, v, 15, l. 83), and above all Cato the Younger, Julius Caesar's heroic opponent. Although Rome's ultimate destiny was Empire, there is no opposition here between the republican and imperial epochs: Rome's virtue shines throughout both. And when the Roman Empire did finally come about, through God's will, it had no genuine predecessors or rivals: for all their military successes, Ninus the Assyrian, Vesoges the Egyptian, the Persian kings Cyrus and Xerxes, even Alexander the Great of Macedon only achieved partial sovereignty. The Romans alone held sway over all the world.

Book II's final chapter (xi) is intended to clinch all the preceding points by focusing on the historical conjunction of Christ's life on earth and the universal sovereignty and jurisdiction of Rome. The significance of His birth under Augustus has already been touched on (*Mon.* I, xvi, 1–2, ll. 1–14; cf. *Conv.* IV, v, 3–8). Now His death too is powerfully brought into the discussion. For Christ's crucifixion in the reign of Tiberius was a punishment for the sins of mankind, and had He suffered under an illegitimate authority His death would have been nothing more than violent injury, as opposed to punishment. But the Roman Emperor's authority was lawful, and moreover his jurisdiction extended over all men; had Christ died under a lesser monarch, the atonement would have been invalid, for He bore the sins of us all. The crucifixion, Dante is here asserting, was Rome's highest achievement and the supreme proof of its legitimacy. The negative side of the crucifixion, which under another aspect is an outrage against the Godhead, was entirely the fault of the Jews.

*Monarchia* III is quite different from the preceding books: whereas Book I has a series of philosophical arguments, and II is primarily historical (with some theology at the end), III addresses the relationship between Church and State in theological terms. Its theme and arguments are at no point adumbrated in the *Convivio*. The opening is combative: once again we begin with a dramatic biblical quotation, telling of Daniel's survival in the lions' den. The relevance of this becomes clear when Dante declares his intention to go into the arena and fight for truth. He will champion the true doctrine of the parallel yet independent authority of Pope and Emperor, each in his own discrete sphere. The enemies of this truth, the papalist promulgators of error, are of three kinds. First, there is the Pope himself, and other churchmen who 'perhaps' out of excessive zeal for Peter's keys ('zelo *fortasse* clavium'—III, iii, 7, ll. 23–24) have gone astray. Second, and far more reprehensible, are an undefined group (probably certain secular rulers) whose support for the Papacy is rooted in greed; they claim to be true sons of the Church, but their real father is the devil. Finally, there are the decretalists, those canon lawyers who, ignorant of philosophy and theology, perversely expound not the Scriptures but miscellaneous papal decrees, all in the cause of the popes' claims to power. They are beneath contempt and should be ejected from the arena: 'de presenti gignasio totaliter excludantur' (III, iii, 11, ll. 42–43).

Dante devotes most of Book III (Chapters iv–ix) to those papalist arguments based on Scripture. His examples are from both Old and New Testaments, and all are commonplaces of the hierocratic or papalist tradition. They involve a figurative meaning allegedly latent in the biblical texts. Now Dante has no quarrel with this kind of exegesis *per se*; what he disputes are the particular interpretations in question. The first he discusses is the most famous of all: the so-called argument of the two luminaries (see p. 187). Genesis 1.16 tells how God created the sun and the moon, and many had sought to draw out from that text an analogy with the respective source and status of imperial power: just as the moon is the lesser luminary, deriving its light from the sun, so the Emperor derives his authority from the Pope. This analogy probably goes back to a papal letter of Innocent III (30 October 1198). But although Dante had earlier accepted it in his fifth and sixth letters, he will have none of it now. In the first place it would be simply inappropriate for the sun and moon to have any reference to the Pope and the Emperor: God created them on the fourth day, whereas man did not make his appearance till Day Six. And even then he started off in a state of innocence; it was only because of his subsequent sin that the

202

Papacy and the Empire were necessary at all. For both these institutions are remedies against the sickness of sin: 'remedia contra infirmitatem peccati' (III, iv, 14, ll. 70–71). But Dante has not yet finished. On astronomical grounds he denies the moon's dependence on the sun: its very being and motion are quite independent of the greater luminary, and even though much of its light is derived from the sun's, it also generates some light of its own (so Dante believed). And in any case, the analogy between light and authority is just wrong. All the hierocrats' other Scriptural arguments are then refuted by Dante, either on the grounds of some inherent defect, or because in his view the texts are not susceptible of, nor were intended to have, an allegorical meaning. Augustine, after all, had warned against trying to subject every single line of the Bible to this kind of treatment.[19]

Chapter X turns to the papalists' use of historical events, as distinct from hidden biblical messages. While mention is made of Charlemagne's coronation by Pope Leo III (Dante mistakenly says Adrian I) the chief focus here is on the Donation of Constantine. It was generally believed in the Middle Ages that the Emperor Constantine, having been cured of leprosy by Pope Sylvester I, and having transferred the seat of Empire from Rome to Constantinople, delegated all temporal power in the west, and more particularly in Italy, to Sylvester. And to Sylvester's successors. The Donation was to become the rock upon which the papalists erected their false notion of the Church. But the document attesting Constantine's gift was a forgery (probably concocted some 500 years after his death) though this was not to be known until the fifteenth century; Dante, like his adversaries, thought it to be genuine. In his view Constantine, though well intentioned, had made a terrible mistake, the source of untold woe, as is very clear from the *Inferno* (XIX, 115–17). And here in the *Monarchia* the very validity of Constantine's action is denied: no emperor has the right to delegate to another man, even a pope, power and jurisdiction that reside in their entirety in him alone. By transferring a part of his authority Constantine was sundering the universal Empire, which ought to be indivisible, as seamless as Christ's garment which even the Roman soldiers dared not divide.[20] And equally the Church has no right to accept temporal power or wealth. Did not Christ expressly forbid the apostles to own gold and silver (Matthew 10.9–10)? Distributing alms to the poor is quite another matter.

Having countered the hierocratic arguments, Dante sets out his own view in the *Monarchia*'s closing chapters. This amounts to a very firm assertion of the separate and independent jurisdiction of Pope and Emperor. The role of each is to promote the attainment of two quite distinct human goals. For man, being both body and soul, holds a unique place in the scheme of things, straddling, so to speak, the material and spiritual realms, the corruptible and the incorruptible: 'homo solus in entibus tenet medium corruptibilium et incorruptibilium' (III, xv, 3, ll. 9–10). Therefore Providence has assigned two ends, or goals, for mankind: the beatitude of this earthly life (symbolized in the Earthly Paradise) and the beatitude of eternal life, consisting in the vision of God. By the former Dante does not imply hedonism or self-indulgence: so far from recommending the pleasures of the senses, he is referring to the practice of the moral and intellectual virtues. And the second, heavenly beatitude is attained through the theological virtues: Faith, Hope and Charity. God has appointed two guides for us: the Emperor's role is to lead us towards temporal happiness, in accordance with the teachings of philosophy ('secundum phylosophica documenta'—III, xv, 10, l.49), whilst the Pope's is to direct us towards eternal life, according to the truths of revelation. Of course temporal and eternal happiness are not on an equal footing; indeed earthly beatitude 'in some sense' ('quodammodo') is geared to that of the afterlife. That is why in the very last sentence of the *Monarchia* Dante says that the Emperor should have a certain reverence towards the Pope, the kind of reverence that a first-born son ought to show to his father; so that, illuminated by paternal grace, he may the more effectively enlighten the world. The precise import of these lines is unclear. Some have seen in them a palinode, or retraction of Dante's earlier position; yet it seems to me that they by no means diminish the central contention of Book III, that the Emperor's power comes direct from God, and is therefore not subordinate to the Pope's.[21]

There is no doubt that the *Monarchia*, whilst in one sense promoting an ideal world order with relevance for all of human history to come, is also a polemical contribution to contemporary debate, a debate sharpened of course by events, not least Henry VII's failed enterprise and the policies of Clement V and John XXII. And it was not long before the treatise fell foul of churchmen. It is perhaps curious that it was not so much the *Comedy*, with its popes in Hell, that provoked ecclesiastical wrath, as this forthright refutation of papal suprematism. The earliest, and most famous, attack on the *Monarchia* is by a Dominican, Guido Vernani. It dates from the late 1320s and is addressed to Graziolo de' Bambaglioli, Chancellor of the Commune of Bologna, and the author of one of the very earliest commentaries on the *Divine Comedy*. Vernani's distinctly acerbic comments appeared during a time of heightened tension between Church and Empire: John XXII was engaged in a bitter struggle with Emperor Lewis IV ('the Bavarian'), protector of Ghibellines and the radical Franciscan spirituals alike, and champion of the anti-Pope 'Nicholas V'. Lewis' chief propagandist was Marsilius of Padua, whose *Defensor Pacis* (1324) had attacked the Church's claims to temporal power in terms that went far beyond anything to be found in the *Monarchia*. Vernani's *De reprobatione Monarchiae Dantis* has to be seen in this historical context. Whilst he was clearly concerned to refute Dante's antipapalist political theory and his exaltation of the Emperor, he also strongly attacked his view of human nature, on specific theological grounds. Here two of Dante's chapters are singled out. I, iii had argued that mankind's intellectual potential is not fully actualized in any one person. It had also referred to Averroes' commentary on the Aristotelian *De Anima*. Vernani pounced. Dante was here subscribing to the very worst of errors: the denial of a personal, immortal soul possessed by each of us. (This was the most notorious notion of Averroes and of his followers in the medieval Christian west.) But although Dante finds an honourable place for Averroes in *Inferno* IV—the Limbo of the great ancient, and medieval, non-Christians—he is no Averroist. The error of monopsychism, which holds that there is one collective soul for the whole species, is respectfully but firmly rejected in the *Purgatorio* (XXV, 61–66). Although the chronology I have adopted in this study (the *Purgatorio* predating the *Monarchia)* may be wrong, that is irrelevant apropos of Vernani. His attack on Dante's 'Averroism' is mistaken; the *Monarchia* text simply does not say what he claims it does.[22]

Vernani's other chief criticism is directed against Dante's closing chapter. It is the dualism, the assertion that God has ordained for us two goals (in scholastic parlance two 'final causes') that he cannot accept. For, he objects, God has assigned one end alone to us, and that is the eternal happiness of heaven. However elevated temporal happiness may be, it never suffices to satisfy man's desire. However much the virtues may be involved, their exercise here on earth is directed to a greater purpose hereafter. There simply is no final cause for us intrinsic to and attainable in our earthly lives. So Vernani is quite unimpressed by the 'quodammodo' in Dante's closing sentence: even a somehow subordinate temporal goal is inadmissible.[23] The *Monarchia* was in fact condemned to be burnt in 1329 by Cardinal Bertrand de Pouget, John XXII's legate in Lombardy. It continued to attract hostility during the fourteenth century, and when at the time of the Counter-Reformation the Church first drew up a formal Index of banned books, the *Monarchia* was included: it appears in Paul IV's Index of 1559 and again in the Council of Trent's (1564). 1559 in fact saw the first printed edition of Dante's treatise, but this was at Basel—Protestant territory. The *Monarchia* was removed from the Index only in 1881.

Dante probably left Verona in 1318. The reasons for his departure are obscure, but there may have been growing tensions between him and some of Can Grande's courtiers and soldiers, perhaps even with Can Grande himself. There is more than a hint of this in several fourteenth-century sources.[24] Verona was a far from uncivilized city; indeed while Dante was there pre-humanists such as Benzo d'Alessandria (who later became Can Grande's chancellor) were active. And of course Can Grande himself was a young man of great intelligence and artistic appreciation. At the same time though, he seems to have had a coarse sense of humour, something which Dante did not share. As Anderson puts it 'Can Grande, as a great warlord, had to entertain his soldiers and he shared their roughest pleasures'.[25] Dante's proud, aloof character may well have jarred with the frivolity and clowning of the court. On the other side, so to speak, Dante may have been attracted by the prospect of a move to Ravenna, where Guido Novello's smaller and quieter court included a number of intellectuals and men of letters. Whatever Dante's reasons, he left Can Grande, with much work still to be done on the *Paradiso*. Petrocchi suggests that roughly half of the final *cantica* was finished by 1318, and more precisely that the high praise of Can Grande in Cacciaguida's Canto XVII speech may be seen as a grateful tribute to Dante's benefactor as he was about to leave for his final place of asylum.[26]

# 11

# Ravenna
## (1318–1321)

Ravenna seems to have been the most intellectually congenial and stimulating environment of Dante's exile. Not that he was dependent at this stage—if he ever was—on the stimuli of others around him. What he needed now above all was tranquillity, for the completion of the Sacred Poem. And this Guido Novello was able to provide. Indeed, if Dante did arrive at his court in 1318, more than two years were to elapse before any serious political or military crisis threatened Ravenna.

But external problems apart, Dante's final years, as a guest of Guido, seem to have been relatively untroubled; his two pastoral Eclogues depict an atmosphere of personal calm and friendship that transcends and pierces through literary convention. Guido himself was a modest vernacular poet, and a man of roughly Dante's own age: an ageing friend and patron. And he did tend to stay put in Ravenna (whereas the young Can Grande's military campaigns meant he was often away from his court and his protégés). There is every reason to suppose Guido wanted Dante to finish the *Comedy* under his patronage and protection. It is true that in the last year of his life (with the *Paradiso* complete, or all but so) Dante acted in a diplomatic capacity for his patron, and he may have done so previously on an *ad hoc* basis. But he was never a paid employee of Guido Novello, no more than he was in any formal sense (whether or not stipendiary) a teacher of rhetoric at the Ravenna *studium* (university). It is only on the basis of remarks by Boccaccio (and one or two other fourteenth-century sources) that we have the legend of Dante the professor at Ravenna.[1] Despite his phenomenal powers of mental concentration, his ability to work at one and the same time on diverse tasks, often in the most rebarbative circumstances, he would surely now more than ever have welcomed peace and quiet; and that is what Guido would have sought for him.

Having said this, in no sense was Dante kept in isolation. Whilst not a university teacher, he would undoubtedly have had the opportunity to enlighten other members of Guido's circle on all manner of subjects: the traditional picture of a small but devoted group (lawyers, physicians and other educated men) centred around the poet whose *Inferno* and *Purgatorio* were now becoming known seems a highly plausible one. Who were these people? A few names have come down to us: Dino Perini, another Florentine exile, much younger than Dante; Fiduccio de' Milotti, another Tuscan, and a medical man; Guido Vacchetta, also a physician; Pier Giardini, a lawyer; Bernardino Canaccio, a Bolognese Ghibelline whom Dante may first have met at Can Grande's court; Menghino Mezzani, a lawyer and poet whose literary correspondents included Antonio da Ferrara and Petrarch himself.[2]

Dante was also joined in his final place of exile by several members of his immediate family. His children Pietro, Iacopo and Antonia were there, and his wife Gemma may have been (on this last point there is no compelling evidence either way). Pietro and Iacopo had almost certainly already been reunited with their father after his 1302 banishment, perhaps in several different cities. Lucca has been suggested and both sons were very probably in Verona at some time during Dante's stay with Can Grande. Both had close and enduring ties with that city: Can Grande gave financial assistance to help them continue their studies; after Dante's death Pietro pursued a successful judicial career there; and Iacopo enjoyed the financial advantages of a canonry and other ecclesiastical benefices in Verona. While in Ravenna Pietro at least enjoyed church preferment there, though he failed to discharge all his obligations. On 4 January 1321 a local ecclesiastical court excommunicated him, and other holders of benefices, for non-payment (despite several requests) of dues owed to the papal legate Bertrand de Pouget, the same man who eight years later was to order the *Monarchia* to be burnt. Dante's daughter Antonia was also involved, and rather more seriously, in Ravenna's religious life: it is generally held that she became a nun at the convent of Santo Stefano degli Ulivi. The name she took was Beatrice.

Dante's literary output while at Ravenna includes two minor works, both in Latin, which while overshadowed by the *Paradiso*, are both of interest.

## (i) The *Quaestio de aqua et terra*

Also known as the *De situ et forma aque et terre*, this short Latin prose work is a scholarly disquisition upon a problem of geography and cosmology. The 'Quaestio' of the title means rather more than the English 'question' might suggest; it is really short for *Quaestio disputata*, the 'disputed question' that is a familiar feature of medieval scholasticism, being typically an elaborated and formalized written account of what had originated as a verbal debate.[3] Indeed, Dante tells us that while on a visit to Mantua (the date and purpose of which are unknown) he heard a number of arguments concerning the relative position of the spheres of earth and water in our sublunary world. In his view, the matter had not been satisfactorily resolved, and the arguments were in fact fallacious. The purpose of the *Quaestio* is to provide a detailed refutation of them, together with a definitive solution. It is probably an *ad hoc* work, though a consummately eloquent and assured one. It was read aloud by Dante himself in Verona, in the little church of Sant' Elena on Sunday 20 January 1320—it may be that Dante had recently left Mantua, pausing awhile in the city that was his *primo rifugio e ostello* (first refuge and lodging) before returning to Ravenna. Although Can Grande is mentioned at the end of the *Quaestio* with great reverence, it is not known whether he was present that day in Sant' Elena. But Dante certainly had a good audience—virtually all the *clerus* of Verona, by which is meant not the clergy but the intelligentsia, whether priests and religious, or laity.

The point at issue arises from a geographical anomaly. For all educated men of Dante's age the universe was a series of concentric spheres, with the earth at its centre. And the earth moreover consisted of the four elemental spheres of fire, air, water and, in a more restricted sense, earth, the last being the lowest, the closest to the centre. The anomaly arose from the fact that at some points on the globe's surface the sphere of earth (dry land, in fact) projects above the sea. This posed something of a threat to the orderly medieval cosmos. The precise question debated at Mantua was whether in any part of the globe the ocean's surface is higher than the excrescent land. Dante says he had heard a number of arguments to the effect that it was; some of these are unworthy of discussion, but he sets out five of the better ones, all of which he proceeds to demolish, using the methods of medieval dialectic with confidence and some satisfaction. No, he concludes, the sea is not at any point higher than dry land: in the 'quarta habitabilis' (the 'habitable quarter', all of it in the northern hemisphere) the earth has indeed risen above the entire sphere of water, not just about the surface of the local sea. But how? It had been suggested that the spheres of earth and water had two different centres, but this Dante cannot support, for it would introduce a fundamental and unacceptable asymmetry. For Dante both these elemental spheres, like all the others outside them, elemental, planetary and stellar, have one centre, the very centre of the universe. And most of the sphere of earth, three-quarters of it, does lie under that of water. Yet it was part of Nature's purpose that there should be a mingling, as distinct from a strict separation of these two elements, so that all possibilities might be actualized: hence the emergence of the dry land, without which animal and human life—all part of the divine plan—would have been impossible. Dante's explanation of the land's emergence is cosmological: he attributes it to the influence of the Eighth Heaven, which contains the Fixed Stars. These differ in magnitude and power, and some of them have 'drawn out' the land from beneath the ocean's surface. (This is quite a different account, of course, from that of the *Inferno* (XXXIV, 121–26), an eminently theological one according to which the fall of rebellious Lucifer from Heaven to the depths of Hell caused the land originally in the southern hemisphere to 'flee' from him, emerging on the opposite side of the globe.)

The *Quaestio* is by no means as arid as is sometimes maintained. It is certainly marginal to Dante's work as a whole (though by no means unrelated to it[4]), yet it bears witness to a fascination with the structure of the world, allied with a mastery of the natural sciences of his time, that is quite typical of him. And the tone of the closing lines (which make deliberate use of the *cursus* so as to heighten the style, once the strictly scientific business is done with) is utterly Dantean. 'I, Dante Alighieri,' he says, 'the least among philosophers ('phylosophorum minimus'[5]) have resolved this question in the fair city of Verona in the presence of nearly all its men of learning—save a few, over-endowed with charity and humility, who have felt unable to attend' (a typically pungent aside). And the dispute has taken place in the reign of Can Grande della Scala, that unconquered Lord (his first military setback, at the hands of the Paduans, occurred only in August 1320) who wields power in the name of the sacrosanct Roman Empire. This phrase refers to Can Grande's status as imperial vicar in Verona and Vicenza, originally bestowed on him by Henry VII and confirmed in 1317 by Frederick of Austria, one of the rivals for the imperial throne. Dante's insistence on this title here probably has a polemical antipapal thrust, given that Pope John XXII had declared all such imperial appointments null and void.[6]

## (ii) The *Eclogues*

Perhaps the last poetry Dante wrote was not in Italian but in Latin. This would be his second Eclogue to Giovanni del Virgilio, the closing poem in a four-stage exchange that may have started as early as the beginning of 1319 and finished as late as the summer of 1321. Giovanni (*Magister Ioannes*) held the only Chair of (Latin) Poetry at Bologna University, an accomplished classicist in an ambience that was predominantly jurisprudential. Indeed the 'del Virgilio' is almost surely a sobriquet, a nickname signifying his devotion to and mastery of the classical Virgil's works. He is commonly referred to as a pre- (or proto-) humanist, and had close links with a new kind of classicism centred on Padua: the 'movement' founded by Lovato Lovati (died 1309) and linked above all with the name of Albertino Mussato, whom Giovanni greatly revered. Italian Humanism, that resurgence of interest in classical literature, which not only sought to recover the values of antiquity but was also a potent literary catalyst, is associated in its beginnings with Petrarch especially. Yet even before him the first stirrings of a new kind of engagement with the ancient world are detectable. Giovanni del Virgilio was part of this. That is why he wrote to Dante in Ravenna. For in his Latin verse letter 'Pyeridum vox alma' ('Sacred voice of the Muses') he respectfully chides Dante for confining his astounding and novel poetic talent to the vernacular. Giovanni refers specifically to all three realms of the *Comedy* (though at this stage he may not have read any of the *Paradiso*): Dante has plumbed the hellish depths, brought his penitents through the healing forgetfulness of Lethe, and soared to the highest heaven with the blessed.

These are momentous themes, and to Giovanni's mind the choice of Italian as a medium is bizarre. In the first place the 'vulgus' or 'gens idiota' (those who are in fact literate but un-Latinate) simply

211

cannot appreciate such things: even Plato had found it difficult to extract from the heavenly spheres their secrets. Worse still, the vernacular can offer no protection from the masses, with the result that bits of the sublime poem end up being garbled by some unkempt comedian at street corners! In any case scholars would spurn the vernacular, even if did not have the fault of variety. And as for Dante's own literary heroes among the ancients, that quintet who welcomed him in Limbo, and the man he is now following heavenwards (Statius)—none of them wrote in the language of the marketplace. Moreover, Giovanni complains, Dante is depriving the learned of so much. He does not have the impertinence to suggest Dante translate the *Comedy* into Latin, but he does long for a new epic Latin poem. There are plenty of excitingly topical themes to hand, and Dante alone could do justice to them. Why not tackle Henry VII, that 'Iovis armiger' (weapon-bearer of Jupiter) now ascended to the heavens? Or Uguccione, who recently vanquished the Tuscan Guelphs? Or Can Grande with his successes against Padua? Even more exciting perhaps, and certainly topical, is Giovanni's final suggestion: the struggle between King Robert and the Ghibelline Visconti of Milan for possession of Genoa. (The spectacular seven-month blockade of that port, beginning in July 1318, was compared by Villani to the siege of Troy.[7]) If he were to write such a poem, or poems, Dante's fame would transcend Italian parochialism and reach the four corners of the world (provided of course that he did write in Latin). And talking of fame, surely Dante does not intend to content himself with the judgement of the crowd. Let him come to learned Bologna, where it would be a pleasure for Giovanni to present him to the scholars, his brow adorned with the scented laurel. It would be just like a herald preceding a triumphant general. In other words, and not unduly anachronistic ones, the Professor is offering himself in the role of Public Orator, presenting Dante for an honorary degree. Giovanni's letter ends by admitting he is a mere goose cackling to a swan, but he hopes for a positive response.

Dante, though still intensely preoccupied with the *Paradiso*, was happy to rise to Giovanni's challenge—not to come to Bologna however, but at least to reply. And so we have the first Dantean Eclogue. This reply to Giovanni del Virgilio must have surprised his Bolognese admirer as much as it still does, or should do, today. For Dante did not, fortunately, embark on a Latin epic: he chose instead a bucolic eclogue, a poem of a kind that was simply not being written then in Italy, or anywhere else, having practically fallen into desuetude since antiquity. Mussato had recently revived classical tragedy, after the manner of Seneca: Dante in his reply to Giovanni wittily revives the eclogue, that idyllic, and usually pastoral, literary form whose veneer of shepherds and their shepherdly concerns typically concealed a moral or socio-political message. Dante's message here will be a literary one. He presents himself and his friends, and Giovanni too, as shepherds; all the pastoral names, most of which can be related with some confidence to real individuals, are taken from Virgil's *Eclogues*. Dante is Tityrus (just as Virgil styled himself in his first Eclogue), Dino Perini is Meliboeus and Giovanni is Mopsus. Tityrus and Meliboeus find themselves under an oak tree. Meliboeus is anxious to know the contents of Mopsus' letter. At first Tityrus is laughingly (though affectionately) dismissive: 'Get back to your goats!' is roughly his advice. Perini, it seems, was out of his depth in the area of Latin poetry. But when pressed further, Tityrus explains: Mopsus, a long-standing devotee of the Muses, wants to honour him as a poet, and in Bologna. When Meliboeus suggests he accept the invitation (why remain an uncrowned rustic recluse?) Tityrus declines, declaring that he hopes still to receive the laurel, but in Florence, once the *Paradiso* is finished. In the meantime, not wishing to be discourteous to Mopsus, he will send him a present, something that might change his view of the vernacular. For Tityrus has a favourite ewe, its udders overflowing with milk; it is a lone creature, not part of any flock, not confined in any sheep-pen. It always comes spontaneously to be milked, and Tityrus will send ten pails of its milk ('decem vascula') to Mopsus. The general view, well founded surely, is that Dante is here referring to ten cantos of the *Paradiso*. What is said figuratively of the 'favourite ewe' aptly describes the final *cantica*: that it stands apart from other poetry is obvious; and rich and prompt inspiration is by no means at odds with subsequent arduous craftsmanship, so the famous *Paradiso* line (XXV, 3) telling how Dante has become wasted with writing the *Comedy* presents no obstacle to this interpretation.

Dante's poem was probably written in the summer of 1319 and it seems that the following spring he received Giovanni del Virgilio's reply. This is another eclogue, in which Tityrus is praised for relaunching the bucolic genre; he is addressed as a divine old man ('divine senex'), a second Virgil, or even Virgil himself ('if we are to believe Pythagoras' doctrine' of the transmigration of souls, i.e. re-incarnation). The suggestion of new Latin epic poetry is now dropped, but Mopsus reiterates the invitation to come to Bologna. Not, however, to be crowned, but simply so that Mopsus and his associates may be honoured and instructed by so illustrious a presence. As for the poetic laurel, Mopsus fully understands Tityrus' desire to receive it in his native city and rebukes the Florentines for their ingratitude towards him. But meanwhile, why does Tityrus not come and visit Mopsus? They can make poetry together, the host albeit playing a subsidiary part. The hospitality of Mopsus' home and of the Bolognese *studium* awaits him; Giovanni proceeds to paint an alluringly idyllic picture of his city, drawing heavily on Virgil's second Eclogue (by contrast, Dante's bucolic poem, apart from the proper names, is far more original).

But Mopsus knows his invitation may be unrealistic: after all, the urbane and congenial Iollas (i.e. Guido Novello) may not let Tityrus go. Yet such is Mopsus' admiring affection that he still hopes. If Tityrus spurns his offer, however, he will have to slake his thirst in the Musone (a stream in Padua). What exactly Giovanni means here has been the subject of some debate. A punning allusion to Albertino Mussato seems more than likely, in which case Giovanni is saying he will offer friendship and esteem to his other contemporary hero. Whether this means that he intends literally to go to Padua is doubtful. In fact Mussato had arrived in Bologna in September 1319, in a political role. Padua was now threatened more than ever by Can Grande, and Mussato and others embarked upon a series of diplomatic missions designed to elicit support from Guelph Bologna, Florence and Siena against the great Ghibelline warlord. Wicksteed and Gardner thought Giovanni was proposing a meeting with Mussato, were Dante to accept the Bologna invitation.[8] Apart from textual difficulties, this interpretation seems odd: would it have been appropriate to arrange an encounter between Dante and a fierce opponent of Can Grande? After all, there is no evidence of any diminution in Dante's esteem for Can Grande, nor of any wavering in his Ghibelline sympathies.

Dante's reply, the final poem in the exchange, may have appeared more than a year after he received Giovanni's second piece—at least that is what a gloss in the famous Laurentian manuscript, most of which is in Boccaccio's own hand, tells us.[9] And it may well be that throughout 1320 and beyond Dante was bent on finishing the *Paradiso*, to the exclusion of all else—hence the delay. But he did in due course find time to reply to Giovanni, in an eclogue of ninety-seven lines, exactly the same number (and not fortuitously) as in Giovanni's poem. The chief character in this eclogue is the shepherd Alphesiboeus (apparently Milotti the medic). Leaning on his crook, he declares that no paradox surprises him as much as does Mopsus' choice of abode: a cave in Sicily, under volcanic Etna, the lair of the Cyclops. Alphesiboeus, by figuratively describing Bologna in these terms, is undermining in advance the idyll fashioned by Giovanni in his second poem. 'In advance', because according to Dante's fiction young Meliboeus at this point turns up armed with a rustic reed—an instrument which then miraculously recites, by itself, all ninety-seven verses from Bologna. The senior shepherds listen. Alphesiboeus then praises Tityrus in the most compelling terms: surely the venerable and fortunate old man will not abandon the pastures and flocks of Ravenna. The mountains and rivers and nymphs, and all the rest, would weep: Tityrus must not deprive them of his immortal name. In reply Tityrus reassures them, adding however that he would not be averse simply to paying Mopsus a visit; it is the presence of Polyphemus that deters him. If 'Polyphemus', the brutal one-eyed cave-dweller of classical myth, is meant to signify some tyrannical individual associated with Bologna (and not all critics agree that this is so[10]), then there would seem to be two especially plausible candidates: King Robert and Fulcieri da Calboli. It should be stressed that Bologna, always a Guelph city, was by now very staunchly so. Its equivalent of the Florentine Blacks had been in power since 1306, and at the time of Dante's exchange with Giovanni, the links with Robert of Naples were particularly close. His representative there in 1318–19 was none other than Ranieri di Zaccaria, who had sentenced Dante and his sons to decapitation in 1315. Fulcieri da Calboli was elected *capitano del popolo* of Bologna early in 1321 (his term of office spanned the second half of that year) and he was another veritable *bête noire* for Dante. In 1303, when *podestà* of Florence, he had acted with egregious cruelty towards those alleged to be in collusion with the White exiles: his repression is grimly recalled in the *Purgatorio* (XIV, 58–66). If Dante's second Eclogue is as late as 1321, Polyphemus could be a topical allusion to Fulcieri, a man unlikely to welcome the renowned Ghibelline sympathizer and friend of Can Grande. In any event, Tityrus will not be going to Bologna, to the great relief of his friends, and the smiling approbation of Iollas who, unseen, has overheard the whole conversation.

Dante's two Eclogues are of undoubted intrinsic interest, not least for their charm and literary expertise. Wicksteed and Gardner were no doubt exaggerating when they described the first poem as 'surely one of the most precious and revealing documents which ever threw light on the character of a great man',[11] but they certainly had a point. For the real importance of both Eclogues lies in what they have to tell us about Dante in Ravenna, how he saw himself and his art—both what he had achieved and what he still had to do. They throw some light, albeit tangential, upon Guido Novello and Dante's circle, but more importantly they re-affirm Dante's supreme self-confidence as an artist. Of course he can turn his hand to Latin poetry, and he does so here with courtesy as well as enthusiasm and skill; yet not the least of his purposes in so doing is to proclaim his resolve to stand by the Sacred Poem and thus to stand by the vernacular in its highest form yet achieved.

### (iii) The Mission to Venice; Dante's Death

The final episode in Dante's life was not literary but diplomatic. Early in August 1321, or perhaps at the end of July, he took part in an embassy sent by Guido Novello to the Republic of Venice, Ravenna's powerful maritime neighbour to the north. Tension between the two cities had been mounting (because of a dispute over customs dues) and the Adriatic had witnessed several clashes, in which Ravenna's ships had done rather well. Venice was not prepared to put up with this, and by the summer all-out conflict threatened. It was to avert this that Guido despatched his ambassadors. Dante's precise role in the negotiations is tantalizingly obscure. Petrocchi does not rule out the possibility that he had no specific brief from his patron, Guido's purpose being simply to include in the peacemaking embassy a by now respected personage, whose mere presence (even passive) would bolster its *bona fides*.[12] That may be. Certainly we know nothing of what Dante may have said, and indeed he may have said nothing—nothing at all, if Filippo Villani is to be believed.[13] Modern *Dantisti* choose not to believe him, but his tale is well worth a mention. Writing at the very end of the fourteenth century, Filippo (grandson of the chronicler Giovanni Villani) tells us that Dante was scheduled to speak on behalf of Ravenna, but the Venetians would not allow him to say a word, so alarmed were they at the prospect of his eloquence. More than that, they would not let him return to Ravenna by sea, lest he should subvert their admiral of the fleet! So he was forced to make part of the return journey overland. And so, in the marshy malarial terrain *en route*, he contracted his final malaise. Villani's account at once affirms Dante's great reputation as an orator, and seeks to denigrate the Venetians, even implicating them in his death. Improbable perhaps, but nonetheless well invented. Certainly Dante fell ill, and fatally so, on his way to Venice, or in Venice, or on his way back. A document dated 20 October states that ambassadors from Ravenna were on that day in Venice. They might have stayed there since July/August (Dante returning early because of his illness) or there might have been two separate embassies on behalf of Guido Novello. But in any case by 20 October Dante had been dead for over a month. Nothing whatever is known of the last few weeks of his life. The most widely accepted date for his death is 14 September, the Feast of the Exaltation of the Holy Cross. However, the two contemporary epitaphs by Giovanni del Virgilio and Menghino Mezzano have 13 September, and it may be that Dante died on the evening of that day.[14] It does not seem to matter much: the fact is that in September 1321 one of the greatest men who ever lived died.

Dante was buried with splendid ceremonial in Ravenna's Franciscan Church of San Pier Maggiore (subsequently dedicated to St Francis himself), the laurel crown finally upon his brow. It has often been suggested that Guido Novello had intended for some time to confer this great poetic honour upon Dante, once the *Paradiso* was completed, and had perhaps delayed doing so until the Venetian crisis had been resolved.[15] Be that as it may, he crowned him now in death and delivered the funeral oration, which alas does not survive but which Boccaccio described as 'ornato' and 'esquisito'.[16] He also planned to erect a fine tomb for Dante and invited a number of poets to compose epitaphs to be inscribed upon it. Unfortunately Guido was deposed by his cousin (in September 1322) and his project was never carried out. Dante's sarcophagus now stands in a small purpose-built neo-classical chapel dating from the late eighteenth century. The inscription on the tomb,

217

beginning 'Jura Monarchiae superos Phlegetonta lacusque lustrando cecini' ('The righteousness of Empire, the heavens, the lakes of Hell—these have I probed in my song') was long thought to have been composed by Dante himself (most unlikely).[17] By far the most famous, and interesting, epitaph is Giovanni del Virgilio's (which at no time, it seems, was ever inscribed on the sarcophagus). Giovanni pays glowing tribute to Dante's great learning and achievements both in Italian and Latin, specifically referring to the *Comedy*, the *Monarchia* and the *Eclogues*—these last, he notes with a kind of sad satisfaction, were what Dante had most recently turned to, only to be cut off by death.[18] His fame has reached the ends of the earth, and his appeal is to the learned and the masses alike. Ravenna's compassionate welcome is contrasted with the ingratitude of Florence. The epitaph begins 'Theologus Dantes, nullius dogmatis expers', and may be translated thus:

> Here lies the theologian Dante, well versed in every branch of learning that philosophy may nurture in her shining bosom, the glory of the Muses, and an author loved by the unlearned: with his fame he strikes both poles. It is he who has assigned the dead to their places and defined the roles of the twin swords [i.e. the Empire and the Papacy] and this both in Italian and Latin ('laicis rhetorisque modis'). Most recently he was playing his Pierian pipes in the pastures; but envious Atropos, alas, cut short that joyous work. Ungrateful Florence, a cruel fatherland, rewarded her bard with the bitter fruit of exile; but compassionate Ravenna is glad to have received him in the bosom of Guido Novello, its revered leader. In the year of Our Lord one thousand three hundred and thrice seven, on the Ides of September, then did he return to his stars.

So Dante was laid to rest in Ravenna, and there he remains. But it was not very long before the Florentines tried to reclaim his bones; their vain attempts to do so, albeit very sporadic, lasted till 1864.[19] Towards the end of the fourteenth century Dante's prestige had grown immensely and the *Comedy* was being read aloud and glossed just like a sacred text in Bologna, Pisa and numerous other cities, not least Florence itself. The Florentines were now anxious to atone for their past ingratitude and injustice; a letter of 1378 from the Veronese Chancellor to a friend in Ravenna indicates that they had already asked the Ravennese for Dante's remains, but to no avail. In 1396 Florence initiated an ambitious, though abortive, project for monuments in the Duomo to five of its greatest scholars and *litterati*: Francesco d'Accorso (the famous jurist who, incidentally, is found among the sodomites of *Inferno* XV); Zanobi da Strada (crowned poet laureate in 1356); Petrarch; Boccaccio; and Dante. None of these was buried in Florence, and the plan was to try to recover their bones. But the whole project was abandoned, in Dante's case presumably because Ravenna's proud determination to hold on to the remains of its most illustrious guest was unabated.

And so it continued. In 1428 or early 1429 Leonardo Alighieri, the poet's great-grandson, visited Florence together with certain other gentlemen of Verona, and was honourably received by Bruni, the Florentine Chancellor. This visit may have prompted a fresh attempt by the Florentine Signoria, in 1429, to have Dante reinterred in his native city. But Obizzo da Polenta, the ruler of Ravenna, would have none of it. Prospects seemed brighter in the 1470s when Bernardo Bembo (father of the famous literary scholar Pietro) was Venetian ambassador to Florence. A letter of 1476 suggests that he had promised Lorenzo the Magnificent to help the Florentines regain Dante (it should be explained that by this time Ravenna was ruled by Venice). But whatever the precise reasons, this promise was never fulfilled; indeed when Bernardo became the Venetian governor in Ravenna, he commissioned a new mausoleum for Dante (1483). The Florentines, thwarted in their long-cherished aims, even tried to get an Alighieri in the flesh: in 1495 they invited Dante III Alighieri (a direct descendant of the poet) to remove from Verona to Florence. But he declined.[20]

The most dramatic moment in the saga of Dante's bones occurred during the reign of Pope Leo X, the Florentine Giovanni de' Medici. He was also ruler of Ravenna, which in 1509 had passed from Venetian to Papal control. Two letters written on Leo's behalf in 1515 show that he had acceded to Florentine requests to be allowed to transfer Dante's remains. In October 1519 an attempt was made to put this into practice: the Medicean Academy of Florence wrote to the Pope, solemnly urging him to expedite the matter. Michelangelo himself added a postscript, offering to construct a tomb worthy of the great poet. Two papal emissaries were despatched to Ravenna, with full authority from Leo, only to find the tomb empty. The Franciscans had removed the bones from

219

the sarcophagus, no doubt with widespread approval, if not con-
nivance. Enquiries were fruitless. Despite an anonymous sonnet[21]
dated 1522 urging Clement VII (the next Medici pope) to be
resolute and pursue the matter where Leo had been weak (he should
have used torture to extract from the Ravennese their secret), the
mystery of the bones remained. In all probability they were replaced
in the sarcophagus once the threat of a Florentine initiative with
papal backing had receded. But in 1677 the friars were in conflict
with the government of Ravenna over their plans to rebuild and
expand the church of San Francesco, plans that would have entailed
demolishing the Dante mausoleum. During their dispute the
Franciscan Antonio Santi thought it prudent to remove and hide
the bones once more. He placed them in a small wooden coffin
which he proceeded to brick up in an adjacent chapel. There they
remained until May 1865, when they were discovered in the course
of repair work. They were at once the subject of detailed historical
and scientific examination, before being rehoused in a new lead-
covered walnut coffin and replaced at last in the sarcophagus. Only
the previous year Florence had made its final appeal for the return
of Dante's remains, but Ravenna had once more refused and was
now able to make the telling point that the poet's last resting-place
could no longer be seen as a prolongation of his exile, owing to the
'happily changed destinies of Italy'[22]: the process of Italian unifi-
cation was then nearing its final stages. In other words, Ravenna
could now lay claim to the custody of Dante's remains in the name
of the new Italy, where the old divisions between city-states no
longer obtained.

# Conclusion

On the whole this study offers few hard-and-fast answers as to when Dante was where he was, and if it does so it has not always been able to say just why he was there then. A good many details of chronology, topography and motivation remain elusive, given the paucity of surviving documentation, and so, as in many other studies, there has been a fair amount of cautious conjecture. This is especially true apropos of the earlier part of Dante's exile. Yet despite the many uncertainties as to external aspects of his life, I have tried to bring out the inner evolution of an artistic, intellectual and religious personality that is both rooted in the tumultuous events of its age and also richly nourished by classical antiquity alongside more than a millennium of Christian history and thought. A public man of action certainly, when given the chance, but also an intensely introspective, private one. Yet the fruits of this introspection are wonderfully transparent, such is the communicative power of Dante's language. And behind his urge to communicate lies a deeply serious educative purpose. This assumes a moral, indeed a salvific form in the *Comedy* of course, but in other ways it is also present in, especially, certain of the *Rime*, the *De Vulgari*, the *Convivio*, the political letters and the *Monarchia*.

Over 150 years ago Carlyle, in typically provocative vein, wrote in praise of Cante de' Gabrielli, the man who condemned Dante: but for him, Dante would have become just a prominent Florentine politician, and the world would never have had the gift of his post-exiliar writings. As to that, who can tell? In one sense, of course, the man of action was thwarted by events and failed, whilst the man of letters triumphed. Yet what counts as action? Few literary lives have been active in the way Dante's was. His long and deep reflection on his own society and his passionate engagement with the past—all that is dynamically set forth in a unique legacy of highly original and powerful works in every genre he turned to: lyric poetry, not least the *canzoni*; treatises, whether literary, philo-

221

sophical or political; letters; and lastly, and for ever *sui generis*, the *Comedy*, with its army of interpreters and no true imitators.

What we do know for certain of Dante's life is fascinating enough, but in the end what matters is that he rose above the bitter tribulations, the wanderings and the isolation to leave us a vision of an ordered, purposeful and ultimately harmonious universe, for all the strife of its human inhabitants. Perhaps any general study of Dante, whether chiefly or only partially biographical, should end by returning to the *Comedy*'s vast scheme, with its messianic message of hope: a structure at once ethical and cosmological, and inseparably so. It is the product of a great mind and, to recall Foster, a mind in love with its Creator.

# Notes

### Guelph and Ghibelline, a Prefatory Note

1.  Barely a hundred years after the first occurrence of the terms Guelph and Ghibelline in Italian sources, the German background had been forgotten. Two mid-fourteenth-century writers, a Venetian Doge and a Lombard chronicler, give wildly different but equally fanciful etymologies for these political labels: Andrea Dandolo (the Doge) tells us that Gibellinus and Guelphus were two noble brothers from Tuscany; Pietro Azario (the chronicler) not unreasonably brings in the powers of darkness in the shape of two enemy demons, Gibel and Gualef. See D. Waley, *The Italian City-Republics* (London: Weidenfeld and Nicolson, 1969), p. 208. Pages 200–18 of this study are as good a short comment on the Guelphs and Ghibellines as can be found anywhere in English.
2.  By the time Dante wrote the *Paradiso* he felt able, through the mouth of the Emperor Justinian, to criticize both sides even-handedly for their partisan abuses (*Par.* VI, 100–08).
3.  Ugo Foscolo, *Dei Sepolcri*, l. 174.

### 1 A Florentine Childhood (1265–1283)

1.  R.I. Moore (1981), Map 28, pp. 58–59; cf. Hyde (1973), pp. 153–55 and Map 5 (which shows the position *c.*1340).
2.  The definitive corpus of documents is in Piattoli (1950, 2nd Edn).
3.  Petrocchi, 'Biografia' (1978); Petrocchi (1983) is a revised and expanded version of the encyclopaedia article.
4.  Villani (1844–45), Vol. III, p. 324.
5.  For an excellent discussion of this, see Davis (1984), pp. 137–65.

### 2 Beatrice and the *Vita Nuova* (1283–1295)

1.  On Brunetto see especially Wieruszowski (1971a), pp. 515–61; and more recently Bolton Holloway (1993).
2.  Wieruszowski (1971b), pp. 589–627 (particularly pp. 604–05).
3.  See Anderson (1980), pp. 418–23—a short Appendix on Dante's use of these four poets.
4.  E. Moore (1969), First Series.
5.  See Contini (1970), II, pp. 895b–901a and his introduction to the critical edition, especially pp. LXXI–CIII and CIX–CXIII; Vanossi (1970), II, pp.

393b–95a.

6. It has indeed been maintained that Brunetto himself was the author both of the *Detto* and the *Fiore*: see Muner (1970–71), pp. 274–320.

7. Took (1990), pp. 32–33.

8. Ibid., p. 41.

9. Ibid., p. 43.

10. Filippini (1929); (e.g.) Rajna (1920), Cochin (1921), Gladstone (1892). Boccaccio had already asserted in the fourteenth century that Dante had been to Paris: Boccaccio (1965) Accessus 34 (p. 8); cf. Villani (1844–45), IX, p. 136.

11. Bruni in Solerti (1904), p. 100.

12. *Purg.* VIII, 46–84; *Inf.* XXVII, 1–132.

13. Benvenuto da Imola (1887), I, pp.88–89.

14. Boccaccio (1965), Canto II (i), §§ 83–84 (p. 114).

15. Hyde (1973), pp. 185–86.

16. Boyde in Limentani (1965), pp. 79–112 (p. 112).

### 3 The Consolation of Philosophy (1290–1296)

1. Of the many excellent histories of Western philosophy in the Middle Ages, special mention may be made of Gilson (1954), Leff (1958), Copleston (1972).

2. Foster in Limentani (1965), pp. 47–78 (p. 59). Among the most important modern studies of Dante in relation to medieval thought are: Nardi (1944), (1949, 2nd Edn), (1960), (1967, 2nd Edn); Gilson (1972, 3rd Edn); Foster (1977); Boyde (1981); Corti (1982), (1983).

3. See Davis (1984), pp. 147–65.

4. Southern (1970), p. 273.

5. Ibid., p. 299.

6. Foster (1965), p. 52.

7. Foster and Boyde (1967), II, pp. 242–43.

8. Ibid., II, p. 243.

9. Apart from the Foster and Boyde edition, see Durling and Martinez (1990).

10. Foster and Boyde (1967), II, p. 274; cf. Took (1990), p. 69.

### 4 Guilds and Government: Dante the Politician (1295–1300)

1. The classic studies of Florentine political and social history at this time are: Salvemini (1966); Davidsohn (1972–73); Ottokar (1962). (On the historiographical relation between Ottokar and Salvemini and Davidsohn, see Catto (1980), pp. 1–17 (pp. 2–3).) More recently, see Raveggi, Tarassi, Medici and Parenti (1978).

2. Mentioned in Waley (1969), p. 211.

3. Piattoli (1950, 2nd Edn), n. 53.

4. Ibid., n. 56.

5. *Trattatello in laude di Dante*, VIII; cf. Barbi (1964–65), I, p. 154.

6. Petrocchi (1978), pp. 19b–20a; (1983), p. 67.

7. Petrocchi (1978), p. 18b; cf. (1983), p. 64.
8. Hyde (1973), pp. 134–36.
9. *Inf.* XVI, 73–78.
10. Compagni (1968), I, xxi, ll. 58–75.
11. *Inf.* XVIII, 28–33; *Purg.* II, 98–99; *Par.* XXXI, 31–36, 103–4.
12. Bruni in Solerti (1904), p. 100.

## 5 Boniface VIII and the Black Coup (1300–1302)

1. Piattoli (1950, 2nd Edn), n. 78.
2. Ibid., nn. 81 and 82.
3. Ibid., nn. 83 and 84.
4. Ibid., n. 88; Petrocchi (1978), p. 28b; (1983), pp. 84–85.
5. Boase (1933), p. 379. In what follows I have relied considerably on this excellent study. Also very valuable is Dupré Theseider (1970).
6. Boase (1933), p. 45.
7. Padoan (1977), pp. 64–102: a thorough survey of critical work on this controversial line in the *Inferno*. (Padoan himself is sceptical about a reference to Celestine.)
8. Boase (1933), p. 176.
9. Ibid., p. 172.
10. Ibid., p. 85.
11. Petrocchi (1978), pp. 29b–30a; (1983), p. 88.
12. Cf. *Purg.* XX, 76–77.
13. Boase (1933), p. 269.
14. Ibid., p. 275.
15. Compagni (1968), II, iii, ll. 1–11.
16. Boase (1933), p. 275.
17. Compagni (1968), II, xi, ll. 1–6 and II, xxv, l. 52.
18. Ibid., II, iv, ll. 18–23.
19. Ibid., II, xi, ll. 1–4.
20. Ibid., II, vii, ll. 17–23.
21. Ibid., II, ix, ll. 1–12.
22. Piattoli (1950, 2nd Edn), n. 90.
23. Ibid., n. 91.
24. Compagni (1968), II, xxv, ll. 41–60.

## 6 Early Exile (1302–1304)

1. Petrocchi (1978), p. 31b; (1983), p. 92.
2. Piattoli (1950, 2nd Edn), n. 92.
3. Petrocchi (1978), p. 32b; (1983), p. 92.
4. See note by Mengaldo in the critical edition (p. 42).
5. However, by the time he came to write the *Paradiso* Dante had changed his mind: there the soul of Adam tells him that the language he spoke had completely died out before the time of Babel (*Par.* XXVI, 124–26).
6. See Marigo's remarks in his edition of the *DVE* (Dante, 1968, 3rd Edn, pp. xc–xcvii).

7. This is the Italian term, conventionally used by critics (Dante's Latin expression is *vulgaris illustris*).
8. Took (1990), p. 133.
9. I, xii, 5; this expostulation of contempt is not found elsewhere in Dante but occurs in the Vulgate Bible (Matthew 5.22).
10. I, xvi, 1. It was a medieval commonplace that the panther exhaled sweetly-perfumed breath, which served to attract its prey; there were numerous allegorizations. See Mengaldo's ample note (1979, pp. 126–27).
11. Foster and Boyde (1967), II, p. 280.
12. Alighieri (1845), pp. 94–95; Foster and Boyde II, pp. 287–88.
13. Took (1990), p. 74.
14. The fifth stanza poses difficult interpretative problems, for which Foster and Boyde's acute analysis is the surest guide (1967), II, pp. 289–91.
15. Foster and Boyde (1967), II, p. 296.
16. For a lively discussion of the Saisset affair, see Boase (1933), pp. 297–300. See also Strayer (1980), pp. 262–67.
17. *Art.* XXVI: 'Of the Unworthiness of the Ministers, which hinders not the effect of the Sacrament'.
18. Bruni in Solerti (1904), p. 103.
19. Toynbee (1920), p. 9.
20. Petrocchi (1978), p. 33b; (1983), p. 96.
21. Ibid., (1978) p. 33b; (1983), p. 97.
22. Petrocchi (1978), p. 34a and (1983), p. 98 surmises that he may well still have been there on 20 July, the day of the Lastra foray, monitoring events from a distance. Petrarch, who was born in Arezzo on that very day, refers to the exiles' military preparations in a much later letter (20 July 1366) to Boccaccio (Petrarch 1554, II, p. 917, *in fine*).

### 7 A One-Man Party (1304–1308)

1. Petrocchi (1978), p. 34a–b; (1983), pp. 98–99.
2. See Petrocchi (1969), pp. 119–41.
3. Benvenuto da Imola (1887), III, p. 313.
4. Foster and Boyde (1967), nn. 84–88a.
5. Ibid., II, p. 328.
6. For an exemplary comment on this, see again Foster and Boyde (1967), II, p. 313.
7. *Inf*.V, 103–5; *Purg.* XVI, 65–84 and XVIII, 40–75—cf *Par.* IV, 76–78 and V, 19–24.
8. Dante refers here to the *De remediis fortuitorum*. Though widely attributed to Seneca in the Middle Ages, this was in fact written in the sixth century by Martin of Braga (Martinus Dumiensis).
9. Both documents are reproduced in Piattoli (1950, 2nd Edn), nn. 98 and 99.
10. Ryan (Dante 1989).
11. Barbi (1965), pp. 48–49; cf. Took (1990), p. 93.
12. Took (1990), pp. 188–89.
13. I, i, 7: 'lo pane de li angeli' (cf. *Par.* II, 10–12). The expression *panis angelorum*

is found in the Psalms (77.25), and this would have been Dante's most obvious source. There has been much critical debate as to the precise import of Dante's phrase here in the *Convivio* (whether he means specifically philosophy as distinct from theology, or wisdom in a more general sense, and so on): Vasoli's note in the critical edition (1988)provides a good short summary, and see also Mellone (1973), pp. 266a–67b.

14. This does not in fact apply to the Book IV *canzone*, which is not allegorical.

15. I, v, 7. On the apparent discrepancy between this and the *DVE* I, i, 3–4, where the vernacular is said to be nobler than Latin, see (among many other studies) the *Convivio* edition by Busnelli and Vandelli (Dante 1968, 2nd Edn), I, pp. 87–89 and Grayson (1965), pp. 54–76.

16. Ryan (Dante 1989), p. 211, makes an apt comparison with the nineteenth-century Russian predilection for the French language.

17. This point is fully developed in II, xi (especially § 9), a chapter in which Dante shows a high consciousness of his own artistry.

18. II, iv, 6. See Bemrose (1983), pp. 117–78.

19. III, xii, 12. Power, Wisdom and Love were traditional Trinitarian attributes, ascribed respectively to the Father, the Son and the Holy Spirit (cf. *Inf.* III, 5–6, where they form part of the inscription above the gate of Hell).

20. III, xiv, 14. See Foster in Limentani (1965), pp. 56–57.

21. III, xv, 5, 18, 16; Wisdom 3.11, 7.26, Proverbs 4.18, 8.27–30.

22. IV, v, 6. Vasoli's note in the critical edition (1988) more or less reproduces that of Busnelli and Vandelli (Dante 1968, 2nd Edn), mentioning Orosius and Vincent of Beauvais. But Ryan (Dante 1989, p. 227) suggests a more immediate source for the David-Aeneas parallel, in Brunetto Latini's *Tresor* I, xxxxiv—in fact, xxxiv, ll. 17–18 (see 1948), p. 43).

23. Notwithstanding these criticisms, Dante has high regard for Frederick's intellect and learning: 'avvegna che ... fosse loico e clerico grande' (IV, x, 6).

24. IV, xvi, 6—for Dante's sources here, see Vasoli's note in the critical edition (1988) and also that of Busnelli and Vandelli (Dante 1968, 2nd Edn).

25. Cf. Purg. XXV, 67–75.

26. Ryan (Dante 1989), p. 235.

27. See especially Foster (1977), pp. 169–77, 212–27, 246–53.

28. Foster and Boyde (1967), II, pp. 334–35.

29. Ibid., pp. 335–36.

30. Took (1990), p. 81.

31. Piattoli (1950, 2nd Edn), Appendice II (pp. 325–26).

32. Barbi (1964–65), II, pp. 347–70.

33. Ibid., p. 357.

34. Boccaccio, *Vita di Dante*, ch. VII; Barbi's expression *sentimento misogino* is not quite right (hence my inverted commas around 'misogyny'): it was wives, not women, that Boccaccio disliked.

## 8 The Sacred Poem: A Survey of the *Divine Comedy* (1308–1321)

1. Petrocchi (1978), p. 46a; (1983), p. 190.

2. The bibliography on the *Comedy* is immense. Here I can do no more than list

the best modern annotated editions and translations. The best Italian edition is *La Divina Commedia*, Bosco and Reggio (1980, 2nd Edn). Still very valuable is *La Divina Commedia*, Sapegno (1968, 2nd Edn). Of bilingual Italian and English versions, the best is *The Divine Comedy*, Singleton (1970–75). On a smaller scale, but still useful, is *The Divine Comedy of Dante Alighieri*, tr. Sinclair (1971, 3rd Edn). Of the many English verse translations, the most helpful are the two in the Penguin Classics series—Sayers and Reynolds (1949–62) and more recently Musa (1984–86). In all these volumes, especially Bosco-Reggio and Singleton, there is a wealth of information, not just for the general reader or beginner. I have therefore limited my own notes to the present chapter. Indispensable for those wishing to enquire deeply into the *Comedy* is the *Enciclopedia dantesca* (1970–78). For those without Italian: Toynbee (1968—still very useful) and Lansing's *Dante Encyclopedia* (2000).

3. Bergin (1965), pp. 213–49; Anderson (1980), pp. 245–72.

4. For me, the best short essay on this first *cantica* is still Foster's classic 'An Introduction to the *Inferno*' (1977), pp. 1–14. Far more extensive, though on a more mundane level, is Fowlie (1981).

5. Notably *Purg.* XX, 10–12; also *Inf.* I, 109–11 and *Purg.* XIV, 50. The *Comedy*'s fourteenth-century commentators were practically unanimous in identifying the leopard with *lussuria* (the sins of uncontrolled passion, that is—'sins of the flesh' would be less accurate), the lion with pride and the wolf with avarice.

6. In understanding 'allegory' in this restrictive sense I am following Lewis (1936), Ch. II—see especially p. 45 for a sharp and succinct contrast between allegory and symbol. But by no means all scholars use the terms in the way Lewis does: apropos of Dante specifically, see also for instance Bergin (1965), Ch. 13 (pp. 250–64); Hollander (1969).

7. This is not to suggest that there is anything obscure about allegories or symbols *per se*: they can be decoded with ease or with difficulty, depending on the author's intention and the reader's intelligence and cultural equipment. Nor should it be thought that apart from its opening canto the *Comedy* is devoid of episodes which on any definition would be termed allegorical or symbolic, the most notable being the mysterious spectacles in the Earthly Paradise, at the summit of Mount Purgatory.

8. Bergin (1965), p. 252.

9. 2 Corinthians 12.4. If Aeneas is the father of the Roman Empire, St Paul may be seen as one of the great founders of the Christian Church. Here we have the first example of one of the *Comedy*'s most powerful motifs: the parallel and complementary character of sacred and profane history, of the Judaeo-Christian and the Graeco-Roman worlds.

10. This is good Trinitarian theology: it is not just God the Father (whom some might regard as a severe, paternalistic 'Old Testament' figure) who is responsible for Hell's creation and maintenance, but the whole Trinity.

11. *Conv.* II, xiii, 6.

12. The notion of neutral angels, though not uncommon in medieval Europe, is not sanctioned by any of the canonical books of the Bible, nor has any place in mainstream Christian theology.

13. Conventionally, I have used the Latin or Anglicized forms of the classical proper names found in the *Comedy*: Dante's medieval Italian equivalents would puzzle some readers.

14. Hell's circles traditionally begin with Limbo, the first beyond the Acheron, the lowest (Cocytus) being the ninth. But with the addition of the vestibule we have a total of ten.

15. *Inf*. XXV, 1–9 (Vanni Fucci); XXXII, 97–111 (Bocca degli Abati); XXXIII, 148–50 (Frate Alberigo).

16. In the *Convivio*, however, Dante praises the ancient philosopher Epicurus (*c*.342–270 BC) and his followers, putting them on a par with the Stoics and the Peripatetics; there is no mention of a denial of the afterlife. For an explanation of this, see Mazzeo (1960), pp. 174–204.

17. Foster (1977), p. 1.

18. Most notably Pézard (1950)—Brunetto's perversion is not sexual but linguistic and cultural; Kay (1978)—the deviation is political and philosophical; Armour (1983a)—the sin of Brunetto and his companions is in a broad sense one of heresy.

19. See especially the *Introduzione* to Canto XXVI in the Bosco-Reggio edition (1980, 2nd Edn), pp. 380–81.

20. The heads are yellow, black and red: they may very well refer, respectively, to impotence, ignorance and hatred, the opposites of the three attributes of the Trinity, namely power (the Father), wisdom (the Son) and love (the Spirit). This is the view of many of the early commentators and modern critics. A quite different exegesis, appearing first in the nineteenth century, and supported by Sayers in her translation, is that Satan's power over the three continents of the known world in Dante's day is here signified, on the basis of the supposedly typical colouring of their inhabitants: the yellow head would refer to Asia, the black one to Africa and the red to Europe. This seems highly unlikely.

21. Among modern studies concentrating on the *Purgatorio*, mention may be made of: Armour (1983b) and (1989), Cervigni (1986); Fergusson (1953); Schnapp (1993), pp. 192–207.

22. Such scriptural passages as might conceivably be held to support the idea of Purgatory are few and far between: Malachi 3.2–3; 2 Maccabees 12.46; 1 Corinthians 3.14–15. The second of these does in fact speak of praying for the dead, that they may be absolved of their guilt, but it should be noted that the two Books of Maccabees are not accepted by the Reformed Churches as authentic parts of the Bible.

23. *Conv*. II, i, 6–7; *Epist*. XIII, § 7(21); cf. *Par*. XXV, 55–57.

24. In fact Foster and Boyde in their 1967 edition of the *Rime* see no reason why Dante should not have intended the poem to be allegorical from the first (II, p. 173). The Bosco-Reggio commentary to the *Purgatorio* (1980, 2nd Edn) strongly disagrees, however: see the *Introduzione* to Canto II (pp. 28–29) and the note to l. 112.

25. This period may however be shortened by the intercessionary prayers of those still on earth (ll. 140–41)—the first mention in the *Purgatorio* of the efficacious solidarity between the living and those waiting to begin their purgation.

26. Brunetto Latini's *Tresor* (1948), for instance, goes into explicit detail as to how Manfred smothered his father (I, 78–79 in Carmody's edition).

27. In these two episodes Dante, for dramatic effect, is drawing on popular, folkloristic traditions. He did not literally believe that any soul's destiny could hang on the outcome of a struggle between good and evil powers: what is decisive, in his view, are the soul's freely-made moral choices.

28. The early chroniclers and commentators who give credence to this story differ as to Charles' motives: see for instance, Toynbee (1968), pp. 614b–15a.

29. Dante's interpretation here of *Aeneid* III, 56–57 appears to distort Virgil's meaning: see the Bosco-Reggio *Introduzione* (1980, 2nd Edn) to Cantos XXI–XXII (p. 357), and the note to XXII, 40–41.

30. The consensus among modern scholars is that the virgin is the mythical Astraea, here a personification of Justice. The infant is in all probability the son of Ausinius Pollio, the writer and statesman, to whom Virgil dedicated the poem, and who was Consul in 43 BC, the year it was written.

31. Forese too was a poet, in a minor way; as we have seen he exchanged a trio of sonnets with Dante, though he is not known to have written anything else.

32. Indeed, Dante's name never occurs anywhere else in his Italian writings. It is however prefixed to six of the letters, and in two of these (XII and XIII) it is found in the body of the text. It also appears at the beginning and end of the *Quaestio de aqua et terra*.

33. Lack of space has precluded any discussion of the Tree and its many differing interpretations. The best study is still Foster (1957).

34. A brief selection of mainly recent works on the *Paradiso:* Freccero (1986), pp. 209–20; Jacoff (1993a), pp. 208–25; Mazzeo (1958); Schnapp (1986).

35. For Dante all the heavenly spheres (save the Empyrean), together with the planets and stars they contain, are material, but their matter is quite different from that of the sublunary regions. Whereas earthly matter is composed of some or all of the four elements Earth, Water, Air and Fire, the heavens consist of a fifth element, or 'quintessence': the Aristotelian *aither*. This can undergo no transmutation or decay, nor any kind of change except that of motion (which in Aristotelian terms is a kind of change).

36. The Heaven of the Sun, and this canto especially, are important for clarifying Dante's position vis-à-vis Aquinas. Modern scholars have established that Dante was not in doctrinal terms a follower of Thomas; Foster, more than anyone, has brought out the true nature of Dante's esteem for him, as a great commentator on Aristotle and as a model of intellectual integrity and method: see especially 'St Thomas and Dante' in Foster (1977), pp. 56–65, and his fundamental study 'Tommaso d'Aquino' (1976) (V, pp. 626b–49a).

37. Looking ahead to Dante's time in Purgatory, it will not be just artistic pride, exemplified by Oderisi, that he will purge on the first terrace, but also pride in ancestry, a fault he shares with Oderisi's companion Omberto Aldobrandesco (*Purg.* XI, 57–69).

38. Dante's position on salvation for pagans is not an isolated one: Aquinas, invoking the notion of 'implicit' faith, maintained that many of them had been granted a revelation of Christ (see, for instance, *Summa theologiae*, II–II, 2,7, ad 3). Foster's treatment of this fascinating question is magisterial: see in par-

ticular 'The Son's Eagle: *Paradiso* XIX' in Foster (1977), pp. 137–55, and also pp. 174–89.

39. Two important studies relating to this last canto: Foster, 'Dante's Vision of God' in Foster (1977), pp. 66–85; Pertile (1981).

40. Not just the medieval west; the Roman Catholic and Reformed Churches alike hold that the Holy Spirit proceeds from the Father *and the Son*. The italicized phrase was not, however, generally adopted before the ninth century, and Orthodox Christians adhere to earlier versions of the Creed, in which the Spirit proceeds from the Father alone.

## 9 Henry VII and Dante's Imperial Dream (1308–1313)

1. Bowsky (1960), p. 25.
2. Ibid., p. 36.
3. Compagni (1968), III, xxxv, ll. 20–29.
4. Bowsky (1960), p. 56, puts these figures into perspective.
5. Ibid., p. 67.
6. Petrocchi (1983), p. 149.
7. Bowsky (1960), p. 40.
8. Compagni (1968), III, xxviii, ll. 1–14.
9. Anderson (1980), p. 211.
10. Bowsky (1960), p. 111 (and p. 142).
11. Piattoli (1950, 2nd Edn) n. 106.
12. Bowsky (1960), p. 140 (and p. 248).
13. Petrarch himself, in a letter of 1359 to Boccaccio, alludes to a childhood sighting of Dante, though he does not specify where it took place: Petrarch (1968), IV, p. 95 (*Familiares* XXI, 15, 7).
14. Petrocchi (1978), p. 43b; (1983), p. 152. In Petrocchi's view the *Inferno* was published in the second half of 1314: (1978), p. 46a; (1983), p. 190.
15. Bowsky (1960), p. 165.
16. Ibid., pp. 155–57.
17. Holmes (1980b), pp. 18–43 (p. 39).
18. Bowsky (1960), p. 204.
19. Anderson (1980), p. 213.
20. Bowsky (1960), p. 211.
21. Petrocchi (1978), p. 44a–b; (1983), pp. 154–55.
22. Ibid., (1978), p. 46a; (1983), p. 190.
23. For a succinct survey, see P.G. Ricci (1971).
24. *Mon.* III, iv, 2–3, ll. 7–14 and 58–102; *Purg.* XVI, 106–8.
25. See Ricci's note in the critical edition (1965), pp. 158–59; cf. Padoan (1981, 2nd Edn), pp. 123–24.
26. Petrocchi (1978), p. 47a; (1983), p. 192. Petrocchi is inclined to follow Ricci's dating (as late as 1317–18).

## 10 The Gentleman of Verona (1312–1318)

1. See Zingarelli (1944, 3rd Edn), pp. 663–64, 677; Anderson (1980), pp. 237, 445.

2. See Wicksteed and Gardner (1902), pp. 34–35.
3. Boccaccio (1965), I, 7, 5.
4. Benvenuto da Imola recounts that when as a boy Can Grande was taken by his father to see his treasury, he urinated over the gold; the onlookers interpreted this *contemptus pecuniarum* as a sign of future *munificentia* (1887), V, p. 197.
5. Petrocchi (1978), p. 47a; (1986), p. 193.
6. Petrocchi (1978), 47b; (1986), p. 194, n. 8. For the 1316 dating, see (e.g.) Toynbee (1968), p. 218b; Anderson (1980), pp. 233–34.
7. Barbi (1964–65) II, pp. 305–28.
8. Holmes (1986), pp. 195–96.
9. Piattoli (1950, 2nd Edn), n. 114.
10. Ibid., n. 115.
11. E.g. Chydenius (1958), pp. 1–159; Auerbach (1959); Singleton (1960), pp. 1–24; Charity (1966), pp. 199–207.
12. E.g. Brugnoli, in the critical edition, (Frugoni and Brugnoli, 1979), pp. 614–23; Barański (1991), pp. 26–55.
13. Toynbee (1920), p. 210, n. 1.
14. D'Ovidio (1901), pp. 448–85. 'The Genuineness of the Dedicatory Epistle to Can Grande' (1903) in E. Moore (1969), Third Series, pp. 284–369.
15. Mazzoni (1955). Nardi (1960).
16. Botterill (1991), p. 117.
17. Hollander (1993).
18. Dronke (1986); Kelly (1989); Hall and Sowell (1989), pp. 89–104; Barański (1991), pp. 26–55.
19. *Mon.* III, iv, 7, ll. 33–36, referring to *De civitate Dei*, XVI, 2 (*in fine*).
20. III, x, 6, ll. 25–28 (cf. I, xvi, 3, ll. 14–16), referring to John 19.23.
21. See Took's excellent comments on these closing lines: (1990), pp. 172–73 and p. 218, n. 25.
22. Nardi (1967, 2nd Edn), pp. 233–40; Gilson (1972, 3rd Edn), pp. 169–70.
23. All these criticisms are eminently Thomist, and are entirely in accord with what Aquinas says in the *De regimine principum*: Gilson (1972, 3rd Edn), pp. 191–93.
24. E.g. Petrarch (1943), II, §83.
25. Anderson (1980), p. 237.
26. Petrocchi (1978), pp. 46a–b.

## 11 Ravenna (1318–1321)

1. See C. Ricci (1965, 3rd Edn), pp. 67–74. Ricci argues that Dante *was* employed by the *studium*; but see Petrocchi (1978), p. 49a–b; (1983), pp. 197–98.
2. Biographical and literary information about Giardini, Mezzani and Canaccio is given by C. Ricci (1965, 3rd Edn), pp. 221–83.
3. Pézard, in his French translation, deliberately chooses the term *Querelle* rather than *Question* (Dante, 1965), pp. 843–44.
4. See Anderson (1980), p. 239.
5. § 87; cf. the phrase *inter vere philosophantes minimus* at the beginning of the treatise: § 1.

6. Padoan (1981, 2nd Edn), p. 112.
7. Villani (1844–45), IX, p. 118 (ed. Sansone-Coen, II, p. 223).
8. Wicksteed and Gardner (1902), pp. 235–38.
9. MS Medicaeo—Laurentiano XXIX. 8 (note that the glosses themselves are not by Boccaccio): see Wicksteed and Gardner (1902), p.127 and pp. 268–73.
10. For instance, Zingarelli (1944, 3rd Edn), p. 760.
11. Wicksteed and Gardner (1902), p. 124.
12. Petrocchi (1978), p. 53a; (1983), p. 222.
13. Villani in Solerti (1904), pp. 86–87.
14. Petrocchi (1978), p. 53b; (1983), pp. 222–23.
15. Ibid., (1978), p. 53b.
16. *Trattatello in laude di Dante* (= *Vita di Dante*), XV; *esquisito* occurs in one of Boccaccio's two later versions of the *Trattatello/Vita* (both passages are in Solerti (1904), p. 31).
17. C. Ricci (1965, 3rd Edn), pp. 291 and 305–6.
18. Text in Wicksteed and Gardner (1902), pp. 174–75. The reference to the *Eclogues* occurs in ll. 7–8, and, as the editors note (p. 244), could mean that Giovanni had not yet received Dante's second poem at the time of his death, or (much less likely) that he hoped Dante would write further eclogues.
19. C. Ricci (1965, 3rd Edn), pp. 416–17.
20. Zingarelli (1944, 3rd Edn), pp. 1360–61.
21. C. Ricci (1965, 3rd Edn), p. 402, reproduces the text. His note (p. 426) points out that the correct date should be 1523 or 1524, since Clement was not elected until 18 November 1523.
22. Zingarelli (1944, 3rd Edn), p. 1366; C. Ricci (1965, 3rd Edn), p. 417.

# Bibliography

Listed below are all those works specifically cited or referred to in the text or notes. I have also added a number of other studies which I have found especially helpful: the choice of these has of necessity been extremely selective. Those entries marked with an asterisk * refer to the critical editions, also listed separately on page xiii. Note that '*ED*' followed by a volume number indicates that the article concerned is from the *Enciclopedia dantesca* (listed in full under 'Bosco').

Alighieri, P., *Super Dantis ipsius genitoris comoediam*, ed. V. Nannucci (Florence: Piatti, 1845).

Anderson, W., *Dante the Maker* (London: Routledge and Kegan Paul, 1980).

Armour, P., 'Dante's Brunetto: The Paternal Paterine?' *Italian Studies* 38 (1983a) pp. 1–38.

Armour, P., *Dante's Griffin and the History of the World* (London: Oxford University Press, 1989).

Armour, P., *The Door of Purgatory: A Study of Multiple Symbolism in Dante's 'Purgatorio'* (Oxford: Clarendon Press, 1983b).

Auerbach, E., '*Figura*', *Scenes from the Drama of European Literature* (New York: Meridian Books, 1959).

Barański, Z.G., '*Comedia*. Notes on Dante, the Epistle to Cangrande, and Medieval Comedy' *Lectura Dantis [virginiana]* 8 (Spring 1991) pp. 26–55.

Barański, Z.G. and Boyde, P. (eds), *The 'Fiore' in Context: Dante, France, Tuscany* (Notre Dame, Indiana: University of Notre Dame Press, 1997).

Barbi, M., *Problemi di critica dantesca, prima serie (1893–1918); seconda serie (1920–37)*, 2 vols (Florence: Sansoni, 1964–65).

Barbi, M., *Vita di Dante* (Florence: Sansoni, 1965—originally publ. 1933; tr. P. Ruggiers as *Life of Dante* (Berkeley-Los Angeles: University of California Press, 1954)).

Bemrose, S., *Dante's Angelic Intelligences: Their Importance in the Cosmos and in Pre-Christian Religion* (Rome: Edizioni di Storia e Letteratura, 1983).

Benvenuto da Imola, *Comentum super Dantis Aldigherij Comoediam*, ed. J.P. Lacaita, 5 vols (Florence: Barbèra, 1887).

Bergin, T.G., *An Approach to Dante* (London: The Bodley Head, 1965).

Boase, T.S.R., *Boniface VIII* (London: Constable, 1933).

Boccaccio, *Decameron*, ed. V. Branca (Florence: Le Monnier, 1965a).

Boccaccio, *Esposizioni sopra la Comedìa di Dante*, ed. G. Padoan (Milan: Mondadori, 1965b—vol. VI of G. Boccaccio, *Tutte le opere*, ed. V. Branca).

Boccaccio, *Vita di Dante* in A. Solerti (ed.) 1904, pp. 8–71.

Bolton Holloway, J., *Twice-told Tales: Brunetto Latino and Dante Alighieri* (New York: Lang, 1993).

Bosco, U. (ed.), *Enciclopedia dantesca*, 6 vols (1970–78): Vol. 1 (A–Cil), 1970; Vol. 2 (Cim–Fo), 1970; Vol. 3 (Fr–M), 1971; Vol. 4 (N–Sam), 1973; Vol. 5 (San–Z), 1976; Vol. 6 (*Appendice*), 1978 (Rome: Istituto dell'Enciclopedia Italiana, 1970–78).

Bosco, U. and Reggio, G. (eds), *La Divina Commedia*, 3 vols (Florence: Le Monnier, 1980, 2nd Edn).

Botterill, S., Review of H.A. Kelly (1989) *Italian Studies* 46 (1991) pp. 117–18.

Bowsky, W.M., *Henry VII in Italy: The Conflict of Empire and City-State, 1310–1313* (Lincoln, Nebraska: University of Nebraska Press, 1960).

Boyde, P., 'Dante's Lyric Poetry' in U. Limentani (ed.) (1965).

Boyde, P., *Dante Philomythes and Philosopher: Man in the Cosmos* (Cambridge: Cambridge University Press, 1981).

Boyde, P., *Perception and Passion in Dante's 'Comedy'* (Cambridge: Cambridge University Press, 1993).

Boyde, P., *Human Vices and Human Worth in Dante's 'Comedy'* (Cambridge: Cambridge University Press, 2002).

Brunetto Latini, *Tresor*, ed. F.J. Carmody (Berkeley and Los Angeles: University of California Press, 1948).

Bruni, L., *Vita di Dante* in A. Solerti (ed.) 1904, pp. 97–107.

Busnelli, G. and Vandelli, G., *see* Dante (1968, 2nd Edn).

Cassell, A.K., *Dante's Fearful Art of Justice* (Toronto-London: University of Toronto Press, 1984).

Catto, J., 'Florence, Tuscany and the World of Dante' in C. Grayson (ed.) (1980).

* Cecchini, E. (ed.), *Egloge, Opere minori* 2 vols (Milan-Naples: Ricciardi, 1979), II, pp. 645–89. Critical edition of *Eclogues*.

Cervigni, D., *Dante's Poetry of Dreams* (Florence: Olschki, 1986).

Charity, A.C., *Events and their Afterlife: The Dialectics of Christian Typology in the Bible and Dante* (Cambridge: Cambridge University Press, 1966).

Chydenius, J., 'The Typological Problem in Dante' *Commentationes Humanarum Litterarum* (Societas Scientiarum Fennica) 25, 1 (Helsinki, 1958) pp. 1–159.

Cochin, H., 'Dante est-il venu à Paris?' *Annuaire Bulletin de la Société de l'Histoire de France* 58 (1921) pp. 91–98.

Compagni, D., *Cronica*, ed. G. Luzzatto (Turin: Einaudi, 1968).

Contini, G., 'Fiore' *ED* 2 (1970), pp. 895b–901a.

* Contini, G. (ed.), *Il Fiore e Il Detto d'Amore attribuibili a Dante Alighieri* (Milan: Mondadori, 1984). Critical edition of *Detto d'Amore* and *Fiore*.

Copleston, F.C., *A History of Medieval Philosophy* (London: Methuen, 1972).

Corti, M., *Dante a un nuovo crocevia* (Florence: Sansoni, 1982).

Corti, M., *La felicità mentale: nuove prospettive per Cavalcanti e Dante* (Turin: Einaudi, 1983).

Cosmo, U., tr. D. Moore, *A Handbook to Dante Studies* (Oxford: Blackwell, 1950). (Originally published as *Guida a Dante*.)

Dante, *Convivio*, ed. G. Busnelli and G. Vandelli (Florence: Le Monnier, 1968, 2nd Edn).

Dante, *Dante: The Banquet, translated with introduction and notes by* C. Ryan (Saratoga, California: ANMA Libri, 1989).

Dante, *Dante: Oeuvres complètes*, tr. A. Pézard (Paris: Gallimard, 1965).

Dante, *De vulgari eloquentia*, ed. A. Marigo (Florence: Le Monnier, 1968, 3rd Edn).

Dante, *De Vulgari Eloquentia*, ed. and tr. S. Botterill (Cambridge: Cambridge University Press, 1995).

Dante, *De Vulgari Eloquentia: Literature in the Vernacular*, tr. S. Purcell (Cheadle, Cheshire: Carcarnet Press, 1981).

Dante, *Dantis Alagherii Epistolae: The Letters of Dante*, ed. P. Toynbee (Oxford: Clarendon Press, 1920).

Dante, *Monarchia*, tr. and ed. P. Shaw (Cambridge: Cambridge University Press, 1995).

Dante, *Vita Nuova*, tr. D.S. Cerrigni and E. Vasta (Notre Dame, Indiana-London: University of Notre Dame Press, 1995).

Dante, *Vita Nuova*, tr. M. Musa (London: Oxford University Press, 1992).

Dante, *Vita Nuova*, eds J. Petrie and J. Salmons (Dublin: Belfield Italian Library, 1994).

Dante, *La Vita Nuova (Poems of Youth)*, tr. B. Reynolds (Harmondswoth: Penguin, 1969).

Davidsohn, R., *Geschichte von Florenz*, 4 vols (Berlin: Mittler, 1896–1927) tr. G.B. Klein as *Storia di Firenze*, 8 vols (Florence: Sansoni, 1972–73).

Davis, C.T., *Dante and the Idea of Rome* (Oxford: Clarendon Press, 1957).

Davis, C.T., 'Education in Dante's Florence' *Speculum* 40 (1965) pp. 415–35, repr. in *Dante's Italy and Other Essays* (Philadelphia: University of Pennsylvania Press, 1984).

De Robertis, D., *Il libro della 'Vita nuova'* (Florence: Sansoni, 1961).

* De Robertis, D. (ed.), *Vita Nuova*, *Opere minori* 2 vols (Milan-Naples: Ricciardi, 1980), I/1, pp. 1–247. Critical edition of *Vita Nuova*.

D'Entreves, A.P., *Dante as a Political Thinker* (Oxford: Clarendon Press, 1952).

D'Ovidio, F., 'L'Epistola a Cangrande' *Studii sulla 'Divina Commedia'* (Milan-Palermo: Sandron, 1901) pp. 448–85.

Dronke, P., *Dante and Medieval Latin Traditions* (Cambridge: Cambridge University Press, 1986).

Dupré Theseider, E., 'Bonifacio VIII, papa' in *Dizionario Biografico degli Italiani* (Rome: Istituto dell' Enciclopedia Italiana, 1960 to present day), 12, (1970), pp. 146a–170a.

Durling, R.M. and Martinez, R.L., *Time and the Crystal: Studies in Dante's 'Rime petrose'* (Berkeley: University of California Press, 1990).

Fergusson, F., *Dante's Drama of the Mind: A Modern Reading of 'Purgatorio'* (Princeton: Princeton University Press, 1953).

Ferrante, J.M., *The Political Vision of the 'Divine Comedy'* (Princeton: Princeton University Press, 1984).

Filippini, F., *Dante scolaro e maestro: Bologna, Parigi, Ravenna* (Geneva, 1929).

Foster, K., *God's Tree: Essays on Dante and other Matters* (London: Blackfriars, 1957).

Foster, K., 'Religion and Philosophy in Dante' in U. Limentani (ed.) (1965).

Foster, K., 'Tommaso d'Aquino' *ED* 5 (1976), pp. 626b–649a).

Foster, K., *The Two Dantes and Other Studies* (London: Darton, Longman and Todd, 1977).

\* Foster, K. and Boyde, P. (eds), *Dante's Lyric Poetry* 2 vols (Oxford: Clarendon Press, 1967). Critical edition of *Rime*.

Fowlie, W., *A Reading of Dante's 'Inferno'* (Chicago and London: Univeristy of Chicago Press, 1981).

Freccero, J., *Dante: The Poetics of Conversion,* ed. R. Jacoff (Cambridge, Mass.: Harvard University Press, 1986).

\* Frugoni, A. and Brugnoli, G. (eds), *Epistole, Opere minori,* 2 vols (Milan-Naples: Ricciardi, 1979) II, pp. 505–643. Critical edition of *Epistolae.*

Gilson, E., *Dante et la philosophie* (Paris: Vrin, 1972, 3rd Edn).

Gilson, E., *History of Christian Philosophy in the Middle Ages* (New York: Random House, 1954).

Gladstone, W.E., 'Did Dante Study in Oxford?' *The Nineteenth Century* (June 1892) pp. 1032–42.

Grayson, C., '*"Nobilior est vulgaris"*: Latin and Vernacular in Dante's Thought' Oxford Dante Society (1965).

Grayson, C. (ed.), *The World of Dante* (Oxford: Clarendon Press, 1980).

Hall, R.G. and Sowell, M.V., '*Cursus* in the Can Grande Epistle: A Forger Shows His Hand' *Lectura Dantis [virginiana]* 5 (Fall 1989) pp. 89–104.

Hollander, R., *Allegory in Dante's 'Commedia'* (Princeton: Princeton University Press, 1969).

Hollander, R., *Dante's Epistle to Cangrande* (Ann Arbor, Michigan: University of Michigan Press, 1993).

Holmes, G., *Dante* (Oxford: Clarendon Press, 1980a).

Holmes, G., 'Dante and the Popes' in C. Grayson (ed.) (1980b).

Holmes, G., *Florence, Rome and the Origins of the Renaissance* (Oxford: Clarendon Press, 1986).

Hyde, J.K., *Society and Politics in Medieval Italy: The Evolution of the Civil Life, 1000–1350* (London: Macmillan, 1973).

Jacoff, R., '"Shadowy Prefaces": an introduction to *Paradiso'* in R. Jacoff (ed.) 1993.

Jacoff, R. (ed.), *The Cambridge Companion to Dante* (Cambridge: Cambridge University Press, 1993).

Jacoff, R. (ed.), *Dante: The Poetics of Conversion* (Cambridge: Cambridge University Press, 1986).

Kay, R., *Dante's Swift and Strong: Essays on 'Inferno'* XV (Lawrence, Kansas: Regents Press of Kansas, 1978).

Kelly, H.A., *Tragedy and Comedy from Dante to Pseudo-Dante* (Berkeley, Los Angeles, London: University of California Press, 1989).

Kirkpatrick, R., *Dante: 'The Divine Comedy'* (Cambridge: Cambridge University Press, 1987).

Lansing, R. (ed.), *Dante Encyclopedia* (New York: Garland, 2000).

Larner, J., *Italy in the Age of Dante and Petrarch, 1216–1380* (London and New York: Longman, 1980).

Leff, G., *Medieval Thought from Saint Augustine to Ockham* (Harmondsworth: Penguin, 1958).

Lewis, C.S., *The Allegory of Love* (London: Oxford University Press, 1936).

Lewis, C.S., *The Discarded Image* (Cambridge: Cambridge University Press,

1968).

Limentani, U. (ed.), *The Mind of Dante* (Cambridge: Cambridge University Press, 1965).

Marigo, A., *see* Dante (1968, 3rd Edn).

Mazzeo, J.A., *Medieval Cultural Tradition in Dante's 'Comedy'* (Ithaca, New York: Cornell University Press, 1960).

Mazzeo, J.A., *Structure and Thought in the 'Paradiso'* (Ithaca, New York: Cornell University Press, 1958).

Mazzoni, F., 'L'Epistola a Cangrande' *Rendiconti della Accademia Nazionale dei Lincei. Classe di scienze morali, storiche e filologiche* Serie 8, 10 (1955) pp. 157–98.

\* Mazzoni, F. (ed.), *Quaestio de aqua et terra, Opere minori* 2 vols (Milan-Naples: Ricciardi, 1979), II, pp. 691–880. Critical edition of *Quaestio de aqua et terra.*

Mellone, A., 'pane de li angeli' *ED* 4 (1973), pp. 266a–67b.

\* Mengaldo, P.V. (ed.), *De vulgari eloquentia, Opere minori* 2 vols (Milan-Naples: Ricciardi, 1979), II, pp. 3–237. Critical edition of *De vulgari eloquentia.*

Migliorini Fissi, R., *Dante* (Florence, *La Nuova Italia*, 1979).

Moore, E., *Studies in Dante*, 4 vols (Oxford: Clarendon Press, 1896–1917; repr. 1969).

Moore, R.I. (ed.), *The Hamlyn Historical Atlas* (London: Hamlyn, 1981).

Muner, M., 'La paternità brunettiana del *Fiore* e del *Detto d'Amore*' *Motivi per la difesa della cultura* 9 (1970–71) pp. 274–320.

Musa, M., *The Divine Comedy* (Harmondsworth: Penguin, 1984–86).

Najemy, J.M., 'Dante and Florence' in R. Jacoff (ed.) (1993).

Nardi, B., *Dal 'Convivio' alla 'Commedia'* (Rome: Istituto storico italiano per il Medio Evo, 1960a).

Nardi, B., *Dante e la cultura medievale* (Bari: Laterza, 1949, 2nd Edn).

Nardi, B., 'Il punto sull'Epistola a Cangrande' *Lectura Dantis Scaligera* (Florence: Le Monnier, 1960b).

Nardi, B., *Nel mondo di Dante* (Rome: Edizioni di Storia e Letteratura, 1944).

Nardi, B., *Saggi di filosofia dantesca* (Florence: La Nuova Italia, 1967, 2nd Edn).

Ottokar, N., *Il Comune di Firenze alla fine del Dugento* (Turin: Einaudi, 1962, 2nd Edn— originally publ. 1926).

Oxford Dante Society, *Centenary Essays on Dante by Members of the Oxford Dante Society* (Oxford: Clarendon Press, 1965).

Padoan, G., '"Colui che fece per viltade il gran rifiuto"' *Il pio Enea, l'empio Ulisse* (Ravenna: Longo, 1977).

Padoan, G., *Introduzione a Dante* (Florence: Sansoni, 1981, 2nd Edn).

Pertile, L., 'Paradiso, XXXIII: l'estremo oltraggio' *Filologia e critica* 6 (1981), 1–21.

Petrarch, *Familiares*, ed. V. Rossi (Florence: Sansoni, 1968).

Petrarch, *Rerum Memorandarum Libri*, ed. G. Billanovich, 2 vols (Florence: Sansoni, 1943).

Petrarch, *'Seniles', Opera omnia* (Basel, 1554), vol. 2.

Petrocchi, G., 'Biografia' *ED* 6 (*Appendice*: 1978) pp. 3a–53b.

\* Petrocchi, G. (ed.), *La Commedia secondo l'antica vulgata* 4 vols (Florence: Casa Editrice le Lettere, 1994, 2nd Edn). Critical edition of *Divina Commedia.*

Petrocchi, G., *Itinerari danteschi* (Bari: Laterza, 1969).

Petrocchi, G., *Vita di Dante* (Bari: Laterza, 1983).

Pézard, A., *Dante Sous la pluie de feu* (Paris: Vrin, 1950).

Pézard, A., *see* Dante (1965).

Piattoli, R., *Codice diplomatico dantesco* (Florence: Gonnelli, 1950, 2nd Edn) with addenda in *Studi danteschi* 30 (1951) pp. 203–6; 42 (1965) pp. 393–417; 44 (1967) pp. 223–68; and *Archivio storico italiano* 127 (1969) pp. 3–108.

Quinones, R.J., *Dante Alighieri* (Boston: Twayne, 1979).

Rajna, P., 'Per la questione dell'andata di Dante a Parigi' *Studi danteschi* 2 (1920) pp. 75–87.

Raveggi, S., Tarassi, M., Medici, D. and Parenti, P., *Ghibellini, Guelfi e popolo grasso: I detentori del potere politico a Firenze nella seconda metà del Dugento* (Florence: La Nuova Italia, 1978).

Reynolds, B., *Dante: The Poet, the Political Thinker, the Man* (London-New York: I.B. Tauris, 2006).

Ricci, C., with additions by E. Chiarini, *L'ultimo rifugio di Dante* (Ravenna: Longo, 1965, 3rd Edn—originally publ. 1891).

Ricci, P.G., 'Monarchia' *ED* 3 (1971), pp. 1000b–1002a.

* Ricci, P.G. (ed.), *Monarchia* (Milan: Mondadori, 1965). Critical edition of *Monarchia*.

Runciman, S., *The Sicilian Vespers* (Harmondsworth: Penguin, 1960).

Ryan, C., *see* Dante (1989).

Salvemini, G., *Magnati e popolani in Firenze dal 1280 al 1295* (Milan: Feltrinelli, 1966—originally publ. 1899).

Sapegno, N. (ed.), *La Divina Commedia*, 3 vols (Florence: La Nuova Italia, 1968, 2nd Edn).

Sayers, D. and Reynolds, B., *The Divine Comedy* (Harmondsworth: Penguin, 1949–62).

Schevill, F., *History of Florence from the Founding of the City through the Renaissance* (New York: Harcourt Brace, 1936).

Schnapp, J.T., 'Introduction to *Purgatorio*' in R. Jacoff (ed.) (1993).

Schnapp, J.T., *The Transfiguration of History at the Center of Dante's 'Paradise'* (Princeton: Princeton University Press, 1986).

Sinclair, J.D. (tr.), *The Divine Comedy of Dante Alighieri*, 3 vols (London: Oxford University Press, 1971, 3rd Edn).

Singleton, C.S., *Dante's 'Commedia': Elements of Structure,* Dante Studies 1 (Cambridge, Mass.: Harvard University Press, 1954, repr. Baltimore: The Johns Hopkins University Press, 1977a).

Singleton, C.S. (ed. and tr.), *The Divine Comedy*, 6 vols (Princeton: Princeton University Press, 1970–75).

Singleton, C.S., *An Essay on the 'Vita nuova'* (Cambridge, Mass.: Harvard University Press, 1949, repr. Baltimore: The Johns Hopkins University Press, 1977b).

Singleton, C.S., 'In exitu Israel de Aegypto' *77th Annual Report of the Dante Society* (1960) pp. 1–24.

Singleton, C.S., *Journey to Beatrice,* Dante Studies 2 (Cambridge, Mass.: Harvard University Press, 1958, repr. Baltimore: The Johns Hopkins University Press,

1977c).

Solerti, A. (ed.), *Le vite di Dante, Petrarca e Boccaccio scritte fino al secolo deci-mosesto* (Milan: Vallardi, 1904).

Southern, R.W., *Western Society and the Church in the Middle Ages* (Harmondsworth: Penguin, 1970).

Starn, R., *Contrary Commonwealth: The Theme of Exile in Medieval and Renaissance Italy* (Berkeley, Los Angeles, London: University of California Press, 1982).

Strayer, J.R., *The Reign of Philip the Fair* (Princeton: Princeton University Press, 1980).

Took, J.F., *Dante, Lyric Poet and Philosopher: An Introduction to the Minor Works* (Oxford: Clarendon Press, 1990).

Toynbee, P., revised by C.S. Singleton, *A Dictionary of Proper Names and Notable Matters in the Works of Dante* (Oxford: Clarendon Press, 1968).

Toynbee, P., *see* Dante (1920).

Vanossi, L., *Dante e il 'Roman de la Rose': saggio sul 'Fiore'* (Florence: Olschki, 1979).

Vanossi, L., 'Detto d'Amore' *ED* 2 (1970), pp. 393b–95a.

* Vasoli, C. and De Robertis, D. (eds), *Convivio, Opere minori* 2 vols (Milan-Naples: Ricciardi, 1988), I/2. Critical edition of *Convivio*.

Villani, G., *Cronica*, ed. F.G. Dragomanni, 4 vols (Florence: Sansone-Coen, 1844–45).

Waley, D., *The Italian City-Republics* (London: Weidenfeld and Nicolson, 1969).

Wicksteed, P.H., *The Early Lives of Dante translated by Philip H. Wicksteed, MA* (London: Moring, 1904) [contains the Lives by Boccaccio and Bruni].

Wicksteed, P.H. and Gardner, E.G., *Dante and Giovanni del Virgilio* (London: Constable, 1902).

Wieruszowski, H., 'Brunetto Latini als Lehrer Dantes und der Florentiner' *Archivio italiano per la storia della pietà* 2 (1958–59) pp. 171–98, repr. in *Politics and Culture in Medieval Spain and Italy* (Rome: Edizioni di Storia e Letteratura, 1971a).

Wieruszowski, H., 'Rhetoric and the Classics in Italian Education of the Thirteenth Century' *Studia Gratiana* 11 (1967), pp. 169–208, repr. in *Politics and Culture in Medieval Spain and Italy* (Rome: Edizioni di Storia e Letteratura, 1971b).

Zingarelli, N., *La vita, i tempi e le opere di Dante*, 2 vols (Milan: Vallardi, 1944, 3rd Edn—originally publ. 1904).

240

# Index